Deep Value

Deep Value

Why Activist Investors and Other
Contrarians Battle For Control of
"Losing" Corporations

TOBIAS E. CARLISLE

WILEY

Published by John Wiley & Sons, Inc., Hoboken, New Jersey.
Published simultaneously in Canada.

For general information on our other products and services or for technical support, please contact our Customer Care Department within the United States at (800) 762-2974, outside the United States at (317) 572-3993, or fax (317) 572-4002.

Wiley publishes in a variety of print and electronic formats and by print-on-demand. Some material included with standard print versions of this book may not be included in e-books or in print-on-demand. If this book refers to media such as a CD or DVD that is not included in the version you purchased, you may download this material at http://booksupport.wiley.com. For more information about Wiley products, visit www.wiley.com.

Library of Congress Cataloging-in-Publication Data:

Carlisle, Tobias E., 1979–
    Deep value : why activist investors and other contrarians battle for control of losing corporations / Tobias E. Carlisle.
        pages   cm. — (Wiley finance series)
    Includes index.
    ISBN 978-1-118-74796-4 (cloth);   ISBN 978-1-118-74785-8 (ebk);
    ISBN 978-1-118-74799-5
    1. Stockholders. 2. Corporate governance. 3. Investments. 4. Valuation. I. Title.
HD2744.C47 2014
338.6—dc23

                                                                    2014012263

Printed in the United States of America.

10 9

For my ladies luck, Nickole and Stella.

Contents

CHAPTER 10

Preface

"The directors of such [joint-stock] companies, however, being the managers rather of other people's money than of their own, it cannot well be expected, that they should watch over it with the same anxious vigilance with which the partners in a private copartnery frequently watch over their own."

—Adam Smith, *The Wealth of Nations* (1776)

Deep value is investment triumph disguised as business disaster. It is a simple, but counterintuitive idea: Under the right conditions, *losing* stocks—those in crisis, with apparently failing businesses, and uncertain futures—offer unusually favorable investment prospects. This is a philosophy that runs counter to the received wisdom of the market. Many investors believe that a good business and a good investment are the same thing. Many value investors, inspired by Warren Buffett's example, believe that a good, undervalued business is the best investment. The research seems to offer a contradictory view. Though they appear intensely unappealing—perhaps *because* they appear so intensely unappealing—deeply undervalued companies offer very attractive returns. Often found in calamity, they have tanking market prices, receding earnings, and the equity looks like poison. At the extreme, they might be losing money and headed for liquidation. That's why they're cheap. As Benjamin Graham noted in *Security Analysis*, "If the profits had been increasing steadily it is obvious that the shares would not sell at so low a price. The objection to buying these issues lies in the probability, or at least the possibility, that earnings will decline or losses continue, and that the resources will be dissipated and the intrinsic value ultimately become less than the price paid." This book is an investigation of the evidence, and the conditions under which *losing* stocks become asymmetric opportunities, with limited downside and enormous upside.

At its heart, deep value investing is simply the methodical application of timeless principles proven by over 80 years of research and practice. The intellectual basis for it is Graham's *Security Analysis*, the foundational document for the school of investing now known as *value investing*. Through his genius and his experience, Graham understood intuitively what other researchers would demonstrate empirically over the eight decades since his book was first published: That stocks appear most attractive on a fundamental basis at the peak of their business cycle when they represent the worst risk-reward ratio, and least attractive at the bottom of the cycle when the opportunity is at its best. This has several implications for investors. First, the research, which we discuss in the book, shows that the magnitude of market price discount to intrinsic value—the *margin of safety* in value investing parlance—is more important than the rate of growth in earnings, or the return on invested capital, a measure of business quality. This seems contradictory to Buffett's exhortation to favor "wonderful companies at fair prices"—which generate sustainable, high returns on capital—over "fair companies at wonderful prices"—those that are cheap, but do not possess any economic advantage.

In the book, we examine why Buffett, who was Graham's most apt student, sometime employee, long-time friend, and intellectual heir, evolved his investment style away from Graham's under the influence of his friend and business partner, Charlie Munger. We examine why Munger prompted Buffett to seek out the wonderful company, one that could compound growth while throwing off cash to shareholders. We analyze the textbook example of such a business to understand what makes it "wonderful," and then test the theory to see whether buying stocks that meet Buffett's criteria leads to consistent, market-beating performance over the long term. Do Buffett's wonderful companies outperform without Buffett's genius for qualitative business analysis, and, if so, what is the real cause? We know that a wonderful company will earn an average return if the market price reflects its fair value. To outperform, the price must be discounted—the wider the discount, or margin of safety, the better the return—or the business must be more wonderful than the market believes. Wonderful company investors must therefore determine both whether a superior business can sustain its unusual profitability, and the extent to which the stock price already anticipates its ability to do so. This is a difficult undertaking because, as we'll see, it is the rare company that does so. And we don't well understand what allows it to do so. In most cases competition works on high quality businesses to push their returns back to average, and some even become loss makers. What appears to be an unusually strong business tends to be one enjoying unusually favorable conditions, right at the pinnacle of its business cycle.

The problem for investors is not only that high growth and unusual profitability don't persist. Exacerbating the problem in many cases is that the market overestimates the business's potential, bidding the price of its stock too high relative to its potential. The stock of high quality companies is driven so high that long-term returns are impaired *even assuming the high rates of growth and profitability persist*. The corollary is also true: A company with an apparently poor business will generate an excellent return if the market price underestimates its fair value *even assuming the low growth or profitability persists*. These findings reveal an axiomatic truth about investing: investors aren't rewarded for picking winners; they're rewarded for uncovering mispricings—divergences between the price of a security and its intrinsic value. It is mispricings that create market-beating opportunities. And the place to look for mispricings is in disaster, among the unloved, the ignored, the neglected, the shunned, and the feared—the losers. This is the focus of the book.

If we want rapid earnings growth, and the accompanying stock price appreciation, the place to look for it is counterintuitive. It is more likely to be found in undervalued stocks enduring significant earnings compression and plunging market prices. How can this be so? The reason is a pervasive, enduring phenomenon known as *mean reversion*. It can be observed in fundamental business performance, security prices, stock markets, and economies. It returns high-growth stocks to earth, and pushes down exceptional returns on investment, while lifting moribund industries, and breathing new life into dying businesses. Though Graham described the exact mechanism by which mean reversion returned undervalued stocks to intrinsic value as "one of the mysteries of our business," the micro-economic theory is well understood. High growth and high returns invite new entrants who compete away profitability, leading to stagnation, while losses and poor returns cause competitors to exit, leading to a period of high growth and profitability for those business that remain.

Though it is ubiquitous, we don't intuitively recognize the conditions for mean reversion. Time and again investors, including value investors, ignore it and consequently reduce returns. We can show that a portfolio of deeply undervalued stocks will, on average, generate better returns, and suffer fewer down years, than the market. But rather than focus on the experience of the class of deeply undervalued stocks, we are distracted by the headlines. We overreact. We're focus on the short-term impact of the crisis. We fixate on the fact that any individual stock appears more likely to suffer a permanent loss of capital. The reason is that even those of us who identify as value investors suffer from cognitive biases, and make behavioral errors. They are easy to make because the incorrect decision—rejecting the undervalued stock—feels right, while the correct decision—buying stocks with anemic, declining earnings—feels wrong. The research shows that our untrained instinct is to naïvely extrapolate out a trend—whether it be in fundamentals like revenues, earnings, or cash flows, or in stock prices. And when we extrapolate the fundamental performance of stocks with declining earnings, we conclude that the intrinsic value must become less than the price paid. These biases—ignorance of the base case and, by extension, mean reversion—are key contributors to the ongoing returns to deep value investment.

In the book we also examine how the public stock market, by making possible an involuntary exchange of management control, creates a means for disciplining underperforming managers, and improving poorly performing businesses. Where high-return businesses attract competitors, low-return businesses attract outside managers. Through acquisition, or activism, these external managers—typically financial buyers like private equity firms, activist investors, and liquidators—compete for control of corporate resources with underexploited potential in the *market for corporate control*. The *principal-agent conflict*—caused by the separation of ownership and management in publicly traded companies—leads management to put its own interests ahead of the shareholders. Activists seek to resolve this conflict by pressuring boards to remove underperforming managers, stop value-destroying mergers and acquisitions, optimize capital structures, or press for a sale of the company, and earn a return doing so. They are thus incentivized to foment catalysts in otherwise neglected stocks, and are an important participant in the market for deeply undervalued, underperforming stocks.

As a portfolio, deeply undervalued companies with the conditions in place for activism offer asymmetric, market-beating returns. Activists exploit this property by taking large minority stakes in these stocks and then agitating for change. What better platform than a well-publicized proxy fight and tender offer to highlight mismanagement and underexploited intrinsic value, and induce either a voluntary restructuring or takeover by a bigger player in the same industry? Activist investing can be understood as a form of arbitrage. Activists invest in poorly performing, undervalued firms with underexploited intrinsic value. By remedying the deficiency or moving the company's intrinsic value closer to its full potential, and eliminating the market price discount in the process, they capture a premium that represents both the improvement in the intrinsic value and the removal of the market price discount. We scrutinize the returns to activism to determine the extent to which they are due to an improvement in intrinsic value, or simply the returns to picking deeply undervalued stocks. Finally, we examine valuation metrics used to identify the characteristics that typically attract activists—undervaluation, large cash holdings, and low payout ratios. These metrics favor companies with so-called *lazy* balance sheets and hidden or unfulfilled potential due to inappropriate capitalization. Activists target these under-valued, cash-rich companies, seeking to improve the intrinsic value and close the market price discount by reducing excess cash through increased payout ratios. We analyze the returns to these metrics and apply them to two real world examples of activism. The power of these metrics is that they identify good candidates for activist attention, and if no activist emerges to improve the unexploited intrinsic value, other corrective forces act on the market price to generate excellent returns in the meantime.

The book is intended to be a practical guide that canvasses the academic and industry research into theories of intrinsic value, management's influ-ence on value, and the impact of attempts to unseat management on both market price and value. Each chapter tells a different story about a charac-teristic of deep value investing, seeking to illustrate a genuinely counterin-tuitive insight. Through these stories, it explores several ideas demonstrating that deeply undervalued stocks provide an enormous tail wind to investors, generating outsized returns whether they are subject to activist attention or not. We begin with former arbitrageur and option trader Carl Icahn. An avowed Graham-and-Dodd investor, Icahn understood early the advantage of owning equities as apparently appetizing as poison. He took Benjamin Graham's investment philosophy and used it to pursue deeply underval-ued positions offering asymmetric returns where he could control his own destiny. More than any other, Icahn's evolution as an investor mirrors the evolution of activism. In the following chapters we step through the look-ing glass to examine the theories of deep value and activist investing from Graham to Buffett to Icahn and beyond.

Acknowledgments

I was the beneficiary of a great deal of assistance in the production of the manuscript for *Deep Value*. First and foremost, I'd like to thank my wife, Nickole, who took over the primary parental responsibilities for our newborn, Auristella, whose arrival marked the midpoint of the preparation of the first draft. I'd like to thank the early reviewers of that primordial first draft: Scott Reardon, Taylor Conant, Travis Dirks, PhD, Peter Love, Toby Shute, and my mother and father, Drs. Wendy and Roger Carlisle. I'd like to thank Jeffrey Oxman, PhD for his assistance with backtesting the various strategies discussed in the book. Finally, I appreciate the assistance of the team at Wiley Finance, most especially Bill Falloon, Lia Ottaviano, Angela Urquhart, Tiffany Charbonier, and Meg Freeborn, who provided guidance and advice along the way.

Tobias Carlisle is the founder and managing director of Eyquem Investment Management LLC, and serves as portfolio manager of Eyquem Fund LP. He is best known as the author of the well regarded web site Greenbackd.com, and co-author of *Quantitative Value: A Practitioner's Guide to Automating Intelligent Investment and Eliminating Behavioral Errors* (2012, Wiley Finance). He has extensive experience in business valuation, portfolio management, investment research, public company corporate governance, and corporate law. Prior to founding Eyquem in 2010, Tobias was an analyst at an activist hedge fund, general counsel of a company listed on the Australian Stock Exchange, and a corporate advisory lawyer. As a lawyer specializing in mergers and acquisitions he has advised on transactions across a variety of industries in the United States, the United Kingdom, China, Australia, Singapore, Bermuda, Papua New Guinea, New Zealand, and Guam. He is a graduate of the University of Queensland in Australia with degrees in Law (2001) and Business (Management) (1999).

CHAPTER 1

The Icahn Manifesto

Corporate Raider to Activist Investor

"Had we but world enough, and time,
This coyness, Lady, were no crime...
                    —Andrew Marvell, *To His Coy Mistress* (c. 1650)

bouleversement *bool-vair-suh-MAWN*\, *noun:*
Complete overthrow; a reversal; an overturning; convulsion;
turmoil.
                    —Comes from French, from Old French *bouleverser,*
            "to overturn," from *boule*, "ball" (from Latin *bulla*) + *verser,*
            "to overturn" (from Latin *versare*, from *vertere*, "to turn").

Over the fall of 1975, Carl Icahn and his right-hand man, Alfred Kingsley, hashed out a new investment strategy in the cramped offices of Icahn & Company. Located at 25 Broadway, a few steps away from the future site of the *Charging Bull*, the iconic 7,000-pound bronze sculpture erected by Arturo Di Modica following the 1987 stock market crash, Icahn & Company was then a small, but successful, discount option brokerage with a specialty in arbitrage. Kingsley, a graduate of the Wharton School with a master's degree in tax from New York University, had joined Icahn in 1968. Immediately impressed by his ability to quickly grasp complex transactions, Icahn had asked Kingsley what he knew about arbitrage. "Not a thing," Kingsley had replied.[1] Soon Kingsley was spending most of his days arbitraging the securities of conglomerates like Litton Industries, LTV, and IT&T. Arbitrage is the practice of simultaneously buying and selling an asset that trades in two or more markets at different prices. In the classic version, the arbitrageur buys at the lower price and sells at the higher price, and in doing so realizes a riskless profit representing the ordinarily small difference between the two. Icahn had Kingsley engaged in a variation known as convertible arbitrage, simultaneously trading a stock and its convertible securities, which, for liquidity or market psychology reasons, were sometimes mispriced relative to the stock. Litton, LTV, IT&T, and the other conglomerates had issued an alphabet soup of common stock, preferred stock, options, warrants, bonds, and convertible debt. As an options broker, Icahn used his superior market knowledge to capitalize on inefficiencies between, say, the prices of the common stock and the warrants, or the common stock and the convertible debt. The attraction of convertible arbitrage was that it was market-neutral, which meant that Icahn & Company's clients were not subject to the risk of a steep decline in the market.

Icahn and Kingsley shortly progressed to arbitraging closed-end mutual funds and the securities in the underlying portfolio. A closed-end mutual fund is *closed* because it has a fixed number of shares or units on issue. Unlike open-end funds, management cannot issue or buy back new shares or units to meet investor demand. For this reason, a closed-end fund can trade at a significant discount or, less commonly, a premium to its net asset value. Icahn and Kingsley bought the units of the closed-end funds trading at the widest discount from their underlying asset value, and then hedged out the market risk by shorting the securities that made up the mutual fund's portfolio. Like the convertible arbitrage strategy, the closed-end fund arbitrage was indifferent to the direction of the market, generating profits as the gap between the unit price and the underlying value narrowed. It was not, however, classic riskless arbitrage.

As it was possible for a gap to open up between the price of the mutual fund unit and the underlying value of the portfolio, it was also possible for that gap to widen. When it did so, an investor who had bought the units of the fund and sold short the underlying portfolio endured short-term, unrealized losses until the market closed the gap. In the worst-case scenario, the investor could be forced to realize those losses if the gap continued to widen and he or she couldn't hold the positions, which could occur if he or she failed to meet a margin call or was required to cover the short position. Unwilling to rely on the market to close the gap, Icahn and Kingsley would often take matters into their own hands. Once they had established their position, they contacted the manager and lobbied to have the fund liquidated. The manager either acquiesced, and Icahn and Kingsley closed out the position for a gain, or the mere prospect of the manager liquidating caused the gap to wholly or partially close. The strategy generated good returns, but the universe of heavily discounted closed-end funds was small. Icahn and Kingsley saw the potentially far larger universe of prospects emerging in public companies with undervalued assets. This was the new investment strategy they were shaping at 25 Broadway in 1975.

Already moribund after a decade of stagflation, an oil crisis, and a failing U.S. economy, Wall Street was sent reeling from the knockout punch delivered by the 1974 stock market crash, the worst since the Great Depression. Out of the bear market punctuating the end of the Go-Go 1960s, the stock market had rallied to a new all-time high in early 1973. From there it was brutally smashed down to a trough in October 1974 that was some 45 percent below the January 1973 peak. (The market would repeat this wrenching up and down cycle until November 1982, at which point it traded where it had in 1966, fully 16 years before.) Stocks that had become cheap in 1973 had proceeded to fall to dust in 1974. Bonds, ravaged by runaway inflation, were described by wags as "certificates of confiscation."[2] Investors were still shell shocked in 1975. Even if they could be persuaded that they were getting a bargain, most seemed unwilling to re-enter the market, believing that undervalued stocks could start dropping again at any moment. If they would take a call from their broker, they simply wanted "the hell out of the market."[3]

Although few could sense it, a quiet revolution was about to get under way. Icahn and Kingsley had seen what many others had missed—a decade of turmoil on the stock market had created a rare opportunity. After trading sideways for nine years, rampant inflation had yielded a swathe of undervalued stocks with assets carried on the books at a huge discount to their true worth. Recent experience had taught most investors that even deeply discounted stocks could continue falling with the market, but Icahn and Kingsley were uniquely positioned to see that they didn't need to rely on the whim of the market to close the gap between price and intrinsic value. Kingsley later recalled:[4]

> We asked ourselves, "If we can be activists in an undervalued closed-end mutual fund, why can't we be activists in a corporation with undervalued assets?"

As they had with the closed-end mutual funds, Icahn and Kingsley would seek to control the destiny of public companies. Their impact on America's corporations would be profound.

ICAHN'S WALL STREET REFORMATION

Icahn's progression from arbitrageur and liquidator of closed-end funds to full-blown corporate raider started in 1976 with a distillation of the strategy into an investment memorandum distributed to prospective investors:[5]

> It is our opinion that the elements in today's economic environment have combined in a unique way to create large profit-making

opportunities with relatively little risk. [T]he real or liquidating value of many American companies has increased markedly in the last few years; however, interestingly, this has not at all been reflected in the market value of their common stocks. Thus, we are faced with a unique set of circumstances that, if dealt with correctly can lead to large profits, as follows: [T]he management of these asset-rich target companies generally own very little stock themselves and, therefore, usually have no interest in being acquired. They jealously guard their prerogatives by building 'Chinese walls' around their enterprises that hopefully will repel the invasion of domestic and foreign dollars. Although these 'walls' are penetrable, most domestic companies and almost all foreign companies are loath to launch an 'unfriendly' takeover attempt against a target company. However, whenever a fight for control is initiated, it generally leads to windfall profits for shareholders. Often the target company, if seriously threatened, will seek another, more friendly enterprise, generally known as a 'white knight' to make a higher bid, thereby starting a bidding war. Another gambit occasionally used by the target company is to attempt to purchase the acquirers' stock or, if all else fails, the target may offer to liquidate.

It is our contention that sizeable profits can be earned by taking large positions in 'undervalued' stocks and then attempting to control the destinies of the companies in question by:

a) trying to convince management to liquidate or sell the company to a 'white knight'; b) waging a proxy contest; c) making a tender offer and/or; d) selling back our position to the company.

The "Icahn Manifesto"—as Icahn's biographer Mark Stevens coined it—was Icahn's solution to the old corporate principal-agency dilemma identified by Adolf Berle and Gardiner Means in their seminal 1932 work, *The Modern Corporation and Private Property.*[6] The principal-agency problem speaks to the difficulty of one party (the principal) to motivate another (the agent) to put the interests of the principal ahead of the agent's own interests. Berle and Means argued that the modern corporation shielded the agents (the boards of directors) from oversight by the principals (the shareholders) with the result that the directors tended to run the companies for their own ends, riding roughshod over the shareholders who were too small, dispersed, and ill-informed to fight back. According to Berle and Means:[7]

It is traditional that a corporation should be run for the benefit of its owners, the stockholders, and that to them should go any profits which are distributed. We now know, however, that a controlling group may hold the power to divert profits into their own pockets. There is no longer any certainty that a corporation will in fact be run primarily in the interests of the stockholders. The extensive separation of ownership and control, and the strengthening of the powers of control, raise a new situation calling for a decision whether social and legal pressure should be applied in an effort to insure corporate operation primarily in the interests of the owners or whether such pressure shall be applied in the interests of some other or wider group.

Berle and Means gave as an example the American Telephone and Telegraph Company (AT&T), which they said had assets of $5 billion, 454,000 employees, and 567,694 shareholders, the largest of whom owned less than one percent of the company's stock:[8]

Under such conditions control may be held by the directors or titular managers who can employ the proxy machinery to become a self-perpetuating body, even though as a group they own but a small fraction of the stock outstanding. In each of these types, majority control, minority control, and management control, the separation of ownership from control has become effective—a large body of security holders has been created who exercise virtually no control over the wealth which they or their predecessors in interest have contributed to the enterprise. In the case of management control, the ownership interest held by the controlling group amounts to but a very small fraction of the total ownership.

Icahn cut straight to the heart of the matter, likening the problem to a caretaker on an estate who refuses to allow the owner to sell the property because the caretaker might lose his job.[9] His manifesto proposed to restore shareholders to their lawful position by asserting the rights of ownership. If management wouldn't heed his exhortations as a shareholder, he would push for control of the board through a proxy contest—a means for shareholders to vote out incumbent management and replace them with new directors. In a proxy contest, competing slates of directors argue why they are better suited to run the company and enhance shareholder value. If he didn't succeed through the proxy contest, he could launch a tender offer or sell his position back to the company in a practice known as *greenmail*. A neologism possibly created from the words *blackmail* and *greenback*, greenmail is a now-unlawful practice in which the management of a targeted company pays a ransom to a raider by buying back the stock of the raider at a premium to the market price. Warren Buffett, who said of greenmail that it was "odious and repugnant," described the nature of the transaction in his 1984 *Chairman's Letter* in characteristically colorful terms:[10]

> *In these transactions, two parties achieve their personal ends by exploitation of an innocent and unconsulted third party. The players are: (1) the "shareholder" extortionist who, even before the ink on his stock certificate dries, delivers his "your-money-or-your-life" message to managers; (2) the corporate insiders who quickly seek peace at any price—as long as the price is paid by someone else; and (3) the shareholders whose money is used by (2) to make (1) go away. As the dust settles, the mugging, transient shareholder gives his speech on "free enterprise", the muggee management gives its speech on "the best interests of the company", and the innocent shareholder standing by mutely funds the payoff.*

Icahn accepted greenmail on several occasions prior to it being outlawed, on one such occasion attracting a class-action lawsuit from the shareholders of Saxon Industries, a New York-based paper distributor that fell into bankruptcy following the transaction. The lawsuit charged that Icahn had failed to disclose to the market that he had requested greenmail in exchange for not undertaking a proxy contest. When Saxon Industries announced that it had paid Icahn $10.50 per share as greenmail, giving him a substantial profit on his $7.21 per share average purchase price, the stock fell precipitously. According to a lawsuit filed against Icahn, upon the sudden announcement by Saxon that it had purchased Icahn's stock, the market price of Saxon's stock nosedived to $6.50. While the bankruptcy of Saxon Industries was arguably more directly the result of its chairman Stanley Lurie's accounting fraud, the complaint demonstrated two ideas: First, the inequity of greenmail. The substantial premium paid to the greenmailer comes at the cost of all shareholders remaining in the company. Second, the complaint illustrates the power of the activist campaign. Icahn's threat of a proxy contest had pushed the stock price from around $6 to $10.50. Absent the possibility of a proxy contest, the stock fell back to its average pre-campaign price of $6.50.

While gaining control gave him discretion over the operating and capital allocation decisions of the company, Icahn's experience with the closed-end funds had taught him a valuable lesson—simply calling attention to the company's market price discount to its underlying and underexploited intrinsic value would attract the attention of other investors. He hoped that by signaling to the market that the company was undervalued, leveraged buy-out firms or strategic acquirers would compete for control and, in so doing, push up the market price of his holding. Icahn could then sell into any takeover bid by tipping his shares out onto the market or delivering them to the bidder. It was the classic win-win situation Icahn sought—even if he didn't win a seat on the board, the proxy contest would act as a catalyst, signaling to other potential bidders in the market the company's undervaluation and mismanagement.

Theory into Activism: Tappan Stove Company in Play

Icahn's first target was Tappan Stove Company, a sleepy range and oven maker still chaired by a member of its eponymous founding family, Dick Tappan, almost a century after it was founded in 1881. Tappan stock was already depressed along with the rest of the stock market following the crash in 1974. It fell off a cliff when it posted its first loss in 40 years following a disastrous move into a new market for Tappan—heating and cooling—and a slump in its old home building market. Kingsley, who identified it as an attractive candidate, said:[11]

> *At the time we took our position in Tappan, everyone else was hot on Magic Chef, but I said, "The multiples on Magic Chef are too high. Where is it going to go from here? Magic Chef was at the top of its cycle and Tappan was at the bottom. That's where I preferred to stake our claim."*

At Kingsley's suggestion Icahn started acquiring the stock in 1977 when it was selling for $7.50 per share. He saw that Tappan, as a niche player in a market dominated by the likes of General Electric and Westinghouse, was an attractive candidate for strategic acquisition by one of those behemoths. With a book value of around $20 per share, Icahn figured his potential upside was around $12.50 per share, or about 170 percent. In what would become a typical Icahn analysis, he saw that the discount in the stock provided limited downside risk, and the potential for a significant gain if he could chum the waters enough to foment a takeover. Tappan made an ideal first target for his new strategy: If the coin fell heads, he would win big; if tails, he wouldn't lose much.

Icahn built his position in Tappan through 1977 and then, in early January 1978, he and Kingsley placed a call to Tappan's president, Donald Blasius, to alert him of their presence. Icahn told Blasius that he had acquired between 10,000 and 15,000 shares of Tappan and was considering making a "substantial additional investment." Seemingly oblivious to Icahn's overtures, Blasius noted in a subsequent memo to Dick Tappan, Tappan's chairman, that Icahn "seemed pleased that we took the time to talk to them about the company." In an effort to keep up the pressure, Icahn and Kingsley called Blasius again in late February, by which time they had acquired 70,000 shares of Tappan stock, to let Blasius know that Icahn was interested in Tappan for its potential as a takeover candidate. As he had after the first call, Blasius dutifully sent a memo to Dick Tappan in which he noted that Icahn had told Blasius that he "had made a lot of money in buying low-priced stocks that were in the process of turnaround. In some cases, the turnaround improved the value of the stock, but in other cases a buy-out was completed which approximately doubled the stock price." Blasius further noted that "they consider [Tappan] a good possibility for this occurring, which is added incentive for their investment."[12]

Icahn continued to build his holding in Tappan stock to several hundred thousand shares—a sizeable position, but still too small to require him to file a *Schedule 13D* notice with the SEC. The Schedule 13D notice lets the market know the intentions of a shareholder who owns more than 5 percent of a company's outstanding stock and who proposes to undertake some corporate action, including a takeover, liquidation, or other change-of-control event. Icahn had hoped that his continued purchases might alert others to the situation developing at Tappan, including risk arbitrageurs—investors who bet on the outcome of takeovers—other potential strategic acquirers, and their investment bankers. In the 1980s, risk arbitrageurs with a position in a stock would often turn a rumor about a takeover into a self-fulfilling prophecy. Unfortunately for Icahn, the explosion of takeover activity that followed in the 1980s hadn't yet kicked off and, in the absence of a 13D filing that might draw attention to Tappan, the stock languished for the next nine months.

Icahn opted to take matters into his own hands, setting up a May 1978 lunch between Blasius and Fred Sullivan, the chairman of the conglomerate Walter Kidde & Co., who owned a large block of Tappan stock. Icahn hoped that Sullivan might want to bolt Tappan's stove business onto its *Faberware* division. He had, however, neglected to mention to Blasius that anyone else would be at the lunch. Blasius was enraged when he discovered on the morning of the lunch that Sullivan would be attending and, further, that he was interested in acquiring Tappan. At the lunch, Blasius made it clear that the company was not for sale. Taken aback, Sullivan told Blasius and Icahn that he wouldn't entertain a hostile takeover, so the acquisition was a non-starter. Blasius's post-lunch memo noted that Sullivan "understood that we were not for sale and, therefore, would not go any further. Then he added without any suggestion on my part, 'If anyone comes along that you are not interested in, or you would like to come to a friendly port, we would be very happy to talk to you.'"[13] If Blasius was relieved when he heard Sullivan say that he wouldn't take the Tappan acquisition any further, Icahn heard that a Tappan acquisition was in the offing if he could find a buyer prepared to proceed on a hostile basis. Blasius's memo also noted that "[Icahn] repeated that this was not an attempt to accomplish, or the beginning of a buy-out—that they felt the stock was undervalued at approximately $8 and had good growth potential. He also indicated that we should not be worried if a [13D] were filed as it would not be intended as the beginning of a takeover attempt."[14]

Icahn stepped up his attempts to find a buyer for Tappan, but without success. He also continued buying Tappan stock. By late November 1978 Icahn's position was big enough that he was required to file a 13D with the SEC, and Wall Street finally got the news that Tappan was "in play." The stock surged and, in January 1979, Icahn let Blasius know that if the shares were to rise two or three more dollars he would be a seller. He also teased Blasius that an anonymous strategic acquirer had approached him to buy him out for between $15 and $17 per share. He reminded Blasius that Sullivan stood ready to serve as a "white knight," a friendly acquirer who might retain existing management. Icahn viewed his shareholding as being large enough to qualify him for a tenth seat on the board to be created just for him, and said as much to Blasius. Blasius rejected the request out of hand. In Blasius's memo to the board, he noted:[15]

> *I explained that our board was limited to nine members with only two being representatives of management and that the number had been fixed by the board either last year or the year before. I also gave him an outline of the board strength that I felt was represented and that I really believe we have an efficient board match—independent, very capable and doing a good job and that I, personally, saw no need or desire to add a tenth member.*

The company, now fully apprehending the threat Icahn presented, moved to issue preferred stock in an effort to block any hostile interest. Icahn found out about the move along with the other shareholders. Said Kingsley, "We first learned of the serially preferred tactic through a proxy statement that came in the mail. As soon as I saw it I said, 'If we're going to do something, Carl, we had better do it now.'"[16] The risk, as Kingsley saw it, was that the preferred stock could be used to derail any hostile tender offer. If Icahn couldn't use his major shareholding as a catalyst to sell the company, much of his influence would be gone.

Icahn responded by launching a media campaign to defeat the preferred stock issue and have Tappan sold at full value. In the face of Icahn's towering indignation, the board folded almost immediately, agreeing to withdraw its proposal for the issue. Icahn pressed on regardless. In an April 1979 letter to Tappan shareholders he argued for a seat on the board and the sale of the company at a substantial premium to the prevailing market price:[17]

> *I am writing this letter to ask you to elect me to the Board of Directors at the Annual Meeting of Shareholders on April 23, 1979. As the largest shareholder of Tappan, I would like to see our company acquired or tendered for at a price close to its December 31, 1978, book value of $20.18.*

Channeling Berle and Means, Icahn argued that management was insulated from Tappan's poor performance by their overly generous compensation package:[18]

> *During the past five years Tappan, under its current management, has lost $3.3 million on sales of $1.3 billion and during the same period [Dick] Tappan and [Donald] Blasius, Tappan's Chairman of the Board and President, respectively, received salaries and bonuses totaling $1,213,710.*

The letter contained a chart comparing Tappan's earnings and Dick Tappan and Blasius's salaries on an annual basis. Referring to the chart, Icahn said:[19]

> *If I personally owned a business with these operating results and which had a substantial net worth, I would certainly seek to sell that business. I believe the same logic should apply in the case of Tappan.*

Taking advantage of any lingering doubts shareholders might hold about the motives of management, Icahn resurrected the specter of the withdrawn preferred stock issue. Saying that management had admitted that such an issue "might have the effect of discouraging some future attempt to take over the company by a cash tender offer or otherwise," Icahn pledged that, if elected to the board, he would "discourage any such future proposals in their embryonic stages."[20]

> *As a director of Tappan my first act will be to recommend that we retain an investment banking firm (unaffiliated with me) to solicit proposals from third parties to acquire our company at a price near its book value, which at December 31, 1978, was $20.18.*
>
> *Although management has stated to me that they do not desire the acquisition of Tappan by another company, I assure you that, if I am elected, I will inform would-be suitors that at least one*

member of the Board does not share management's views with respect to the acquisition of Tappan by another company. I will attempt to see to it that shareholders are made aware of any indications of interest or actual offers to acquire our company, which are received from third parties.

The letter had the desired impact, and Icahn won his seat on the board. As a director, he moved quickly to sell Tappan's assets. At the first board meeting he pushed for the liquidation of the company's money-losing Canadian subsidiary, Tappan-Gurney, which owned valuable real estate in Montreal, and for the sale of Tappan's Anaheim, California, factory. He also pressed on for the sale of the entire company, shopping Tappan to leveraged buy-out firms and strategic acquirers. Recognizing that Icahn had won, and would shortly find a buyer, management moved to find their own white knight. Tappan and Blasius met with the giant Swedish appliance maker AB Electrolux and offered Tappan up on a platter. Electrolux bit, bidding $18 per share. The bid delivered a $2.7 million profit on Icahn's 321,500 shares, representing an almost 90 percent gain on his $9.60 per share average purchase price.

In a surprising move, Dick Tappan was so impressed with Icahn's strategy that he subsequently became an investor in Icahn's partnership:[21]

We held a final board meeting, at which time the directors approved the company's sale to Electrolux. Icahn attended that meeting and sometime during the course of the evening I said, 'Icahn has done us a favor. We got a 50 percent premium over the company's market value, and Electrolux is going to make capital investments in Tappan.' I said, 'If you have any deals you want to cut me in on—' That's when Icahn said, 'Yes, I have one going on now.'

And so Dick Tappan became a limited partner, investing $100,000 in the Carl C. Icahn Partnership. It would prove to be a great investment for the former chairman.

Tappan would become the template for Icahn's later sorties. In Tappan, the theory outlined in the *Icahn Manifesto* had been proven correct in stunning fashion: Acquire a shareholding in a deeply undervalued company sufficiently large to influence management; draw the market's attention to the wide discount between market price and intrinsic value; and push management for a catalyst, like a sale of the company, a liquidation, or some other value-enhancing act. If management remained intransigent and the proxy contest didn't draw the attention of other bidders, Icahn could move to put the company in play by making a tender offer, which put him in a win/win position. On one hand, it created a price floor in the stock. Icahn could then wait to see if other financial or strategic buyers stepped in with a higher bid to create a liquidity event for his position. If no other bidder emerged, Icahn could take the company private himself, providing liquidity to the other shareholders, and, presumably, getting it for cheap after demonstrating that no other bidder wanted such a moribund business. It was value investing in which the investor controlled his own destiny, and, as Icahn's experience in Tappan and other early campaigns documented in a later Icahn partnership memorandum demonstrated, it worked:[22]

TABLE 1.1   Icahn Partnership Memo: "Stock Prices During Unfriendly Maneuvers"

Target Company	Three Months Prior to Attempt at Target ($)	High After Attempt ($)
Warner Swasey	29	80
National Airlines	15	50
Wylain	13	28½
Flintkote	30	55
Fairchild Camera	29	66
Tappan	8	18

GRAHAMITE PROTO-ACTIVISM

What drew Icahn to Tappan? What did Kingsley see that others had missed? The stock had been savaged after it had posted its first loss in 40 years, the new business seemed to be a loser, and it was a tiny player in a market led by General Electric and Westinghouse, behemoths both. To understand Tappan and the strategy outlined by Icahn and Kingsley in the *Icahn Manifesto* that they used to such powerful effect, we need to begin with the great value investor and investment philosopher Benjamin Graham. Icahn and Kingsley owed an intellectual debt to Graham, whose own investment strategy was quite different from one that might be suggested by his *Dean of Wall Street* sobriquet, more red-in-tooth-and-claw than professorial or academic. Graham was a forceful and eloquent advocate for the use of shareholder activism to foment change in deeply undervalued companies. The very first edition of his magnum opus, *Security Analysis*, published in 1934, devoted an entire chapter to the relationship between shareholders and management, which Graham described as "one of the strangest phenomena of American finance."[23] "Why is it," he wondered, "that no matter how poor a corporation's prospects may seem, its owners permit it to remain in business until its resources are exhausted?" In answering his question, Graham wrote that it was a "notorious fact . . . that the typical American stockholder is the most docile and apathetic animal in captivity:"[24]

> *He does what the board of directors tell him to do and rarely thinks of asserting his individual rights as owner of the business and employer of its paid officers. The result is that the effective control of many, perhaps most, large American corporations is exercised not by those who together own a majority of the stock but by a small group known as "the management."*

He saw deep undervaluation as a prod impelling shareholders to "raise the question whether it is in their interest to continue the business," and "management to take all proper steps to correct the obvious disparity between market quotation and intrinsic value, including a reconsideration of its own policies and a frank justification to the stockholders of its decision to continue the business."[25]

Graham published *Security Analysis* just two years after Berle and Means, who had identified the principal-agent problem in public corporations, released their work. He cited Berle and Means's work with some agitation. They had submitted that it was "apparent to any thoughtful observer" that the effect of the separation of ownership and control was that the corporation had ceased to be a "private business device" and had become a public "institution:"[26]

> *[The] owners of passive property, by surrendering control and responsibility over the active property, have surrendered the right that the corporation should be operated in their sole interest—they have released the community from the obligation to protect them to the full extent implied in the doctrine of strict property rights. At the same time, the controlling groups, by means of the extension of corporate powers, have in their own interest broken the bars of tradition which require that the corporation be operated solely for the benefit of the owners of passive property.*

Graham rejected Berle and Means' argument that a corporation be regarded as something like community property that "serve not only the owners or the control group but all society." He doubted that the shareholders had intentionally "surrendered the right that the corporation should be operated in their sole interest,"[27] contending that the American stockholder had abdicated by default. Graham's view was "that corporations are the mere creatures and property of the stockholders who own them; that the officers are only the paid employees of the stockholders; and that the directors, however chosen, are virtually trustees, whose legal duty it is to act solely on behalf of the owners of the business."[28] All that was required to reverse course was to "reassert the rights of control which inhere in ownership."[29]

It was no coincidence that the discussion on shareholder rights in *Security Analysis* followed on the heels of the chapter on calculating liquidation value, the dourest assessment of a company's prospects. Liquidation value is the residue remaining after all of a company's liabilities have been satisfied and the company has been wound up. Graham described it as simply "the money which the owners could get out of it if they wanted to give it up."[30] To Graham, a stock price below liquidation value was clear evidence that the company's management was pursuing a "mistaken policy," and should take "corrective action, if not voluntarily, then under pressure from stockholders:"[31]

> *In its simplest terms the question comes down to this: Are these managements wrong or is the market wrong? Are these low prices merely the product of unreasoning fear, or do they convey a stern warning to liquidate while there is yet time?"*

In 1932—two years before the publication of *Security Analysis*—Graham authored a series of articles for *Forbes* magazine highlighting the large number of stocks that continued to trade well below liquidation value fully three years after the 1929 stock market crash. The solution, proposed Graham, was that investors become "ownership conscious:"[32]

> *If they realized their rights as business owners, we would not have before us the insane spectacle of treasuries bloated with cash and their proprietors in a wild scramble to give away their interest on any terms they can get. Perhaps the corporation itself buys back the shares they throw on the market, and by a final touch of irony, we see the stockholders' pitifully inadequate payment made to them with their own cash.*

Graham practiced what he preached. The employees of Graham-Newman, his investment partnership, spent their days poring through the 10,000 pages in the *Standard and Poor's* or *Moody's Manuals* looking for net nets. Among them was a future star who Graham had been initially reluctant to take on, the young Warren Buffett. Graham's philosophy was also eagerly embraced by a clutch of investors in the 1940s, 1950s, and 1960s, including Thomas Mellon Evans, Louis Wolfson, and Leopold Silberstein—the so-called *White Sharks of Wall Street*[33]—who rose to prominence using proxy contests and media campaigns to unseat entrenched managements. Evans was the prime mover of his day, taking Graham's liquidation value analysis and using it to wreak havoc on the gray flannel suits of the 1940s and 1950s. He waged numerous takeover battles using tactics that are forerunners of those employed by many of the modern-day activists. Born September 8, 1910, in Pittsburgh and orphaned at the age of 11, Evans grew up poor. Despite his famous middle name—his grandmother's first cousin was Andrew Mellon, the industrialist and Secretary of the Treasury under Presidents Harding, Coolidge, and Hoover—he began his financial career at the bottom. After graduating from Yale University in 1931 in the teeth of the Great Depression, he landed a $100-a-month clerk job at Gulf Oil. While his friends headed out in the evening, Evans would stay home reading financial statements and looking for promising companies, those he could buy for less than liquidation value.

In *Security Analysis* Graham had outlined a clever short cut to calculating liquidation value, which examined a company's working capital as a rough, but usually conservative, proxy for the liquidation value. Graham called this calculation the *net current asset* value. Employing Graham's technique, Evans found stocks selling for less than liquidation value by calculating their net quick assets, another name for the most liquid portion of Graham's net current asset value. His friends teased him about his obsession, so much so that they gave him the nickname "Net Quick" Evans.[34] In 1939 Evans got control of the dilapidated H. K. Porter Co., a builder of industrial locomotives, by buying its distressed bonds at 10 to 15 cents on the dollar. He reorganized the company, converting his bonds into equity, and became president at age 28. From then on, "Net Quick" Evans was the "slick-haired, aggressive"[35] terror of the sleepy boardrooms of the era, much like the stereotype of the corporate raiders in the 1980s.

Even Warren Buffett, Graham's most apt student, tried his hand as a liquidator, briefly turning to Graham-style shareholder activism in his own investment partnership. He obtained control of Dempster Mill Manufacturing Company[36] in the early 1960s through a majority shareholding and board seat before almost completely liquidating it. In the process he incurred the wrath of the town of Beatrice, Nebraska, when he proposed to liquidate the plant there. After a vitriolic campaign waged by the townsfolk and supported by the local paper, Buffett eventually sold Dempster at book value—its almost wholly liquidated assets consisting of just cash, marketable securities, and the plant in Beatrice—to the founder's grandson and his investor group. While it was a typically profitable investment for Buffett, he was scarred by the animosity directed at him, and vowed never to do it again.[37]

Like Graham, Icahn had no such qualms. Icahn's biographer Mark Stevens, describing his rapid ascent from discount options broker to "formidable raider and financial tactician," said that Icahn "combined an extraordinary intellect with a battering-ram personality to exploit a glaring weakness in the American corporate establishment, earning enormous sums as he attacked the likes of Tappan." At the zenith of his influence in the 1980s, he controlled billions in capital and his reach extended to the giants of the public markets, including Texaco, the "Big Red Star of the American Highway" for which he bid $12.4 billion, and U.S. Steel, the world's first billion-dollar corporation, then sporting a market capitalization of $6 billion. Other investors took notice, and a cottage industry of so-called corporate raiders sprang up. For a brief period, news of their exploits would extend beyond the business pages and into popular culture, most notably in Michael Douglas's character Gordon Gecko in *Wall Street* (1987), Richard Gere's Edward Lewis in *Pretty Woman* (1990), and Danny Devito's Larry "The Liquidator" Garfield in *Other People's Money* (1991), notable for a memorable scene in which DeVito draws Graham's net current asset value formula on a blackboard. Their influence waxed and waned with the market. Following the 1987 stock market crash, they gradually retreated again from the public consciousness.

A new breed of activist investors emerged in the wake of the dot-com bust in the early 2000s, chasing the cashed-up failures of the information technology and communications boom. As Evans and Icahn had before them, the new activist investors rediscovered the power of the public media campaign, the proxy contest, and the tender offer. The new activists moved in some cases to civilize shareholder activism, allowing institutionalization that attracted new capital, and rendered countless new innovations, from web-based campaigns and "public" private equity. Others resisted civilization and institutionalization, maintaining the freebooting ways and anti-glamour machismo of their corporate raider forebears. Perhaps it is a necessary response to the goings on in the stocks found in the netherworld of the market. Far from the glare of analysts and the media, blatant fraud, outright theft, and flagrant oppression of minority investors flourishes. The sheriffs on this frontier are the activists and short sellers, and who can blame them if *the horror, the horror* drives them to write Hunter S. Thompson *Gonzo*-style poison-pen letters, drafted as if Mistah Kurtz had to file his "Exterminate all the brutes!" pamphlet with the SEC.

Icahn's evolution from liquidator to corporate raider reflected the underlying philosophical shift in the broader world of value investment and shareholder activism. Graham's approach, which identified targets by their discount to liquidation value, was appropriate to the time and extremely effective, but those opportunities had largely disappeared from the investment landscape by the 1980s. In response, modern activists have adapted, employing a wider lens to assess value and exploiting a broader array of tools to achieve their ends. Icahn took his place alongside them, bigger and better capitalized than ever, and, as he had in the 1980s, he would straddle the most recent epoch of shareholder activism and stand again at the fore-front of large capitalization shareholder activism in the 2000s.

Notes

1. Mark Stevens. *King Icahn*. (New York: Penguin Group) 1993.
2. Spencer Jakab. "Fears of return to the 1970s are overdone," *Financial Times*, April 29, 2011. Available at http://www.ft.com/intl/cms/s/0/8f773248-727f-11e0-96bf-00144feabdc0.html#axzz29bATsOYq.
3. Tom Lauricella. "Flashbacks of the 1970s for Stock-Market Vets." *The Wall Street Journal*, April 18, 2009. Available at http://online.wsj.com/article/SB124001598168631027.html.
4. Stevens, 1993.
5. Ibid.
6. Adolf Augustus Berle and Gardiner Coit Means. *The Modern Corporation and Private Property*. (New Brunswick: Transaction Publishers) 1932.
7. Ibid.
8. Ibid.
9. Anon, "'If He Ruled the World': Carl Icahn's Take on Time Warner and Corporate America," Knowledge@Wharton, February 22, 2006, Available at http://knowledge.wharton.upenn.edu/article.cfm?articleid=1392.
10. Warren Buffett. "Chairman's Letter." *Berkshire Hathaway, Inc. Annual Report*, 1984.
11. Stevens, 1993.
12. Ibid.
13. Ibid.
14. Ibid.
15. Ibid.
16. Ibid.
17. Ibid.
18. Ibid.
19. Ibid.
20. Ibid.
21. Ibid.
22. Ibid.
23. Benjamin Graham and David Dodd. *Security Analysis*. (New York: *McGraw Hill*) 1934.
24. Ibid.
25. Ibid.
26. Berle and Means.
27. Graham and Dodd, 1934.
28. Ibid.
29. Ibid.

30. Ibid.
31. Ibid
32. Benjamin Graham. "Inflated Treasuries and Deflated Stockholders." *Forbes*, 1932. Available at http://www.forbes.com/forbes/1999/1227/6415400a.html.
33. Diana B. Henriques. *The White Sharks of Wall Street: Thomas Mellon Evans and the Original Corporate Raiders.* (New York: Lisa Drew Books) 2000.
34. *Time Magazine.* "Young Tom Evans." March 27, 1944. Available at http://www.time.com/time/magazine/article/0,9171,803258,00.html.
35. Ibid.
36. Warren Buffett. "Partnership Letters." Buffett Partnership. Available at http://csinvesting.org/wp-content/uploads/2012/05/dempster_mills_manufacturing_case_study_bpls.pdf.
37. Alice Schroeder. *The Snowball.* (New York: Bantam) 2009.

CHAPTER 2

Contrarians at the Gate

The Dean of Wall Street on Liquidations, Activism, and the Great Mean-Reverting Mystery of Value Investment

Chairman: "... One other question and I will desist. When you find a special situation and you decide, just for illustration, that you can buy for 10 and it is worth 30, and you take a position, and then you cannot realize it until a lot of other people decide it is worth 30, how is that process brought about—by advertising, or what happens?"
Graham: "That is one of the mysteries of our business, and it is a mystery to me as well as to everybody else. We know from experience that eventually the market catches up with value. It realizes it in one way or another."
—Benjamin Graham, "Stock Market Study. Hearings Before The Committee on Banking and Currency, United States Senate, Eighty-Fourth Congress, First Session on Factors Affecting the Buying and Selling of Equity Securities." (March 3, 1955)[1]

In 1927, 31-year-old Benjamin Graham started teaching a night class at Columbia University called "Security Analysis." Graham discussed in the lectures a new method he had developed for analyzing securities. The young lecturer, who had turned down offers to undertake doctorates in the philosophy, mathematics, and English departments when he graduated from there 13 years earlier, proposed the radical idea that a stock's price and its intrinsic value were distinct quantities. A stock's *intrinsic value*, he taught, could be deduced through careful fundamental analysis of the financial statements and business prospects, and that intrinsic value compared to the price available in the market. If the stock price traded at a sufficient discount to the intrinsic value to provide a margin of safety, the stock could be purchased. Given time, the market price would revert toward the intrinsic value, at which time the stock should be sold. Where the intrinsic value exceeded the price or where it didn't offer a sufficient margin of safety the stock should be avoided. Simplicity itself. With David Dodd, a Columbia Business School professor who as a student had taken Graham's first class, Graham converted those lectures in 1934 into *Security Analysis*, a book universally regarded as the foundational document for value investment.

To Graham, who had been brought close to ruin in the 1929 stock market crash, the best estimate of intrinsic value was the most conservative one, and the most conservative estimate of intrinsic value was a stock's liquidation value. It was also the easiest to calculate, requiring little analysis beyond the application of a simple, purely quantitative rule. Graham used the so-called "net current asset value" calculation—so eagerly embraced by Thomas "Net Quick" Evans and the other White Sharks of Wall Street—to examine a company's working capital and deliver an inexact, but typically conservative, proxy for the liquidation value. Graham's objective when employing the net current asset value method was not to determine the exact liquidation value of the company, but to form a rough idea of that value in order to ascertain whether or not the shares were selling for less than the shareholders could take out of the business:[2]

> *A company's balance sheet does not convey exact information as to its value in liquidation, but it does supply clues or hints which may prove useful. The first rule in calculating liquidating value is that the liabilities are real but the assets are of questionable value. This means that all true liabilities shown on the books must be deducted at their face amount. The value to be ascribed to the assets however, will vary according to their character.*

Graham determined the net current asset value by calculating the company's current assets, and then deducting from that calculation *all* liabilities, both current and long term. Long-term asset values—for example, intangible assets and fixed assets like plants—were totally excluded from the calculation. In ordinary times, and for the vast majority of companies, the net current asset value calculated after conducting such an examination was negative, indicating a surplus of liabilities over current assets. For a small number of stocks, however, the net current asset value would be positive, indicating a surplus of cash, receivables, and inventory over all liabilities. To be considered for purchase, Graham required that a company with a net current asset surplus trade at a market capitalization no higher than two-thirds of the net current asset value. Graham found that companies satisfying the criteria—sometimes described as *net nets* because the market capitalization was *net* of the net current asset value—were often priced at significant discounts to estimates of the value that stockholders could receive in an actual sale or liquidation of the entire company.

Graham's insistence on a purchase price no more than two-thirds of the net current asset value illustrates an important element of Grahamite value investment: the margin of safety. Graham wrote in *The Intelligent Investor*:[3]

> *In the old legend the wise men finally boiled down the history of mortal affairs into the single phrase, "This too will pass." Confronted with a like challenge to distill the secret of sound investment into three words, we venture the motto, MARGIN OF SAFETY. This is the thread that rounds through all the preceding discussion of investment policy—often explicitly, sometimes in a less direct fashion.*

The *margin of safety* is the market price discount from our estimate of intrinsic value. Graham's insistence on a purchase price no more than two-thirds of net current asset value means, for example, that the margin of safety for the archetypal net-net stock at acquisition is no less than one-third of the purchase price, and our estimate of net current asset value can fall by one-third before rendering a permanent impairment of capital. The margin of safety therefore theoretically provides protection from significant permanent loss, even in liquidation scenarios where the business has little or no ongoing intrinsic value. The margin of safety also provides the opportunity for an advance as the discount between a stock's net current asset value and its market price closes. The greater the market price discount from intrinsic value, the greater the margin of safety, and the greater the possibility for investment return. If the second point sounds like a repetition of the first, it is because it is essentially the same idea considered from another perspective. The greater the margin of safety—calculated as the discount from intrinsic value—the lesser the risk of permanent impairment of capital, and the greater the possibility for return. This dual principle—lower risk equates to greater return—is axiomatic to value investment, but an impossibility under orthodox finance theory.

Why do companies trade at a discount to liquidation value? In the years following the 1929 crash a large number of companies continued to trade well below liquidation value, prompting Graham to write a series of articles for *Forbes* magazine in 1932—two years before the publication of *Security Analysis*—considering the phenomenon. Ordinarily a rare occurrence, Graham discussed a study he had commissioned in 1932 at *Columbia University School of Business* that estimated 200 of the 600 industrial companies—fully one in three—then listed on the New York Stock Exchange sold for less than their net current assets. More than 50 sold for less than their cash and marketable securities, and dozens more sold for less than the cash they held at the bank. Graham noted that this implied that in the "best judgment of Wall Street," those businesses were *"worth more dead than alive"* (emphasis Graham's).[4] One reason for the indiscriminate selling, Graham suggested, was that investors weren't paying attention to the companies' assets—not even their cash holdings. Value was associated only with earning power, and "reported earnings—which might only be temporary or even deceptive."[5] He wondered whether investors selling such deeply under-valued stocks were aware that they were disposing of their interest at "far less than its scrap value." He concluded that many investors who might have realized this could have justified the too-low sales price on the basis that the company had no intention of liquidating. Why discuss liquidation values if a company won't liquidate? The answer, according to Graham, was that, while stockholders do not have it in their power to make a business profit-able, they do have the power to liquidate it. "At bottom, he wrote, "it is not a theoretical question at all; the issue is both very practical and very pressing."[6] "Is it true," he asked, "that one out of three American businesses is destined to continue losing money until the stockholders have no equity remaining?"[7]

> *Liquidation after insolvency is, of course, more frequent, but the idea of shutting up shop before the sheriff steps in seems repugnant to the canons of Wall Street.*

More than just forgetting to look at balance sheets, wrote Graham, stockholders seemed to have forgotten also that they were *"owners of a business* and not merely owners of a quotation on the stock ticker." It was high time that the millions of American shareholders asked whether their money "should be tied up unproductively in excessive cash balances while they themselves are in dire need of funds." "These are not management problems," wrote Graham, "these are *ownership problems*," and the solu-tion was to become "ownership conscious."[8]

Graham believed it to be fundamentally illogical for a company to con-tinuously trade at a discount to liquidation value. It was a signal from the market that either the price was too low or the company should be wound up. In either case, the stock was too cheap, and therefore offered an attrac-tive area for security analysis and, potentially, an attractive purchase oppor-tunity. He likened such stocks to gold dollars with strings attached:[9]

> *If gold dollars without any strings attached could actually be pur-chased for 50 cents, plenty of publicity and plenty of buying power*

would quickly be marshaled to take advantage of the bargain. Corporate gold dollars are now available in quantity at 50 cents and less—but they do have strings attached. Although they belong to the stockholder, he doesn't control them. He may have to sit back and watch them dwindle and disappear as operating losses take their toll. For that reason the public refuses to accept even the cash holdings of corporations at their face value.

He allowed, however, that stocks trading at a discount to liquidation value did so because they "almost always have an unsatisfactory trend of earnings:"[10]

If the profits had been increasing steadily it is obvious that the shares would not sell at so low a price. The objection to buying these issues lies in the probability, or at least the possibility, that earnings will decline or losses continue, and that the resources will be dissipated and the intrinsic value ultimately become less than the price paid.

Graham responded to these objections that, while these outcomes occurred in individual cases, there was a much wider range of potential developments that would result in a higher stock price. Graham's list of developments reads like a modern activist investor's list of demands, and it included the following:[11]

1. *The creation of an earning power commensurate with the company's assets. This may result from:*
   a. *General improvement in the industry.*
   b. *Favorable change in the company's operating policies, with or without a change in management. These changes include more efficient methods, new products, abandonment of unprofitable lines, etc.*
2. *A sale or merger, because some other concern is able to utilize the resources to better advantage and hence can pay at least liquidating value for the assets.*
3. *Complete or partial liquidation.*

Graham proposed that the discerning analyst would lean toward those stocks for which she saw a fairly imminent prospect of one of these favorable developments emerging, or else she would look for other attractive statistical features like current earnings and dividends or a high average earning power in the past. The analyst would avoid issues that were rapidly dissipating their current assets and showed no definite signs of ceasing to do so. Even so, he wrote, there was "scarcely any doubt that common stocks selling well below liquidating value represent on the whole a class of undervalued securities."[12]

Other investors have been less effusive than Graham about the prospects for liquidation value stocks. *Baupost Group* Chairman Seth Klarman in his wildly popular but out-of-print book, *Margin of Safety*, reminds us that, when emulating Graham in approximating liquidation value, this assessment must be made with imperfect information, requiring several assumptions:[13]

> *As long as working capital is not overstated and operations are not rapidly consuming cash, a company could liquidate its assets, extinguish all liabilities, and still distribute proceeds in excess of the market price to investors. Ongoing business losses can, however, quickly erode net-net working capital. Investors must therefore always consider the state of a company's current operations before buying. Investors should also consider any off-balance sheet or contingent liabilities that might be incurred in the course of an actual liquidation, such as plant closing and environmental laws.*

Legendary investor and prolific author Marty Whitman, founder of value investor Third Avenue Management, illustrated some of the difficulties to which Klarman referred:[14]

> *We do net nets based more on common sense. As, for example, you have an asset, a Class A office building, financed with recourse finance, fully tenanted by credit-worthy tenants, that, for accounting purposes, is classified as a fixed asset, but, given such a building, you pick up the telephone and sell it, and really it's more current than K-Mart's inventories, for example, which is classified as a current asset.*

Warren Buffett has written that he regards the acquisition of net nets as "foolish" unless you are a liquidator, and referred to sub-liquidation stocks as "cigar butts:"[15]

> *If you buy a stock at a sufficiently low price, there will usually be some hiccup in the fortunes of the business that gives you a chance to unload at a decent profit, even though the long-term performance of the business may be terrible. I call this the "cigar butt" approach to investing. A cigar butt found on the street that has only one puff left in it may not offer much of a smoke, but the "bargain purchase" will make that puff all profit.*
> *Unless you are a liquidator, that kind of approach to buying businesses is foolish. First, the original "bargain" price probably will not turn out to be such a steal after all. In a difficult business, no sooner is one problem solved than another surfaces—never is there just one cockroach in the kitchen. Second, any initial advantage you*

secure will be quickly eroded by the low return that the business earns. For example, if you buy a business for $8 million that can be sold or liquidated for $10 million and promptly take either course, you can realize a high return. But the investment will disappoint if the business is sold for $10 million in ten years and in the interim has annually earned and distributed only a few percent on cost. Time is the friend of the wonderful business, the enemy of the mediocre.

Despite Klarman's, Whitman's, and Buffett's reservations, the research into the performance of net-net stocks seems to bear out Graham's assertion that there is "scarcely any doubt that common stocks selling well below liquidating value represent on the whole a class of undervalued securities." Buying stocks that meet Graham's net current asset value proxy for liquidation value is a remarkably well-performed investment strategy. In an interview given in 1976, Graham estimated that his net-net strategy had generated an average yearly return of 20 percent over the 30-year life of Graham-Newman, his investment management firm.[16]

We used this approach extensively in managing investment funds, and over a 30-odd year period we must have earned an average of some 20 per cent per year from this source. For a while, however, after the mid-1950s, this brand of buying opportunity became very scarce because of the pervasive bull market. But it has returned in quantity since the 1973–74 decline. In January 1976 we counted over 300 such issues in the Standard & Poor's Stock Guide—about 10 per cent of the total.

Henry Oppenheimer, then an associate professor of finance at the State University of New York at Binghamton, examined the returns to Graham's net current asset value strategy over a 13-year period from December 31, 1970, through December 31, 1983.[17] Oppenheimer's study assumed that all stocks meeting the investment criterion were purchased on December 31 of each year, held for one year, and replaced on December 31 of the subsequent year by stocks meeting the same criterion on that date. The total sample size was 645 net-net selections. The smallest annual sample was 18 stocks and the largest was 89 stocks—many fewer than Graham found in his 1932 study. Oppenheimer's conclusion about the returns to such a strategy is nothing short of extraordinary. He found that the average return over the 13-year period he examined was 29.4 percent per year versus 11.5 percent for the market. To put a compound return of that magnitude in perspective, Oppenheimer wrote that $1 million invested in the net current asset value portfolio on December 31, 1970—the start of the examination—would have increased to $25,497,300 by December 31, 1983—the end of his study. By comparison, $1 million invested in the market would have increased to just $3,729,600.

With Jeffrey Oxman and Sunil Mohanty, I tested the performance of Graham's net current asset value strategy over the 25 years from the end of Oppenheimer's data in December 31, 1983 to December 31, 2008.[18] We found the net current asset value rule returned on average 35.3 percent yearly for the full period, outperforming the market by an average of 22.4 percent yearly, and a comparable Small Firm Index portfolio by an average of 16.9 percent yearly. The fewest selections were found in 1984, with only 13 stocks meeting the criteria. We found the most in 2002, when 152 stocks met Graham's rule. These are astonishing returns, and they are not unique to the United States.

Other studies of Graham's net current asset value rule have found the same market-beating form in major international markets. A study of the Japanese market from 1975 to 1988 found that Graham's criterion led to average returns in excess of the market of approximately 13 percent per year.[19] A similar study of net-net stocks listed on the London Stock Exchange over the period 1981 to 2005 found average returns in excess of the market of 19.7 percent per year.[20] The paper, from the business school of the University of Salford in the United Kingdom, reported that stocks selected using Graham's strategy substantially outperformed the London Stock Exchange main market over holding periods of up to five years. Adopting Oppenheimer's method, the authors found that £1 million invested in the net current asset value portfolio starting on July 1, 1981, would have increased to £432 million by June 2005, which is an extraordinary 29 percent per year compounded. By comparison, £1 million invested in the entire UK market would have increased to £34 million by the end of June 2005.

Behavioral finance expert and value investor James Montier examined the returns to a strategy that purchased a portfolio of net-net stocks in all developed markets globally over the period 1985 to 2007.[21] Montier found that the strategy averaged an outstanding 35 percent per year, beating a comparable market portfolio return of 17 percent per year. An annual return of 35 percent over 23 years puts the strategy in elite company indeed. Montier's findings point to some of the common characteristics of net-net portfolios. First, the median portfolio contained 65 stocks, indicating that the universe for net-net stocks globally is relatively few in number. He also found the median market capitalization of net-net stocks in the portfolio to be U.S. $21 million, indicating that the portfolios tended to contain small-to-micro capitalization stocks. Of course, not all net nets are tiny. Apple, Inc. (Nasdaq:AAPL) was a net net in 2002, trading at a split-adjusted $7 per share in October of that year, which gave it a market capitalization of a little over $2.5 billion. At the time it possessed $7.80 per share in cash net of all debt, and was profitable. Ten years later in October 2012 it would trade at $700 per share, close to its all-time peak, and up

100-fold over the decade. Graham's net current asset value strategy yields some extraordinary bargains, and this is the source of its extraordinary returns.

Graham's instinct about the margin of safety turns out to be correct. The greater the discount from net current asset value, the greater the return. Oppenheimer examined this by calculating for each stock its purchase price as a proportion of its net current asset value, and then dividing the population into five portfolios, from the smallest margin of safety to the widest. Oppenheimer's conclusion was clear cut: The portfolios of stocks with the widest margin of safety—or, in other words, the most undervalued— outperformed the next portfolio and so on until the portfolio with the smallest margin of safety delivered the lowest returns. Oppenheimer found that the size of the margin of safety, and therefore the degree of undervaluation, was an important consideration—the most undervalued net nets delivered more than 10 percent a year in additional return over the least undervalued net nets. We replicated Oppenheimer's method, and found essentially the same results, with one caveat that is as significant as it is perplexing. Our findings generally supported Oppenheimer's conclusion—the returns are higher for firms with higher discounts to net current asset value— however, the stocks in the portfolio with the deepest discount from net current asset value had the lowest returns. It's possible that the result is an outlier, and it's worth bearing in mind, but it doesn't change the finding that there is a positive relationship between the size of the discount and returns.

Graham recommended that the "discerning analyst" tend toward those net current asset value stocks likely to attract the attention of an activist or with other attractive statistical features, like current earnings and dividends. Here, Oppenheimer's findings contradict Graham's advice. Graham's ordinarily prescient intuition about the earnings and dividends seems to be wrong, perhaps because this finding is so counterintuitive. Oppenheimer tested Graham's suggestion by dividing the net current asset value stocks into two portfolios—one containing only stocks that had been profitable over the preceding year, and another containing only stocks that had been operating at a loss. He found that the portfolio containing stocks operating at a loss tended to *outperform* the portfolio of profitable stocks. He also found that profitable, dividend-paying stocks generated a lower return than profitable stocks that did not pay a dividend. These findings led Oppenheimer to conclude that choosing only profitable stocks or profitable dividend-paying stocks would lead to lower returns. Our results supported Oppenheimer's conclusion. Profitable net-net stocks significantly underperformed the loss-makers, and profitable dividend payers significantly underperformed the profitable stocks that did not pay dividends.

Graham observed that "[t]he objection to buying these issues lies in the probability, or at least the possibility, that earnings will decline or losses continue, and that the resources will be dissipated and the intrinsic value ultimately become less than the price paid."[22] There seems to be some validity to this concern on an individual company level. In his study, Montier found that an individual stock selected by the net current asset value strategy was more likely to suffer a permanent loss of capital than the average stock. Montier found that about 5 percent of net current asset value stocks declined 90 percent or more in a single year, while only 2 percent of all stocks suffered a similar decline. Paradoxically, it seems that what is true at the individual company level is not true at an aggregate level. The net-net portfolios had fewer down years than the market. Net nets only suffered losses at the portfolio level in three years in the entire 23-year sample Montier tested. By contrast, the overall market witnessed some six years of negative returns.[23] So not only did the strategy outperform over the full period, it had fewer losing years, even though the average net net was two-and-a-half times more likely than the average stock to suffer a terminal decline. These are intriguing results, and demonstrate some of the counterintuitive phenomena—the hallmark of deep value investment—that we'll investigate in detail later.

ONE OF THE MYSTERIES OF OUR BUSINESS

When Graham appeared before the U.S. Senate Committee on Banking and Currency in 1955 to testify in its investigation into the "factors affecting the buying and selling of equity securities," he was asked by the Chairman how it was that undervalued stocks returned to fair value, a question central to value investment:[24]

> When you find a special situation and you decide, just for illustration, that you can buy for 10 and it is worth 30, and you take a position, and then you cannot realize it until a lot of other people decide it is worth 30, how is that process brought about—by advertising, or what happens?

Graham's response is vintage Graham, but it is unlikely to have satisfied the Chairman. "That is one of the mysteries of our business," he explained, "and it is a mystery to me as well as to everybody else. We know from experience that eventually the market catches up with value. It realizes it in one way or another."[25] The Chairman's question is perhaps the most important question for value investors. How does an undervalued stock find its fair value? In his widely sought-after out-of-print book *Margin of Safety*, legendary investor Seth Klarman wrote:[26]

A corporate liquidation typically connotes business failure; but ironically, it may correspond with investment success. The reason is that the liquidation or breakup of a company is a catalyst for the realization of the underlying business value. Since value investors attempt to buy securities trading at a considerable discount from the value of a business's underlying assets, a liquidation is one way for investors to realize profits.

Is the source of the returns the catalyst, an event like a liquidation, merger, or some other cause? Seth Klarman advises that investors seek catalysts, both to generate return and to reduce risk:[27]

Value investors are always on the lookout for catalysts. While buying assets at a discount from underlying value is the defining character-istic of value investing, the partial or total realization of underlying value through a catalyst is an important means of generating prof-its. Furthermore, the presence of a catalyst serves to reduce risk. If the gap between price and underlying value is likely to be closed quickly, the probability of losing money due to market fluctuations or adverse business developments is reduced. In the absence of a catalyst, however, underlying value could erode; conversely, the gap between price and value could widen with the vagaries of the mar-ket. Owning securities with catalysts for value realization is there-fore an important way for investors to reduce the risk within their portfolios, augmenting the margin of safety achieved by investing at a discount from underlying value.

Is it necessary, as Buffett suggests, to be a liquidator to make the strategy profitable? The theoretical basis for the strategy as described by Graham is the shareholder's ultimate right to wind up the company and retrieve his or her capital. Buying stocks for less than liquidation value may only make sense because a legal mechanism exists for recovering more cash than needs to be invested to set this process in motion. For most investors, however, their share-holding will be too small to trigger the legal mechanism, and so their rights are for all intents and purposes not enforceable. Can an investor who is not a liquida-tor, or unable to trigger the legal mechanism, still profit from a net-net strategy? In *Margin of Safety*, Klarman wrote that a "liquidation is, in a sense, one of the few interfaces where the essence of the stock market is revealed:"[28]

Are stocks pieces of paper to be endlessly traded back and forth, or are they proportional interests in underlying businesses? A liqui-dation settles this debate, distributing to owners of pieces of paper

*the actual cash proceeds resulting from the sale of corporate assets
to the highest bidder. A liquidation thereby acts as a tether to reality
for the stock market, forcing either undervalued or overvalued share
prices to move into line with actual underlying value.*

Absent Klarman's "tether to reality," do undervalued stock prices move
into line with actual underlying value? It seems that they do. In fact, it turns
out that most net-net stocks are not liquidated or merged.

As Graham and Klarman have pointed out, liquidation analyses—
including the net current asset value proxy for liquidation value—are
theoretical exercises in valuation. A liquidation is not usually the actual
approach to value realization. The reason is that assets of a company are
worth more as part of a going concern than in liquidation, so liquidation
value is considered the worst-case scenario. Recall that Graham proposed
a wide range of potential developments other than liquidation that would
result in a higher stock price. In my research with Jeffrey Oxman and Sunil
Mohanty, we looked specifically at the range of outcomes for net-net stocks.
We found that very few stocks were liquidated or merged. In fact, of the
1,362 stocks in our sample, only nine firms were delisted due to liquidation
(0.66 percent of the sample), and another five were delisted through merger
(0.37 percent of the sample). Thus, excluding these firms made little difference to our estimate of the returns. It seems that it's not necessary for these
stocks to attract attention from liquidators to advance. What, then, drives
the returns to net-net stocks?

The exact mechanism by which the discount between intrinsic value
and market price closes remains as much of a mystery today as it was in
Graham's day. While a liquidation, like a merger, is one of the catalytic possibilities for value realization, our research shows that it is an exceedingly
rare occurrence. This means that the most likely outcome is earnings generation commensurate with assets. Note that this development occurs in companies that Graham had previously identified as almost always having an
unsatisfactory trend in earnings—"[i]f the profits had been increasing
steadily it is obvious that the shares would not sell at so low a price."[29] What
causes a stock with a poor earnings record to spontaneously begin generating adequate earnings, and to close the market price discount from intrinsic
value? Graham suggested that it might be due to an improvement in the
industry or through a change in the company's operating policies, with or
without a change in management, but that's not really a satisfactory answer.
He knew it, too, and this is why he described it as one of the mysteries of
the business. Whatever its apparent cause, the narrowing of the discount
between price and value is a phenomenon called mean reversion, and it is
fundamental to deep value investment.

MEAN-REVERTING QUALITATIVE ELEMENTS

Graham warned in *Security Analysis* that the inclusion of certain qualitative factors in a valuation without an appreciation of the impact of mean reversion would inadvertently introduce into the analysis errors of overvaluation or, more unusually, undervaluation. Graham classified the elements of a security analysis in two groupings: quantitative and qualitative. The quantitative factors—what Graham described as the stock's *statistical exhibit*—were simply the company's financial statements and other information about the company's production and order book. The qualitative factors included "the nature of the business; the relative position of the individual company in the industry; its physical, geographical, and operating characteristics; the character of the management; and, finally, the outlook for the unit, for the industry, and for business in general."[30] Most of the effort should be "devoted to the figures," wrote Graham, because the qualitative elements would include, "a large admixture of mere opinion," and so should be treated in a "superficial or summary fashion."[31]

To the extent that one would consider qualitative factors, the most important were the nature of the business and the quality of the management, but they were both "exceedingly difficult to deal with intelligently."[32] The reason, argued Graham, was that most people had definite, though erroneous notions as to what constituted a "good" business based on mere conjecture or their own bias.[33] Their assessment of the nature of the business was often based on its very recent performance:[34]

> It is natural to assume that industries which have fared worse than the average are "unfavorably situated" and therefore to be avoided. The converse would be assumed, of course, for those with superior records. But this conclusion may often prove quite erroneous. Abnormally good or abnormally bad conditions do not last forever. This is true of general business but of particular industries as well. Corrective forces are usually set in motion which tend to restore profits where they have disappeared, or to reduce them where they are excessive in relation to capital.

Businesses with good records were likely the beneficiaries of a favorable business environment, and so were likely primed for the intrusion of "corrective forces" and a period of stagnation. Similarly, businesses that had endured poor conditions were more likely to enjoy a period of bounty. The analyst assuming present conditions would persist missed the mean-reverting nature of business conditions and profitability in relation to capital. What about assessing the abilities of management? There, Graham suggested that the analyst would meet with the same difficulty because "[o]bjective tests of managerial ability were few and far from scientific:"[35]

> *In most cases the investor must rely upon the reputation which may or may not be deserved. The most convincing proof of capable management lies in a superior comparative record over a period of time. But this brings us back to the quantitative data.*
>
> *There is a strong tendency in the stock market to value the management factor twice in its calculations. Stock prices reflect the large earnings which the good management has produced, plus a substantial increment for "good management" considered separately.*

Graham described this as "counting the same trick twice," and wrote that it was a frequent cause of overvaluation. The final qualitative factor that Graham warned against was assuming a trend in earnings. In what was then apparently a recent occurrence, but is a common occurrence today, analysts projected a past trend—be it earnings, sales, or some other fundamental measure—into the future and used the projection as the basis for valuing the security. The fact that the process included figures made it appear "mathematically sound" when it was in fact a "definite prediction of either better or poorer results, and it must be either right or wrong:"[36]

> *The factors that we mentioned previously as militating against the maintenance of abnormal prosperity or depression are equally opposed to the indefinite continuance of an upward or downward trend. By the time the trend has become noticeable, conditions may well be ripe for a change.*

Thus, placing too much weight on the trend would lead to errors of overvaluation or undervaluation:[37]

> *This is true because no limit may be fixed on how far ahead the trend should be projected; and therefore the process of valuation, while seemingly mathematical, is in reality psychological and quite arbitrary.*

Graham warned that a trend was merely the statement of an assumption about future prospects in the "form of an exact prediction." Just as conclusions about the nature of the business or the abilities of management, the trend found its chief significance as a forecasting tool when it was difficult to separate it from the prevailing business conditions. All of these qualitative factors suffer from the same basic problem: That it is impossible to determine the extent to which they are already reflected in the price of a given security:[38]

> *In most cases, if they are recognized at all, they tend to be overemphasized. We see the same influence constantly at work in the general market. The recurrent excesses of its advances and declines are due at bottom to the fact that, when values are determined chiefly by the outlook, the resultant judgments are not subject to any mathematical controls and are almost inevitably carried to the extremes.*

Graham suggested that the analyst treat the qualitative and quantitative elements thus: The analyst's conclusions "must rest upon the figures and upon established tests and standards," but they may be "completely vitiated by qualitative considerations of an opposite import."[39] Qualitative factors were important, "But whenever the commitment depends to a substantial degree upon these qualitative factors—whenever, that is, the price is considerably higher than the figures alone would justify—then the analytical basis of approval is lacking."[40] The analyst should be concerned primarily with values that are supported by facts and not with those that depend on expectations. This differentiated the security analyst from the speculator, whose success turned on his or her ability to guess the future, where the analyst sought not to profit from the future, but to guard against it. Graham wrote that the analyst viewed "the business future as a hazard which his conclusions must encounter rather than as the source of his vindication."[41] It was a telling statement, illustrating the extent to which Graham was a product of the 1929 stock market crash. It would take Graham's best student, Warren Buffett, to turn this advice on its head.

Notes

1. United States Government Printing Office. Washington. 1955. Available at http://www4.gsb.columbia.edu/filemgr?file_id=131668.
2. Benjamin Graham and David Dodd. *Security Analysis: The Classic 1934 Edition.* (New York: McGraw Hill) 1934.
3. Benjamin Graham. *The Intelligent Investor: A Book of Practical Counsel.* (New York: HarperBusiness) 2006. (First published 1949).
4. Benjamin Graham. "Inflated Treasuries and Deflated Stockholders." *Forbes,* 1932. Available at http://www.forbes.com/forbes/1999/1227/6415400a.html.
5. Benjamin Graham. "Should Rich but Losing Corporations Be Liquidated?" *Forbes,* 1932. Available at http://www.forbes.com/forbes/1999/1227/6415410a.html.
6. Graham and Dodd.
7. Graham, "Inflated Treasuries." 1932.
8. Ibid.

9. Benjamin Graham. "Should Rich but Losing Corporations Be Liquidated?" *Forbes*, 1932. Available at http://www.forbes.com/forbes/1999/1227/6415410a.html.
10. Graham and Dodd.
11. Ibid.
12. Ibid.
13. Seth A. Klarman. *Margin of Safety: Risk-Averse Value Investing Strategies for the Thoughtful Investor* (New York: HarperCollins) 1991.
14. "Marty Whitman on Graham and Dodd." July 2008. Available at http://www.youtube.com/watch?v=Hlj3fMUx73c.
15. Warren Buffett. "Chairman's Letter." *Berkshire Hathaway, Inc., Annual Report*. 1989.
16. Graham, 1976.
17. Henry R. Oppenheimer. "Ben Graham's Net Current Asset Values: A Performance Update." *Financial Analysts Journal*, Vol. 42, No. 6 (1986), pp. 40–47.
18. Jeffrey Oxman, Sunil K. Mohanty, and Tobias Eric Carlisle. "Deep Value Investing and Unexplained Returns." (September 16, 2011) Midwest Finance Association 2012 Annual Meetings Paper. Available at SSRN: http://ssrn.com/abstract=1928694 or http://dx.doi.org/10.2139/ssrn.1928694.
19. John B. Bildersee, John J. Cheh, and Ajay Zutshi. "The Performance of Japanese Common Stocks in Relation to Their Net Current Asset Values." *Japan and the World Economy*, Vol. 5, No. 3 (1993), pp. 197–215.
20. Ying Xiao and Glen Arnold. *Testing Benjamin Graham's Net Current Asset Value Strategy in London*. Available at SSRN: http://ssrn.com/abstract=966188 or http://dx.doi.org/10.2139/ssrn.966188.
21. James Montier. "Graham's Net Nets: Outdated or Outstanding." *SG Equity Research*. Societe Generale, 30 September 2008.
22. Ibid.
23. Ibid.
24. United States Government Printing Office. Washington. 1955. Available at http://www4.gsb.columbia.edu/filemgr?file_id=131668.
25. United States Government Printing Office. Washington. 1955. Available at http://www4.gsb.columbia.edu/filemgr?file_id=131668.
26. Klarman, 1991.
27. Ibid.
28. Ibid.
29. Graham and Dodd, 1934.
30. Ibid.
31. Ibid.
32. Ibid.
33. Ibid.
34. Ibid.
35. Ibid.
36. Ibid.
37. Ibid.
38. Ibid.
39. Ibid.
40. Ibid.
41. Ibid.

CHAPTER 3

Warren Buffett: Liquidator to Operator

How Charlie Munger and Phil Fisher's Scuttlebutt Pushed Buffett Beyond Graham

*"It's like a finger pointing at the moon.
Do not concentrate on the finger or you will miss all of the heavenly
glory!"*
— Bruce Lee, *Enter the Dragon* (1973)

Warren Buffett first heard about Charlie Munger on a Sunday afternoon in 1957. He was meeting with two potential investors for his nascent investment partnership, Dr. Edward "Eddie" Davis and his wife, Dorothy, in their home. Sitting in their living room, the young Buffett—he was 26 but looked 18 according to Eddie—laid out the ground rules for an investment in the partnership. For over an hour Buffett described his philosophy on managing money and the unusual terms of his proposed investment partnership— Buffett would have absolute control over the money and would not tell his partners how he was invested; they would get an annual summary of his returns and could only withdraw the money annually on December 31. All the while, Eddie Davis sat in the corner, doing nothing, and not, so it seemed to Buffett, paying attention to him. When Buffett finished his high-speed soliloquy, Dorothy, who had been listening very intently, turned to Eddie and said, "What do you think?"[1] Eddie responded, "Let's give him a hundred thousand dollars." Politely, Buffett replied, "Doctor Davis, you know, I'm delighted to get this money. But you weren't really paying a lot of attention to me while I was talking. How come you're doing it?" Eddie turned to Buffett and said,

"Well, you remind me of Charlie Munger." Buffett replied, "Well, I don't know who this Charlie Munger is, but I really like him." The Davises invested with Buffett, but he and Munger would not meet for another two years. When they did finally meet, the result would be one of the most enduring and successful American business partnerships ever formed.

Buffett had created his first Buffett Partnership on May 1, 1956, after his teacher and mentor, Benjamin Graham, decided to wind up the Graham-Newman Corporation where Buffett was employed. When Graham decided to retire, Buffett simply continued in the Buffett Partnerships as he had at Graham-Newman, thumbing through the same *Standard and Poor's* and *Moody's Manuals*, page by page, looking for classic Graham-style net nets. While Buffett regarded himself as Graham's intellectual heir, and ran the Buffett Partnerships as Graham would, he showed an early intention to develop his own style and slowly moved away from his strict application of Graham's principles. Where Graham liked to diversify, buying many small positions, Buffett preferred to concentrate on his best ideas. Graham had counseled that it was futile to spend time examining the quality of a found cigar butt: The margin of safety was in the discount to liquidation value. Graham knew that a number of the cigar butts would go bust, but he also believed that, on average, the portfolio would work out. Buffett used his prodigious ability to absorb numbers in the *Standard and Poor's* and *Moody's Manuals* to winnow down the universe of net nets into those few that were so cheap as to be almost free. Said Buffett to his biographer Alice Schroeder, "I would pore through volumes of businesses and I'd find one or two that I could put ten or fifteen thousand dollars into that were just *ridiculously* cheap."[2] Where Graham did not like to visit management—he called this "self-help"[3] and felt that an investor should be an outsider who confronted managements rather than rubbed shoulders with them—Buffett liked to become friendly with management. Buffett hoped that he might be able to use his charm to influence the company to do the right thing. Still, he hadn't drifted far from Graham's cigar butt investment philosophy when he finally met Charlie Munger.

Buffett and Munger met on a hot summer Friday in 1959 at the Omaha Club. Charles T. Munger, six years Buffett's senior, didn't know much about the 28-year-old Buffett. Before long, the two were talking simultaneously and understanding each other perfectly. Buffett talked about Graham and value investing. He also described the investment partnerships he ran and his returns to date: up 10 percent in 1957 against a market that was down 8 percent; up 40 percent in 1958 against a return of 38.5 percent for Dow; and he would end up 25.9 percent in 1959, again beating the Dow, up 19.9 percent.[4] Impressed, Munger asked, "Do you think *I* could do something like that out in California?"[5] Buffett replied, "Yeah, I'm quite sure you could do it."[6]

Buffett's biggest position in 1959—taking up more than one-third of the partnerships' capital—was Sanborn Map. Sanborn published extremely detailed maps of power lines, water mains, driveways, building engineering, roof composition, and emergency stairwells for all the cities of the United States. Fire insurance companies purchased the bulk of Sanborn's maps, and they used them to conduct national underwriting activities from a central office. For 75 years the business operated as a virtual monopoly, with profits realized in each year and no need for strenuous sales activity. Buffett explained in his 1961 partnership letter that Sanborn was a vintage Graham stock: The business was shrinking as insurance companies merged—profitability was down from $500,000 annually in the 1930s to around $100,000 annually in 1958 on sales of $2.5 million—but it owned an investment portfolio worth more than $7 million or $65 per share.[7] The shares traded for $45. Buffett noted that, in 1938, when Sanborn sold for $110 per share, the investment portfolio was worth $20 per share, implying a business value at that time of $90 per share. By 1958, some 20 years later, the $45 stock price then implied that the same map business was worth *negative* $20 per share, or the investment portfolio worth 69 cents on the dollar with the map business thrown in for free.

The Buffett Partnerships bought 46,000 shares out of the 105,000 on issue—enough of Sanborn to have Buffett elected to the board. Prior to Buffett's elevation to the board, dividends had been cut five times in eight years, but, he noted dryly, he "could never find any record of suggestions pertaining to cutting salaries or director's and committee fees."[8] At his first board meeting in March 1959 Buffett learned why the stock was so cheap. The other board members were representatives of the insurance companies, Sanborn's biggest customers, and they held between them only a token 46 shares, one-one thousandth of Buffett's holding. Buffett proposed liquidating the investment portfolio and distributing it to the shareholders. The other board members were opposed, and immediately ruled out the idea. Later, Buffett proposed that the company take out all stockholders who wanted out with portfolio securities at fair value. The board agreed to avoid a proxy fight, which Buffett would have been certain of winning. Around 50 percent of the 1,600 shareholders, representing 72 percent of the stock, accepted the offer. Buffett subsequently noted in his partnership letter that such "control situations" would be infrequent. His "bread-and-butter" business was "buying undervalued securities and selling when the undervaluation is corrected along with investment in "special situations" where the profit is dependent on corporate rather than market action."[9]

Buffett and Munger had continued talking on the telephone an hour or more daily after Munger returned to California. In 1962, Buffett talked him into forming his first investment partnership, Wheeler, Munger & Company. Run out of a tiny mezzanine office on Spring Street near the Skid Row section of Los Angeles, Munger Wheeler raised money by promising to hew closely to Graham's investment precepts. While he was initially a strict Grahamite—buying cigar butts and investing in special situations—differences in his investment philosophy and Graham's were soon apparent. Munger was not as impressed as Buffett with all of Graham's principles, saying, "Ben Graham had blind spots. He had too low an appreciation for the fact that some businesses are worth paying big premiums for."[10] Munger continued to follow Graham's most fundamental teachings—value stocks as a private business owner would, and buy and sell with reference to intrinsic value—but he wasn't interested in Graham's cigar butt stocks. He wasn't interested in bargains for their own sake. Munger thought some businesses were "worth paying up a bit to get in with for a long-term advantage."[11] When analyzing an investment, Munger considered both quality and price. "[T]he trick," according to Munger, "is to get more quality than you pay for in price. It's just that simple." It was simple, but it was also revolutionary.

Munger tried to persuade Buffett to move away from Graham's practice of considering the margin of safety in purely quantitative terms, arguing that a high-quality business provided more margin of safety than a purchase price at a discount from liquidation value. Stocks trading at a discount to liquidation value typically owned poor businesses. Munger had strong opinions on low-quality businesses. He had learned how difficult it was to fix up a struggling business as a director of an International Harvester dealership in Bakersfield, California. The dealership, as painful as it had been to administer, had given Munger an important insight into the difference between high- and low-quality businesses. International Harvester consumed capital. Each new machine had to be purchased before it could be sold, tying up capital that sat just sat on the lot. Munger wanted a business that not only grew without soaking up capital, but threw off cash as it did so. What were the qualities of such a business, he wondered. He asked people, "What's the best business you've ever heard of?"[12] As he explored the idea, he saw the limitations to Graham's investment methodology. In Munger's opinion Graham was too conservative. He saw the future "more fraught with hazard than ripe with opportunity,"[13] which was in stark contrast to Buffett's natural optimism. He expounded to Buffett at length on the virtues of high quality businesses, but found him resistant because of the esteem in which he held Graham. The turning point for Buffett was American Express.

THE AMERICAN EXPRESS CRISIS

In late 1963, American Express was embroiled in the infamous salad-oil fraud perpetrated by a client, commodities trader Anthony "Tino" De Angelis.

De Angelis dealt in soybean oil, which he stored in tanks in his New Jersey warehouse. While American Express's main business was its Traveler's Cheques, and credit cards, it also had a smaller business issuing warehouse receipts, a document that provided proof of ownership of commodities stored for safekeeping in a warehouse. American Express issued De Angelis with warehouse receipts verifying the amount of soybean oil in his tanks, which De Angelis turned around and sold, or used as collateral for loans. At some stage he figured out that he could trick the inspectors into believing he owned more soybean oil than he actually did, and so began to substitute seawater for soybean oil. De Angelis got so good at fooling the inspectors that he eventually controlled more soybean oil than there was in existence.[14] The ruse was discovered when the market moved violently against him, and he was unable to meet margin calls from his broker. De Angelis was immediately wiped out. The position was so big that it also sent his broker into bankruptcy. Facing a fraudulent De Angelis and his bankrupt broker, De Angelis's lenders naturally went looking for some deep pockets to sue. They found American Express, the company that had actually issued the warehouse receipts certifying the soybean oil existed. The sum sought was $175 million—more than 10 times American Express's earnings in 1964— and it wasn't clear that American Express could survive an award of that magnitude. The stock price was cut in half.

His interest piqued, Buffett had his broker, Henry Brandt, find the *scuttlebutt*—rumors or gossip—on American Express. Philip Fisher, a renowned San Francisco-based growth investor, had first used the term in his 1958 book *Common Stocks and Uncommon Profits*.[15] Fisher advocated the use of the *scuttlebutt method* to identify qualitative factors that might give an investor original insight into a potential investment. Gleaned from competitors, customers, or suppliers, these qualitative considerations might include the skill of management; the utility of the research and development or technology; the business's service ability or customer orientation; or the effectiveness of marketing. Fisher used the totality of the information garnered through the scuttlebutt method to determine the business's ability to grow and defend its market against competitors through technological superiority, service excellence, or a consumer franchise.[16] Buffett was concerned that De Angelis's fraud and American Express's potential liabilities might stop other businesses from accepting Traveler's Cheques and American Express cards, which would destroy the franchise. He asked Brandt to find out if restaurants and other businesses that usually took American Express were still accepting them.

This was an unusual question from Buffett, who was usually more interested in quantitative questions about the assets or liabilities of a company, but Brandt undertook to fulfill it with his usual vigor. He staked out banks, restaurants, hotels, American Express cardholders, and delivered to Buffett a foot-high pile of material.[17] Buffett also visited several restaurants in Omaha, and saw that they continued to accept the card. Buffet's assessment of the scuttlebutt was that American Express was temporarily reeling from the effects of a fiscal blow that would not destroy its exceptional underlying economics. It was an "extraordinary business franchise with a localized excisable cancer," and it would survive.[18] Buffett put about 40 percent of the partnerships' capital into the stock. It was the largest investment the partnerships had ever made, and gave Buffett control of more than 5 percent of American Express's stock at a cost of $13 million. American Express settled with the lenders in 1965 for $60 million, and the stock, which had plunged below $35, quickly popped to $49 per share.[19]

American Express was a substantial departure from Graham's purely quantitative method. Where Graham had explicitly warned against considering the nature of the business, Buffett was including it in his assessment. But Buffett hadn't abandoned Graham completely. Two cigar butts—Texas Gulf Producing and Pure Oil—made up another third of the portfolio. The theses for these two were both simply Grahamite statistical undervaluation. Buffett said that the quantitative approach remained his "bread-and-butter,"[20] but he acknowledged it had its limitations. By 1966 such quantitative bargains were few and far between, and when they could be found, they tended to be very small. Like his capital, Buffett was starting to outgrow Graham. His investment in American Express had uncovered another limitation to Graham's purely statistical strategy. American Express's value was not to be found on its balance sheet, but in its business. It was very definitely worth more alive than dead, possessing little in the way of hard assets that could be liquidated, but a great deal of value in the consumer franchise. Buffett saw that the consumer franchise had an advantage over the cigar butt: The consumer franchise would continue to compound, while the cigar butt possessed but a single puff. For this reason, the consumer franchise presented a better investment, but it didn't meet Graham's strict guidelines. By 1967 Buffett had resolved the issue sufficiently in his own mind to discuss it in his partnership letter:[21]

> The evaluation of securities and businesses for investment purposes has always involved a mixture of qualitative and quantitative factors. At the one extreme, the analyst exclusively oriented to qualitative factors would say, "Buy the right company (with the right prospects, inherent industry conditions, management, etc.) and the price will take care of itself." On the other hand, the quantitative spokesman would say, "Buy at the right price and the company (and stock) will take care of itself."

. . .

Interestingly enough, although I consider myself to be primarily in the quantitative school (and as I write this no one has come back from recess—I may be the only one left in the class), the really sensational ideas I have had over the years have been heavily weighted toward the qualitative side where I have had a "high-probability insight." This is what causes the cash register to sing. However, it is an infrequent occurrence, as insights usually are, and, of course, no insight is required on the quantitative side—the figures should hit you over the head with a baseball bat. So the really big money tends to be made by investors who are right on qualitative decisions, but, at least in my opinion, the more sure money tends to be made on the obvious quantitative decisions.

The force of Munger's logic, it seemed, had yielded results. By 1969, Buffett would describe himself in an interview with *Forbes Magazine* as "15 percent Phil Fisher, and 85 percent Benjamin Graham."[22] Buffett now regards *Common Stocks and Uncommon Profits* as a "book that ranks behind only *The Intelligent Investor* and the 1940 edition of *Security Analysis* in the all-time-best list for the serious investor."[23] Says Buffett, "Charlie shoved me on the direction of not just buying bargains, as Ben Graham had taught me. This was the real impact he had on me. It took a powerful force to move me on from Graham's limiting view. It was the power of Charlie's mind."[24] With the philosophical leap made, Buffett would take the final step in his evolution as a value investor with the 1972 acquisition of See's Candies.

SEE'S CANDIES

When Buffett received the call that See's Candies was for sale, his immediate response was, "Call Charlie."[25] Munger had all kinds of scuttlebutt on See's, and was effusive when he spoke to Buffett, "See's has a name that no one can get near in California. . . . We can get it at a reasonable price. It's impossible to compete with that brand without spending all kinds of money."[26] Buffett took a look at the numbers, and agreed that he "would be willing to buy See's at a price."[27] But the price offered, it turned out, was very high. Harry See wanted $30 million for a company that owned just $8 million in assets. The $22 million more than the hard assets were worth bought the See's brand, the trademarks, the goodwill, and a business that would earn just under $2 million after-tax in 1971. Buffett balked. He was, after all, still only 15 percent Fisher, and See was asking an extraordinarily expensive price. Munger was adamant that See's was worth paying up for, and so Buffett countered with a price that would have made Graham blush: $25 million, which equated to a price-to-earnings ratio of 12.5, and a price-to-book-value ratio of 4. See was initially reluctant to lower his price, but Buffett and Munger were at the "exact dollar limit of what [they were] willing to pay."[28] Any higher, and Buffett would have walked. See eventually caved, and on January 31, 1972, Buffett and Munger bought See's Candies for $25 million. Fittingly, the acquisition was undertaken through Blue Chip Stamps, a partially owned Berkshire Hathaway, Inc. subsidiary run by Munger.

Buffett's insight into the valuation of See's Candies, and his willingness to pay such an apparently exorbitant price, was the value of See's consumer franchise. See's chocolate was, according to Buffett, particularly high quality and preferred by lovers of chocolate to candy costing two or three times as much.[29] Additionally, Buffett observed that the quality of See's customer service in company-owned shops was "every bit as good as the product," and "as much a trademark of See's as is the logo on the box."[30] Cumulatively, these qualities created an unassailable consumer franchise that allowed See's to take commodity raw materials—sugar, cocoa beans, and milk—and transform them into a particularly high-margin product. That consumer franchise only grew as See's become part of a tradition for Californians.

Where Graham might have assessed the quantity of tangible assets possessed by the company as warranting a lower purchase price—perhaps a discount to book value, to provide a margin of safety—Buffett had another "high-probability insight." He saw that See's ability to generate high returns on little invested capital made those tangible assets worth a substantial premium to book value. See's high returns on the little capital it employed allowed it to grow rapidly, throwing off cash as it did so, exactly the qualities that Munger had assessed as being the hallmarks of a high-quality business. But what was See's worth? See's had earned just less than $5 million pre-tax in 1971, generating an extraordinary 60 percent return on the $8 million in tangible assets. Assuming a discount rate of between 10 and 12 percent—for comparison, the 10-year treasury rate in January 1972 was 5.95 percent—See's was worth between 5 and 6 times its invested capital, or between $40 and $48 million. Illustrating that, true to his word, Buffett was still 85 percent Graham, the $25 million purchase price was only one-half to two-thirds of See's intrinsic value. Even if Buffett had paid full price, however, See's would still have been an extraordinary investment.

In his 2007 letter to shareholders, Buffett described See's as the "prototype of a dream business."[31] That year it earned for Berkshire Hathaway, Inc. $82 million on just $40 million of capital, generating an extraordinary 195 percent return on capital. The more than sixteen-fold growth in earnings from $5 million to $82 million required only a five-fold growth in its tiny invested capital. This allowed See's to return to Berkshire Hathaway all the earnings it generated between 1972 and 2007—$1.35 billion—less the $32 million required for See's organic growth. By way of comparison, Buffett estimated that an average business would have required an additional $400 million invested in working capital and fixed assets to grow earnings in the same magnitude, and would have been worth less than See's after having done so. Instead, Buffett and Munger were able to redirect most of See's excess earnings to purchasing other high-quality businesses, and Berkshire Hathaway became a financial powerhouse.

In 1989 Buffett would distill the investment lessons he had learned from Graham, Munger, Fisher, and See's into a single sentence, "It's far better to buy a wonderful company at a fair price than a fair company at a wonderful price."[32] It would become a familiar refrain. Graham had established the philosophy of value investment: The concept of intrinsic value as a quantity distinct from price, and the importance of a margin of safety. He had also established a number of ideas about the manner in which intrinsic value could be assessed, and was so expansive in his teachings that he left very little ground uncovered for future value investors. It is apt that the only student of Graham's to receive an A+ in his class would find new ground within Graham's framework, which he achieved by blending Phil Fisher's philosophy with Graham's. Buffett's divergence from Graham's methods was not a rejection of Graham's philosophy, but rather an extension of it. It was prompted by the increasingly large sums of capital he had to invest and Munger's insistence that Graham's view was a limiting one, ignoring pertinent facts like business quality. Buffett has regularly acknowledged Munger's influence on his "wonderful company at a fair price" investment process. In 1989 he said, "Charlie understood this early; I was a slow learner. But now, when buying companies or common stocks, we look for first-class businesses accompanied by first-class managements."[33]

HOW TO RUN A CANDY STORE (AND A FEW THINGS BUFFETT LEARNED ABOUT BUSINESS VALUATION)

The lesson Buffett took from See's is that a business's intrinsic value is a function of the return it generates on the capital invested in it—the higher the return on invested capital, the greater the business's intrinsic value. This was an unusual idea. Shortly after Graham published *Security Analysis* in 1934, John Burr Williams published his 1938 masterpiece *The Theory of Investment Value* in which he described the classic theory of "net present value."[34] On a topic suggested by the great economist Joseph

Schumpeter—most famous for his description of capitalism as "creative destruction"[35]—Williams's thesis closely mirrored Graham's worldview: a security's price and its intrinsic value were distinct properties. William's innovation was that the intrinsic value could be calculated by the present value of its future cash flows. In his 1992 Berkshire Hathaway, Inc. Chairman's Letter, Buffett described Williams's theory as it applies to businesses, stocks, and bonds:[36]

> *In* The Theory of Investment Value, *written over 50 years ago, John Burr Williams set forth the equation for value, which we condense here:* The value of any stock, bond or business today is determined by the cash inflows and outflows—discounted at an appropriate interest rate—that can be expected to occur during the remaining life of the asset. *Note that the formula is the same for stocks as for bonds. Even so, there is an important, and difficult to deal with, difference between the two: A bond has a coupon and maturity date that define future cash flows; but in the case of equities, the investment analyst must himself estimate the future "coupons." Furthermore, the quality of management affects the bond coupon only rarely—chiefly when management is so inept or dishonest that payment of interest is suspended. In contrast, the ability of management can dramatically affect the equity "coupons." The investment shown by the discounted-flows-of-cash calculation to be the cheapest is the one that the investor should purchase—irrespective of whether the business grows or doesn't, displays volatility or smoothness in its earnings, or carries a high price or low in relation to its current earnings and book value. Moreover, though the value equation has usually shown equities to be cheaper than bonds, that result is not inevitable: When bonds are calculated to be the more attractive investment, they should be bought.*

Williams's *discounted cash flow* theory of intrinsic value is the foundation of modern finance, and forms the intellectual basis for a variety of valuation models. Buffett took William's discounted cash flow theory and extended it to properly value growth in a business. According to Buffett, measures traditionally used in business valuation—book value, earnings, and growth—were flawed in their application. Intrinsic business value was "*the measurement that really counts,*" Buffett emphasized in his 1983 *Chairman's Letter*:

> *Book value's virtue as a score-keeping measure is that it is easy to calculate and doesn't involve the subjective (but important) judgments employed in calculation of intrinsic business value.*

It is important to understand, however, that the two terms—book value and intrinsic business value—have very different meanings. Book value is an accounting concept, recording the accumulated financial input from both contributed capital and retained earnings. Intrinsic business value is an economic concept, estimating future cash output discounted to present value. Book value tells you what has been put in; intrinsic business value estimates what can be taken out.

Earnings—central to William's net present value theory—were only useful in context with invested capital. Despite his obvious regard for William's theory, Buffett could show that two businesses with identical earnings could possess wildly different intrinsic values if different sums of invested capital generated those earnings. Most surprising was Buffett's observation that growth in and of itself was not necessarily good, but could in fact destroy value. Only businesses earning a return on invested capital exceeding the rate required by the market should grow. Businesses with returns on capital falling below that threshold were turning dollars in earnings into cents-on-the-dollar in business value.

The valuation of businesses using Buffett's method is a subjective process, falling somewhere between an art and an inexact science. We can, however, extract some rough guidelines. There are two considerations when valuing a business—the quantitative and the qualitative—and each informs the other. The quantitative leg of a theoretical valuation employing Buffett's insight is relatively simple:[37]

The economic case justifying equity investment is that, in aggregate, additional earnings above passive investment returns—interest on fixed-income securities—will be derived through the employment of managerial and entrepreneurial skills in conjunction with that equity capital. Furthermore, the case says that since the equity capital position is associated with greater risk than passive forms of investment, it is "entitled" to higher returns. A "value-added" bonus from equity capital seems natural and certain.

All else being equal, the higher the return on invested capital, the more valuable the business. For example, if we assume all earnings are paid out and we ignore the impact of tax, a business returning 20 percent on invested capital in perpetuity—a "good" business—is four times as valuable as another earning 5 percent on invested capital in perpetuity—a "bad" business. If long-term taxable government bonds yield 10 percent, then the good business earning 20 percent on equity is worth no more than twice

(20 percent ÷ 10 percent = 2×) its invested capital, and the bad business earning 5 percent on invested capital is worth no more than half its invested capital (5 percent ÷ 10 percent = 0.5×). For both the good and bad business the intrinsic value is "no more than" the value calculated. The quantitative value is the ceiling from which we must discount the valuations to account for the degree to which each business can sustain its return on capital and the risk of each business relative to the government bonds.

If the yield on the long-term taxable government bond changes, the intrinsic values of the businesses change too. If the yield on the government bond falls to 5 percent, the value of the bad business rises to no more than its invested capital (5 percent ÷ 5 percent = 1×), and the value of the good business rises to no more than four times its invested capital (20 percent ÷ 5 percent = 4×). On the other hand, if the yield on the government bond rises to say 20 percent, the value of the bad business falls to no more than one-quarter its invested capital (5 percent ÷ 20 percent = 0.25×), and the value of the good business falls to no more than one times its invested capital (20 percent ÷ 20 percent = 1×). "The rates of return that investors need from any kind of investment," wrote Buffett in 1999, "are directly tied to the risk-free rate that they can earn from government securities:"[38]

> *The basic proposition is this: What an investor should pay today for a dollar to be received tomorrow can only be determined by first looking at the risk-free interest rate.*
>
> *Consequently, every time the risk-free rate moves by one basis point—by 0.01%—the value of every investment in the country changes. People can see this easily in the case of bonds, whose value is normally affected only by interest rates. In the case of equities or real estate or farms or whatever, other very important variables are almost always at work, and that means the effect of interest rate changes is usually obscured. Nonetheless, the effect—like the invisible pull of gravity—is constantly there.*

While we initially made the simplifying assumption that all earnings are paid out, in actuality the proportion of earnings reinvested and the proportion paid out as dividends is hugely influential to the valuation. For the purposes of this exercise, let's ignore the impact of taxes. With the long bond earning 10 percent, each dollar of earnings reinvested in the good business earning a 20 percent return on capital will immediately return up to 200 cents on the dollar in business value (20 percent ÷ 10 percent), which is a very good return. Contrast this with the return to the owner of the bad business returning 5 percent on capital. Each dollar of earnings reinvested in that business will become 50 cents on the dollar in business value

(5 percent ÷ 10 percent), thereby chewing up half the value of any dollar invested in it. The owner of the good business earning 20 percent on invested capital wants the business to reinvest, and grow because that growth is profitable. The owner of the bad business earning 5 percent on invested capital wants all the earnings paid out because the "growth" destroys value. In a cruel irony, most good businesses earning high returns on invested capital can't absorb much incremental capital without reducing those high returns, while most bad businesses earning low returns on invested capital require all earnings be reinvested simply to keep up with inflation. Bad businesses that can only earn sub-par returns destroy capital until they are liquidated. The sooner the business is liquidated, the more value that can be salvaged. The longer the good business can maintain a high return on invested capital, the more valuable the business. What then distinguishes the first-class business from the ordinary business? The differentiator is not simply high returns on capital, which, as Graham pointed out, even an ordinary business will earn at some point in the business cycle, but *sustainable* high returns on capital throughout successive business cycles. The sustainability of high returns depends on the business possessing good economics protected by an enduring competitive advantage, or what Buffett describes as "economic castles protected by unbreachable 'moats.'"[39]

First-Class Businesses

A business's intrinsic value turns on its ability to sustain high returns on invested capital and resist reversion to the mean. For it to be worth more than its invested capital, it must have economics that allow it to generate a return greater than its required return and to protect that super-normal return over the course of the business cycle. For most businesses, high returns on invested capital are unlikely to be sustainable for the simple reason that high returns attract competitors and competition erodes high returns (and, by extension, intrinsic value). Their returns will revert to the average return. This is why the moat is so important to the castle:[40]

> *A truly great business must have an enduring "moat" that protects excellent returns on invested capital. The dynamics of capitalism guarantee that competitors will repeatedly assault any business "castle" that is earning high returns. Therefore a formidable barrier such as a company's being the low-cost producer (GEICO, Costco) or possessing a powerful world-wide brand (Coca-Cola, Gillette, American Express) is essential for sustained success. Business history is filled with "Roman Candles," companies whose moats proved illusory and were soon crossed.*

Illustrating the centrality to his investment philosophy of the moat, Buffett has given over a great deal of space in his Berkshire Hathaway, Inc. Chairman's Letters to a meditation on the physiology of competitive advantages. It is the presence or absence of a competitive advantage that allows the enterprise to resist mean reversion in its business and to continue earning super-normal returns on capital. Most businesses succumb to competitive pressures, and this is why Buffett instructs the managers in his controlled businesses to "unendingly focus on moat-widening opportunities."[41] He also seeks the special cases that resist mean reversion—the "economic franchise"—which he distinguishes, a little confusingly, from an ordinary "business" thus:[42]

> *An economic franchise arises from a product or service that: (1) is needed or desired; (2) is thought by its customers to have no close substitute and; (3) is not subject to price regulation. The existence of all three conditions will be demonstrated by a company's ability to regularly price its product or service aggressively and thereby to earn high rates of return on capital. Moreover, franchises can tolerate mismanagement. Inept managers may diminish a franchise's profitability, but they cannot inflict mortal damage.*
>
> *In contrast, "a business" earns exceptional profits only if it is the low-cost operator or if supply of its product or service is tight. Tightness in supply usually does not last long. With superior management, a company may maintain its status as a low-cost operator for a much longer time, but even then unceasingly faces the possibility of competitive attack. And a business, unlike a franchise, can be killed by poor management.*

The so-called *economic franchise* is therefore a special business with unusual, naturally occurring economics that allow it to earn a naturally high return on invested capital over the course of the business cycle and to sustain that return despite the incursions of competitors. Where competition causes the return of the average business—one with a weak or no competitive advantage—to revert to the mean, franchises and first-class businesses resist mean reversion.

Most businesses over the course of a full business cycle will do no better than earn their required return. In peak earnings years they will appear to be good businesses earning a return exceeding the required return, but in trough earnings years they will look like bad businesses generating subnormal returns. While a theoretical valuation might suggest that the decision to retain earnings or pay out dividends in a normal business—one that earns no more than its required return over the full cycle—makes no difference to intrinsic value, it is a vitally important, and often counterintuitive, decision. Reinvestment will appear most attractive in peak years, and folly in trough years, but the reverse is usually the case because trough earnings follow peak earnings, and vice versa. Capital reinvested in peak years earns sub-normal returns as the business cycle moves toward a trough, and so is typically more valuable in shareholders' hands. Capital reinvested in trough years has the opportunity to earn super-normal returns as the business cycle moves toward a peak, but often little incremental capital can be harvested organically because earnings are in a trough. In another cruel irony, businesses find capital in abundance—both from retained earnings and outside investors—when they need it least and scarce when they need it most. Management teams can therefore distinguish themselves through the careful husbanding of capital over the business cycle, anticipating mean reversion at both peaks and troughs, and this is why Buffett insists that first-class businesses be accompanied by first-class management.

First-Class Management

Skilled managers maximize a business's intrinsic value by maximizing its return on invested capital, which means managing both the numerator (the return) and the denominator (the invested capital) over the course of the business cycle. In practice, this means paying out as much of the return as possible, and any fallow invested capital, to minimize the invested capital employed in the business. This reduces the size of the invested capital denominator and increases the ratio of return on invested capital. It also means avoiding investments that might incrementally increase earnings, but offer a return on invested capital below the threshold rate of return set by the market. Most managers, through their employment contracts, bonuses, and option grants, are *de facto* incentivized not to maximize the return on invested capital, but to maximize only the growth in the numerator—the earnings. To illustrate this odd phenomenon, Buffett asked his shareholders in 1985 to imagine a $100,000 savings account earning 8 percent interest and managed by a trustee who could decide each year what portion of the interest they were to be paid in cash.[43] Interest not paid out would be retained earnings added to the savings account to compound. The trustee set the pay-out ratio at one-quarter of the annual earnings. Under these assumptions, the savings account would contain $179,084 at the end of 10 years. Additionally, the annual earnings would have increased about 70 percent from $8,000 to $13,515 under this management. And, finally, their dividends would have increased commensurately, rising regularly from $2,000 in the first year to $3,378 in the tenth year. Buffett wryly observed, "Each year, when your manager's public relations firm prepared his annual report to you, all of the charts would have had lines marching skyward,"[44] but such growth was clearly no great managerial achievement if you could "get the same result personally while operating from your rocking chair:"[45]

> [J]ust quadruple the capital you commit to a savings account and you will quadruple your earnings. You would hardly expect hosannas for that particular accomplishment. Yet, retirement announcements regularly sing the praises of CEOs who have, say, quadrupled earnings of their widget company during their reign—with no one examining whether this gain was attributable simply to many years of retained earnings and the workings of compound interest. If the widget company consistently earned a superior return on capital throughout the period, or if capital employed only doubled during the CEO's reign, the praise for him may be well deserved. But if return on capital was lackluster and capital employed increased in pace with earnings, applause should be withheld.

In Buffett's definition, first-class managements would understand the economics of their businesses and manage the denominator—the invested capital—to maximize the return on it, and, therefore, the intrinsic value. Buffett recognized, however, that there were limits to what management could achieve:[46]

> Good jockeys will do well on good horses, but not on broken-down nags.
>
> . . .
>
> The same managers employed in a business with good economic characteristics would have achieved fine records. But they were never going to make any progress while running in quicksand.
> I've said many times that when a management with a reputation for brilliance tackles a business with a reputation for bad economics, it is the reputation of the business that remains intact.

We can now see the contours of Buffett's *wonderful company* in its entirety. A wonderful company owns a first-class business and is led by a first-class management. A first-class business earns sustainable high returns on invested capital because of its good economics and resistance to competition. The franchise is a special case with unusual economics that allow it to naturally resist competition and earn super-normal returns on capital. First-class managers will maintain and increase high returns on capital by regulating the amount of capital invested in the business and continually widening the business's moat. When these conditions are present, the business's intrinsic value is optimized. These are the elements of Buffett's wonderful companies. The archetypal wonderful company—think See's Candies—grows with minimal incremental reinvestment, compounding the intrinsic value at a high rate while paying out most earnings. Provided that the business continues to earn returns in excess of the required rate of return and sustain its competitive advantage, investors are rewarded for holding wonderful companies for long periods or, as Buffett quips, "[W]hen we own portions of outstanding businesses with outstanding managements, our favorite holding period is forever."[47] This allows the investment to compound without paying capital gains tax and is one of the main reasons that wonderful companies appear to be such attractive investment opportunities.

With this leap made, Buffett had left Graham behind. Where Graham had warned against relying on qualitative matters, Buffett embraced them. Not only that, he embraced two particular factors that Graham had explicitly warned against—the nature of the business and the ability of the management. Graham believed that it was impossible to separate out unusually good returns on capital or uncommonly adept management from a stock enjoying favorable business conditions. "Corrective forces" Graham warned, "are usually set in motion which tend to restore profits where they have disappeared, or to reduce them where they are excessive in relation to capital."[48] Buffett acknowledged Graham's caveat, but believed that there existed some businesses earning high returns on invested capital able to resist Graham's corrective forces due to their extraordinary economics. Able management would only prosper on such high-quality businesses, but was essential in managing the capital tied up in the business and maintaining the competitive advantage. The story does not, however, end here.

Notes

1. Alice Schroeder. *The Snowball*. (New York: Bantam Books) 2008.
2. Ibid.
3. Ibid.
4. Warren Buffett, "The Superinvestors of Graham-and-Doddsville." *Hermes, Columbia Business School Magazine*. Fall, 1984.
5. Schroeder, 2008.
6. Ibid.
7. Warren Buffett, "Partnership Letter: 1960." *Buffett Associates Limited*, 1961.
8. Ibid.
9. Ibid.
10. Janet Lowe. "Damn Right: Behind the Scenes with Berkshire Hathaway Billionaire Charlie Munger." (New York: Wiley, 2003).
11. Lowe, 2003.

12. Schroeder, 2008.
13. Ibid.
14. Ibid.
15. Philip Fisher. *Common Stocks and Uncommon Profits*. (New York: Wiley Investment Classics) 1996.
16. Fisher, 1996.
17. Schroeder, 2008.
18. Buffett, 1980.
19. Schroeder, 2008.
20. Warren Buffett. "Partnership Letter: 1967." *Buffett Associates Limited*, October 9, 1967.
21. Ibid.
22. "The Money Men: How Omaha Beats Wall Street." *Forbes Magazine*, November 1, 1969.
23. Warren Buffett. "Chairman's Letter." *Berkshire Hathaway, Inc. Annual Report*, 2013.
24. Lowe, 2003.
25. Schroeder, 2008.
26. Ibid.
27. Lowe, 2003.
28. Schroeder, 2008.
29. Warren Buffett. "Chairman's Letter." *Berkshire Hathaway, Inc. Annual Report*, 1983.
30. Buffett, 1983.
31. Warren Buffett. "Chairman's Letter." *Berkshire Hathaway, Inc. Annual Report*, 2007.
32. Warren Buffett. "Chairman's Letter." *Berkshire Hathaway, Inc. Annual Report*, 1989.
33. Ibid.
34. J. B. Williams. *The Theory of Investment Value*. (Burlington, Vermont: Fraser Publishing Co.) 1997.
35. Joseph A. Schumpeter. *From Capitalism, Socialism and Democracy*. (New York: Harper) 1975.
36. Warren Buffett. "Chairman's Letter." *Berkshire Hathaway, Inc. Annual Report*, 1992.
37. Warren Buffett. "Chairman's Letter." *Berkshire Hathaway, Inc. Annual Report*, 1981.
38. Warren Buffett and Carol Loomis, "Mr. Buffett on the Stock Market." *Forbes Magazine*, November 22, 1999. Available at http://money.cnn.com/magazines/fortune/fortune_archive/1999/11/22/269071/
39. Warren Buffett. "Chairman's Letter." *Berkshire Hathaway, Inc. Annual Report*, 1995.
40. Warren Buffett. "Chairman's Letter." *Berkshire Hathaway, Inc. Annual Report*, 2007.
41. Warren Buffett. "Chairman's Letter." *Berkshire Hathaway, Inc. Annual Report*, 2012.
42. Warren Buffett. "Chairman's Letter." *Berkshire Hathaway, Inc. Annual Report*, 1991.
43. Warren Buffett. "Chairman's Letter." *Berkshire Hathaway, Inc. Annual Report*, 1985.
44. Ibid.
45. Ibid.
46. Warren Buffett. "Chairman's Letter." *Berkshire Hathaway, Inc. Annual Report*, 1989.
47. Warren Buffett. "Chairman's Letter." *Berkshire Hathaway, Inc. Annual Report*, 1988.
48. Benjamin Graham and David Dodd. *Security Analysis: The Classic 1934 Edition*. (New York: *McGraw Hill*) 1934.

CHAPTER 4

The Acquirer's Multiple

Fair Companies at Wonderful Prices

*"Our statistical screens are merely exploiting a group of underval-
ued stocks that are easily identified and are further protected by
strong balance sheets and large asset values. Additionally, because
of the depressed nature and liquid make-up of the companies
that meet our test criteria, they are often the object of takeover
initiatives."*

—Joel Greenblatt, *How The Small Investor
Beats The Market* (1981)

Joel Greenblatt conducted an experiment in 2002 to see if a computer
could be taught to invest like Warren Buffett. Greenblatt, a renowned
value investor and adjunct professor at the Columbia University Graduate
School of Business, has a long history researching and writing about value
investment strategies. As a 19-year-old student at the Wharton School
he read about Benjamin Graham in an article in *Forbes Magazine* called
"Ben Graham's Last Will and Testament."[1] The article described an interview Graham had given to the *Financial Analysts Journal* months before
his death in 1976 in which he had said that he was "no longer an advocate of elaborate techniques of security analysis in order to find superior
value opportunities." "All that was required," said Graham, "were a few
techniques and simple principles."[2] The most important thing was that
investors "buy groups of stocks that meet some simple criterion for being
undervalued—regardless of the industry and with very little attention to
the individual company."[3] Graham proposed investors use his net current
asset value proxy for liquidation value, which he regarded as a "foolproof

method of systematic investment" and "unfailingly dependable and satis-factory."[4] Greenblatt was intrigued. He decided to test Graham's statistical criteria for stocks selling below liquidation value.

With Wharton classmates Rich Pzena and Bruce Newberg, he labored through a pile of old *Standard and Poor's* stock guides and marked up the returns by hand. Greenblatt wanted to test the strategy's performance through a period of extreme market conditions, so he chose the volatile six-year period beginning April 1972 through April 1978. This period included the great market plunge of late 1974 during which the market almost halved, and the subsequent strong recovery that saw the market double. As they were valuing each company and tracking the returns by hand, they limited their universe to companies with market capitalizations $3 million and above beginning with the letters A or B. This sample included about 750 companies, representing approximately 15 percent of the stocks listed in the *Standard and Poor's* stock guides. After several months of painstakingly test-ing four variations of Graham's criteria, Greenblatt, Pzena, and Newberg had their results. They found that each variation of Graham's formula selected portfolios that beat the market by more than 10 percent yearly, including one that averaged 42.2 percent per year over the full period (for comparison, the market returned 1.3 percent yearly over the same period). Greenblatt wrote up the results, and the article appeared in the *Journal of Portfolio Management* in 1981 as "How the small investor can beat the market."[5]

In the article, Greenblatt et al., asked, "Why does it work?" Perhaps foreshadowing his later research on Buffett's strategy, Greenblatt responded, "We were unable to discover any 'magic' qualities associated with stocks selling below liquidation value:"[6]

> *Simply stated, by limiting our investments to stocks that according to fundamental notions of stock valuation appear severely depressed, we were able to locate more than our share of these inefficiently priced, undervalued securities. In other words, there are probably many more undervalued stocks that are not selling below liquida-tion value.*

More than 20 years after his test of Graham's net current asset value criteria, and following an outstanding career as the co-portfolio manager of Gotham Capital during which it returned 50 percent[7] annually, Greenblatt turned his attention to Buffett. If, as he had surmised in 1981, there were many more undervalued stocks *not* selling below liquidation value, who better than Buffett to help identify them?

Greenblatt proposed to test Buffett's *wonderful company at a fair price* strategy, but such an examination presented a greater challenge than

Graham's statistical criteria had. Buffett's strategy was not designed to be applied algorithmically to select a portfolio, as Graham's was, but appeared to rely on Buffett's uncanny abilities as a business analyst. How could Buffett's strategy be codified, and how would a systematic application of those quantitative elements perform without Buffett's superior insight into the qualitative elements of the business: First-class management and a first-class business, meaning an enduring moat and good economics? Greenblatt read through Buffett's *Berkshire Hathaway, Inc. Annual Report* "Chairman's Letters" to break down his strategy into its component parts—a wonderful company, and a fair price—and to find a quantifiable definition for each.

Buffett's classification of a wonderful company in particular seemed to resist quantification. How could Greenblatt simply identify a first-class business with a first-class management? In his 1977 *Chairman's Letter*, Buffett showed the way:[8]

> *Except for special cases (for example, companies with unusual debt-equity ratios or those with important assets carried at unrealistic balance sheet values), we believe a more appropriate measure of managerial economic performance to be return on equity capital.*

Greenblatt reinterpreted Buffett's *return on equity capital* measure as *return on capital*, which he construed as the ratio of *pre-tax operating earnings* (*earnings before interest and taxes*, or EBIT) to *tangible capital* employed in the business (Net Working Capital + Net Fixed Assets), defined as follows:[9]

Return on Capital = EBIT ÷ (Net Working Capital + Net Fixed Assets)

The use of EBIT for *pre-tax operating earnings* makes the *return on capital* ratio comparable across different capital structures. This is important because the particular mix of debt and equity in a company impacts the interest paid and the tax rate, and therefore reported earnings. (Greenblatt makes the simplifying assumption that maintenance capital expenditures equate to depreciation and amortization, and so can be excluded from the *operating earnings* calculation.) EBIT makes an apples-to-apples comparison possible. For *tangible capital* Greenblatt uses Net Working Capital + Net Fixed Assets, rather than say *total assets*, to determine the amount of capital each company actually requires to conduct its business. Greenblatt's Net Working Capital ratio therefore does not punish a company that carries excess cash (cash beyond the amount required to fund its receivables and inventory). Net Fixed Assets—the depreciated cost of a company's fixed assets—is included in the *tangible capital* calculation because a company must also fund the purchase of its real estate, plant, and equipment. The ratio resulting from the calculation is easy to interpret: The better the business and the harder management works the tangible capital tied up in the company, the higher *operating earnings* will be in relation to *tangible capital*. In other words, the higher the *return on capital* ratio, the more wonderful the company.

To determine a fair price, Greenblatt uses *earnings yield*, which he defines as follows:

$$\text{Earnings Yield} = \text{EBIT} \div \text{EV}$$

Greenblatt's *earnings yield* is like the inverse of the more familiar price/earnings (P/E) ratio, but varies in two important ways. First, Greenblatt substitutes *enterprise value* (EV) for market capitalization (the *price* in the P/E ratio). *Enterprise value* is the cost an acquirer must pay to take over a company in its entirety. It comprises the full market capitalization, including any preferred stock; any debt, which an acquirer must service; any minority interests; and adjusts for excess cash, which an acquirer can redeploy. Enterprise value gives a more full picture of the actual price an acquirer must pay than market capitalization alone. Second, Greenblatt uses EBIT rather than *earnings* for the same reason that he uses it in the *return on capital* ratio: *Earnings* are influenced by a company's capital structure, whereas EBIT is agnostic, allowing us to compare companies on a like-for-like basis. Like the ratio resulting from the *return on capital* calculation, the *earnings yield* is easy to interpret: The higher *operating earnings* are in relation to *enterprise value*, the higher the *earnings yield*, and the better the value.

With Buffett's *wonderful company at a fair price* strategy quantified and therefore codeable, in 2005 Greenblatt asked a young Wharton graduate acquaintance with experience in computer programming to test it. There would be no onerous testing by hand as there had been in the 1970s. Instead, the programmer instructed the computer to do the heavy lifting, and examine the largest 3,500 stocks, excluding certain financial stocks and utilities, in a historical database of stock prices and fundamental data going back to 1988. In each year, the program would assign to each stock in the universe a rank based on its *earnings yield* and another rank based on its *return on capital*. It would then add each stock's *earnings yield* rank and *return on capital* rank to generate a new combined rank for each stock. The program formed an equally weighted portfolio—meaning the theoretical portfolio capital is divided equally among all the stocks—in each year of the 30 stocks with the best combined rank. It then tracked the performance of the portfolio over the following 12 months. Rinse and repeat for each year in the database. When the process was complete Greenblatt examined the results. Quoting Graham, he found them "quite satisfactory."[10]

Over the 17 years tested from 1988 to 2004, portfolios of 30 stocks with the best combination of *earnings yield* and *return on capital* would have returned 30.8 percent per year. To put this in context, wrote Greenblatt, investing at 30.8 percent per year for 17 years would have turned $11,000 into well over $1 million. Over the same period, the market returned just 12.4 percent per year, which would have turned the same $11,000 into just $79,000. Further, Greenblatt found that his portfolios generated those returns while taking much less risk than the overall market. The smallest company in Greenblatt's 3,500 stock universe had a market capitalization of just $50 million. If he limited the universe to the largest 2,500 stocks—this time the smallest company in the universe would have a market capitalization of $200 million—the Magic Formula's average annual return dropped to a still very impressive 23.7 percent, almost double the market's return. In a universe limited to just the largest 1,000 stocks—the smallest company would have a market capitalization in excess of $1 billion—the Magic Formula still generated an average annual return of 22.9 percent. The three computer simulations of Greenblatt's quantified and simplified version of Buffett's *wonderful company at a fair price* investment strategy suggested that it would have substantially beaten the market, and done so with less risk. Greenblatt was so impressed with the results that he called the simple criteria the "Magic Formula," and wrote about it in a 2006 book called *The Little Book That Beats The Market*.[11] Greenblatt has now built his mechanical Buffett. With business partner Robert Goldstein he founded an investment firm, Gotham Asset Management, to systematically implement the Magic Formula in a variety of different investment vehicles.

Many investors, when exposed to the Magic Formula, seem skeptical that such simple criteria could reliably select stocks that beat the market on average, and by such a wide margin. The criticism clusters around two main objections. First, the critics claim the Magic Formula will not work as it did in the test period because it is a product of data mining. Data mining is the repeated examination of a data set to uncover a relationship that exists only coincidentally, and is therefore unlikely to persist outside the data set. The critics imply that Greenblatt tested many different factors and combinations of factors until he found one that beat the market. He then retroactively fitted a plausible-sounding explanation to those factors, and the Magic Formula was the result. The second criticism is that the Magic Formula does select *stocks* that appear to beat the market, but an *investor* could not use it to beat the market because the stocks selected are too small and illiquid. Curious, with Wes Gray, a 2010 Ph.D. graduate from the University of Chicago's Booth School of Business finance program, I analyzed Greenblatt's Magic Formula for our book *Quantitative Value* (2012).[12] We tested the Magic Formula to the academic gold standard, meaning that, among other things, we examined historical data outside the period tested by Greenblatt and controlled for small-capitalization stocks. Our findings surprised us, and revealed a deep truth about value investment, one that is often lost in the scramble to emulate Buffett.

ANALYSIS OF THE MAGIC FORMULA

Our independent investigation into the Magic Formula found that it did outperform the market, and by a wide margin, as Greenblatt claimed, but not in the same magnitude. We also found that the returns were concentrated in smaller market capitalization stocks, but not so small as to be uninvestable for all but the very largest institutional investors. We examined the performance of the Magic Formula over the period 1964 to 2011—considerably longer than the period examined by Greenblatt, and including years both prior to and after his study—and excluded smaller capitalization stocks, which we defined as any stock falling outside the S&P 500 Index. For context, the smallest company in the S&P 500 Index in January 2014 is $3.4 billion, the median market capitalization is $16.5 billion, and the average is $35 billion. These are very large companies. We also weighted the remaining stocks by market capitalization to make the portfolios comparable to the S&P 500 Index, which is market-capitalization weighted, to adjust for any bias to small capitalization stocks. We found that, even under these arduous conditions, Greenblatt's Magic Formula outperformed the S&P 500 Total Return Index (which includes dividends, as does the Magic Formula) over the full sample, returning on average 13.9 percent annually compared to 10.5 percent for the market over the same period. Figure 4.1 shows a logarithmic chart of the performance of the market-weighted Magic Formula and the S&P 500 Total Return Index.

The Magic Formula achieved this 3.3 percent yearly outperformance at approximately the same level of risk (using the academic definition of standard deviation, 16.5 percent for the Magic Formula against 15.2 percent for the market). 330 basis points—3.3 percent yearly—might not look like a big edge, but compounded over the full period, it meant that the Magic Formula earned almost six times the market's return. $10,000 invested in the Magic Formula grew to $12.2 million, while the same amount invested in the market grew to just $2.1 million. The Magic Formula's performance was also quite reliable through the full period, beating the market in 85 percent of rolling 5-year periods, and 97 percent of rolling 10-year periods. We concluded that, while the results were not as impressive as the equal-weighted results claimed by Greenblatt, in the very large capitalization stocks we tested the market-capitalization-weighted Magic Formula

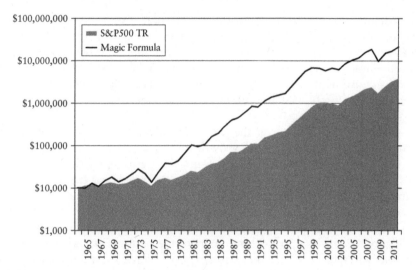

FIGURE 4.1 Logarithmic Chart of Magic Formula and S&P 500 (Total Return) Performance (1964 to 2011)
Source: Eyquem Investment Management LLC.

did substantially and regularly outperform the S&P 500 Index over the full period, and at comparable risk to the market. In short, we concurred with Greenblatt's assessment that the Magic Formula was, to quote Graham, "quite satisfactory."

Further studies examining the returns to the Magic Formula outside the United States have found comparable market-beating results. In 2006 James Montier tested the returns to the Magic Formula in Europe, the UK, and Japan using data from between 1993 and 2005.[13] He limited the universe to stocks comprising the FTSE and the MSCI indices, each of which contains large capitalization stocks. Montier equally weighted the stocks, which has the effect of boosting returns, but controlled for this by comparing the results to equally weighted versions of the indices. Montier found that the Magic Formula outperformed the market by 8.8 percent in Europe (excluding the UK), 7.3 percent in the UK, and 10.8 percent in Japan, and all did so at lower risk than the respective market. Montier concluded that his "results certainly support the notions put forward in the *Little Book*. In all the regions, the *Little Book* strategy substantially outperformed the market, and with lower risk!"[14] The out-of-sample evidence is compelling that the Magic Formula has consistently beaten the market, and at comparable or lower risk. Whether we examine differently sized stocks measured by market capitalization, or different markets geographically and temporally, the Magic Formula has outperformed. But what drives the returns to the Magic Formula? Is it really mimicking Buffett's *wonderful companies at fair prices* strategy, finding first-class businesses with first-class managements, or is something else at work? Eager to know, we devolved the Magic Formula into its constituent parts—*return on capital* and *earnings yield*—and tested each independently over the full data period. The results were, to say the least, a little surprising.

In the United States over the period 1974 to 2011, the Magic Formula generated a compound annual growth rate of 13.94 percent, beating the market's annual average of 10.46 percent.[15] The *earnings yield* alone, however, earned 15.95 percent annually, while the *return on capital* measure earned just 10.37 percent annually. You read that right. The *earnings yield* alone beat out the Magic Formula, and the *return on capital* measure underperformed the market, dragging down the return to the Magic Formula with it. Figure 4.2 shows a logarithmic chart of the performance of the market-weighted Magic Formula, the earnings yield alone, the return on capital measure alone, and the S&P 500 Total Return Index.

Perhaps *return on capital* contributed something else to the Magic Formula, lowering its risk or improving its consistency? Table 4.1 shows the results. The standard deviation of returns to the Magic Formula over the full period was 16.93 percent, against 17.28 percent for the *earnings yield*, and

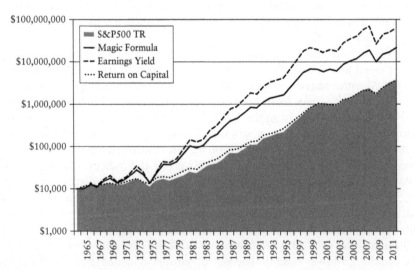

FIGURE 4.2 Logarithmic Chart of Magic Formula (Market Weight), Earnings Yield, Return on Capital, and S&P 500 (Total Return) Performance (1974 to 2011)
Source: Eyquem Investment Management LLC.

TABLE 4.1   Performance Statistics for Magic Formula (Market Weight), Earnings Yield, Return on Capital, and S&P 500 (Total Return) (1974 to 2011)

	Magic Formula	Earnings Yield	Return on Capital	S&P 500 TR
CAGR (%)	13.94	15.95	10.37	10.46
Standard Deviation (%)	16.93	17.28	17.04	15.84
Downside Deviation (%)	12.02	11.88	11.35	11.16
Sharpe Ratio	0.55	0.64	0.35	0.37
Sortino Ratio (MAR = 5%)	0.80	0.96	0.56	0.56
Rolling 5-Year Outperformance (%)	—	15.11	84.38	80.10
Rolling 10-Year Outperformance (%)	—	11.28	89.91	96.44
Correlation	—	0.927	0.806	0.872

Data Source: Wesley Gray and Tobias Carlisle. *Quantitative Value: A Practitioner's Guide to Automating Intelligent Investment and Eliminating Behavioral Errors.* (Hoboken: Wiley Finance) 2012.

17.04 percent for *return on capital.* While the Magic Formula did seem to have a slightly lower standard deviation than the *earnings yield* or *return on capital* alone, if we limited the statistic to just downside deviation, which measures just the extent to which the portfolios deviate below the mean return, we found that the Magic Formula's downside deviation was slightly higher than the *earnings yield* or *return on capital* alone. The Magic Formula's downside deviation was 12.02 percent, against 11.88 percent for the *earnings yield* and 11.35 percent for *return on capital,* which means that the *earnings yield*'s higher standard deviation was tilted toward the upside. For the period tested, the earnings yield had the best volatility-adjusted return ratios, earning a Sharpe ratio of 0.64 against the Magic Formula's 0.55 and *return on capital*'s 0.35, and a Sortino ratio of 0.96 against the Magic Formula's 0.80 and *return on capital*'s 0.56. On every return or volatility measure, the *earnings yield* beat out the Magic Formula, which means that *return on capital* did not reduce volatility. Neither did *return on capital* improve the Magic Formula's consistency. While the returns to the *earnings yield* and the Magic Formula were closely correlated—as one would expect because one is a component of the other—on a rolling 5-year basis, the *earnings yield* beat out the Magic Formula 15.1 percent of the time, and about 11.3 percent of the time on a rolling 10-year basis. What does *return on capital* contribute to the Magic Formula? Startlingly, it seems to add little but poorer returns and elevated volatility.

Montier had similar finding in his research into the performance of the Magic Formula and its constituent parts in Europe (excluding the United Kingdom), the United Kingdom, and Japan, shown in Table 4.2.[16] The *earnings yield* alone outperformed the Magic Formula in each market but Japan. In Europe, the *earnings yield* generated a compound annual return of 22.2 percent (versus 22 percent for the Magic Formula), in the UK the *earnings yield* returned 22.6 percent (versus the Magic Formula's 17 percent), and in Japan the *earnings yield* generated an average annual return of 14.5 percent (versus 18.1 percent for the Magic Formula), but it did so at considerably reduced volatility relative to the Magic Formula. In the UK the *earnings yield* delivered very sizeable gains over the Magic Formula. In Europe *return on capital* contributed little. The *earnings yield* slightly outperformed the Magic Formula, but did so at a slightly elevated volatility. In Japan, the *return on capital* measure improved returns, but did so at higher volatility. Montier concluded that *earnings yield* alone is "very powerful," and bore out his belief as a value investor that "buying bad companies at very low prices is also a perfectly viable strategy, provided, of course, they don't go bankrupt."[17]

Again, the evidence is compelling that the Magic Formula outperforms the market, but not because it identifies wonderful companies at fair prices. Wonderful companies, defined in this context as ones earning a high return on capital, reduce returns. The data suggest that the better bet is fair companies at wonderful prices. The *why* of it reveals two truths about value

TABLE 4.2 Summary Performance Statistics for Magic Formula (Equal Weight), Earnings Yield, Return on Capital, and Market in the US, Europe, the UK, and Japan (1993 to 2005)

	Magic Formula	Earnings Yield	Market
CAGR			
United States (%)	17.1	19.7	13.5
Europe (ex. UK) (%)	22.0	22.2	13.3
United Kingdom (%)	17.0	22.6	9.7
Japan (%)	18.1	14.5	7.3
Standard Deviation			
(Relative to Market)			
United States	0.92	0.66	—
Europe (ex. UK)	0.95	1.12	—
United Kingdom	0.91	0.78	—
Japan	0.87	0.70	—

Data Source: James Montier. "The Little Note that Beats the Market." *DrKW Macro Research*, March 9, 2006.

investment: First, Greenblatt's *earnings yield* is a very good metric for identifying undervalued stocks, and, second, mean reversion is a powerful phenomenon. Let's first examine why the earnings yield performed so strongly and then return to an examination of mean reversion for value investors seeking to emulate Buffett.

THE ENTERPRISE MULTIPLE

Greenblatt's *earnings yield*—known generally as the *enterprise multiple*, or, occasionally as the *acquirer's multiple*—is a highly predictive measure of relative valuation. In fact, various industry and academic studies have found it to be better at identifying undervalued stocks than any other "price-to-a fundamental" ratio, including price-to-book value, price-to-earnings, price-to-operating cash flow, or price-to-free cash flow. The conventional metric for identifying undervalued stocks is price-to-book value. It is widely used for academic research, primarily due to the work of two influential financial economists, Ken Fama and Eugene French, on asset pricing. In 1992, Fama and French identified two anomalous classes of stocks that tended to outperform the market, resisting the application of the traditional asset-pricing model. Those two anomalous classes—small capitalization and low price-to-book value stocks—led Fama and French to propose a new asset-pricing model that explicitly accounted for size and price-to-book value, the so-called "three-factor model." Fama and French maintain that it makes no difference which "price-to-a-fundamental" is employed, but favor price-to-book value:[18]

> *A stock's price is just the present value of its expected future dividends, with the expected dividends discounted with the expected stock return (roughly speaking). A higher expected return implies a lower price. We always emphasize that different price-to-value ratios are just different ways to scale a stock's price with a fundamental, to extract the information in the cross-section of stock prices about expected returns. One fundamental (book value, earnings, or cashflow) is pretty much as good as another for this job, and the average return spreads produced by different ratios are similar to and, in statistical terms, indistinguishable from one another. We like [price-to-book value] because the book value in the numerator is more stable over time than earnings or cashflow, which is important for keeping turnover down in a value portfolio.*
> *Nevertheless, there are problems in all accounting variables and book value is no exception, so supplementing [price-to-book value] with other ratios can in principal improve the information about*

*expected returns. We periodically test this proposition, so far with-
out much success.*

Aswath Damodaran, professor of finance at the Stern School of Business
at New York University, has found that the enterprise multiple, along with
the price-to-earnings ratio and price-to-sales ratio, is the most common relative valuation ratio used by equity analysts.[19] Driven by the popularity of the
enterprise multiple in industry, other researchers have challenged Fama and
French's positions that investors can remain agnostic or that price-to-book
value is the best metric. In 2009, Tim Loughran, the C.R. Smith professor of
finance at the University of Notre Dame, and Jay W. Wellman, the visiting
assistant professor of finance at Cornell University, highlighted serious flaws
with the use of price-to-book value, arguing that the enterprise multiple
was the better metric for several important reasons.[20] The primary reason
is that the enterprise multiple better identified undervalued stocks over the
full period of Loughran and Wellman's research—1963 to 2008—and better
identified undervalued large market capitalization stocks where they found
price-to-book value to be incompetent. Note that Loughran and Wellman
define the enterprise multiple in a slightly different way to Greenblatt,
employing earnings before interest, taxes, depreciation, and amortization
(EBITDA) in place of Greenblatt's EBIT:

$$\text{Enterprise Multiple} = \text{EBITDA} \div \text{EV}$$

As we'll see, whether we employ EBIT or EBITDA makes little difference. The major problem with price-to-book value is that it tends to identify very small, micro-capitalization stocks and stocks that benefit from the
so-called "January effect"—a general increase in stock prices in January,
possibly as a result of tax-loss selling in December. Loughran and Wellman
found that for the largest stocks, which account for about 94 percent of the
stock market's total market capitalization, price-to-book value could not
be used to identify undervalued stocks once they controlled for the January
effect. Thus, conclude Loughran and Wellman, for nearly the entire market
value in the world's largest stock market (the United States), over the most
important time period (post-1963), price-to-book value could not identify
undervalued stocks. Additionally, price-to-book value may not have identified undervalued stocks in the smallest 6 percent of stocks because the wide
bid-ask spreads may have misrepresented the price at which those micro-
capitalization stocks could be traded. Loughran and Wellman also note
that many investment managers are restricted in their ability to buy very
small stocks due to ownership concentration restrictions, and are prohib-
ited from buying low-priced stocks—a stock priced below $5—due to their

"speculative nature." Thus, in practical terms, price-to-book value did not identify undervaluation in the smallest stocks either. They contend that the enterprise multiple succeeds where price-to-book value fails.

For the largest stocks, which accounted for about 94 percent of the market's total capitalization, the enterprise multiple was very good at identifying relatively undervalued stocks over the 1963 to 2008 period examined. This power persisted after the researchers controlled for the January effect and removed low-priced stocks, both of which can bias returns upward. Loughran and Wellman found that the enterprise multiple also did a better job than price-to-book value identifying undervalued stocks in the UK and Japan. The enterprise multiple is the better metric when it comes to identifying undervalued stocks. Rather than being driven by "obscure artifacts of the data"—namely the stocks in the bottom 6 percent of the market by capitalization—and the January effect, the enterprise multiple identified undervalued stocks throughout the entire universe of U.S. stocks.

Our own research confirms that the enterprise multiple has more consistently picked undervalued stocks than any other price-to-value ratio. Note that it isn't strictly correct to describe these ratios as price-to-*value* ratios. As Buffett has observed:[21]

> *Whether appropriate or not, the term 'value investing' is widely used. Typically, it connotes the purchase of stocks having attributes such as a low ratio of price to book value, a low price-earnings ratio, or a high dividend yield. Unfortunately, such characteristics, even if they appear in combination, are far from determinative as to whether an investor is indeed buying something for what it is worth and is therefore truly operating on the principle of obtaining value in his investments. Correspondingly, opposite characteristics—a high ratio of price to book value, a high price-earnings ratio, and a low dividend yield—are in no way inconsistent with a 'value' purchase.*

A more honest description is "price-to-a fundamental" ratio, but it's an unwieldy depiction that obscures rather than elucidates the meaning of the ratios. It's intuitive to understand these ratios as price-to-value ratios—low price-to-value ratios are associated with value stocks while high price-to-value ratios are associated with glamour or growth stocks—even if it's not strictly correct to describe them that way. Buffett's explanation is indisputable, but it's also true that a low price in relation to a fundamental measure is *more likely* to be associated with an undervalued stock than a high price in relation to the same fundamental measure. In conducting the research, we were, to borrow another one of Buffett's favorite phrases, more interested in being vaguely right, than in being exactly wrong. As in Ecclesiastes, the race is not always to the swift, nor the battle to the strong, but as Damon Runyon tells us, that's the way to bet.

In our research we examined data over the period 1964 to 2011 to test the performance of several popular price-to-value ratios (Tables 4.3, 4.4):

- two variations of the enterprise multiple, one employing EBIT and the other employing EBITDA;
- price-to-earnings;
- price-to-book value;
- enterprise value-to-free cash flow, where "free cash flow" was defined as net income + depreciation and amortization – working capital change – capital expenditures;
- enterprise value-to-gross profit, where "gross profit" was calculated as revenues – cost of goods sold; and
- price-to-forward earnings estimates, where forward earnings estimates were defined as consensus Institutional Brokers' Estimate System (IBES) earnings forecast of EPS for the fiscal year (available only from 1982 through 2010).

As before, we conducted the research to the academic gold standard, examining only companies with market capitalizations greater than the fortieth percentile NYSE breakpoint—for context, the smallest company at December 31, 2011, had a market capitalization of $1.4 billion—and weighted the stocks in the portfolios by market capitalization. We formed decile portfolios—each comprising 10 percent of the universe—for both the lowest- and highest-ranked stocks according to each price-to-value ratio (the low price-to-value ratio identifies value stocks and the high price-to-value ratio identifies glamour stocks). Other than the price-to-forward earnings estimates ratio, all other ratios use trailing 12-month data. The portfolios were rebalanced annually on June 30 of year t using lagged fundamental data from December 31 of year $t – 1$.

We found that both variations of the enterprise multiple had the most success identifying undervalued stocks, with the value portfolios of the EBIT form generating a compound annual growth rate of 14.6 percent and the EBITDA form earning 13.7 percent over the full period (for context, the S&P500 Total Return Index earned 9.5 percent). Wall Street's favorite metric—the price-to-forward earnings estimate ratio—was by far the worst performing of the price-to-value ratios, earning a compound annual growth rate of just 8.6 percent and underperforming even the market.

The value premium is the difference in returns to a portfolio of glamour stocks (the most overvalued decile) when compared to a portfolio of value stocks (the most undervalued decile) ranked by price-to-value ratio.

TABLE 4.3 Compound Annual Growth Rates for All Historical Price-to-Value Ratios (1964 to 2011)

| | Enterprise Multiple | | | | | |
	EBITDA Variation	EBIT Variation	Price-to-Earnings	Enterprise Value-to-Free Cash Flow	Enterprise Value-to-Gross Profit	Price-to-Book Value
S&P 500 TR	9.5%					
Value	13.7%	14.6%	12.4%	11.7%	13.5%	13.1%
Glamour	7.6%	7.1%	7.8%	9.1%	7.4%	8.6%
Value Premium	6.2%	7.5%	4.7%	2.6%	6.1%	4.5%

Data Source: Wesley Gray and Tobias Carlisle. *Quantitative Value: A Practitioner's Guide to Automating Intelligent Investment and Eliminating Behavioral Errors.* (Hoboken: Wiley Finance) 2012.

TABLE 4.4 Relative Volatility and Volatility Adjusted Returns for Value Decile of Each Historical Price-to-Value Ratio (1964 to 2011)

| | Enterprise Multiple | | | | | |
	EBITDA Variation	EBIT Variation	Price-to-Earnings	Enterprise Value-to-Free Cash Flow	Enterprise Value-to-Gross Profit	Price-to-Book Value
Standard Deviation Relative to S&P500 TR	1.14	1.13	1.16	1.08	1.21	1.14
Downside Deviation Relative to S&P500 TR	1.08	1.06	1.14	1.03	1.21	1.04
Sharpe Ratio	0.53	0.58	0.46	0.44	0.50	0.50
Sortino Ratio (MAR=5%)	0.82	0.89	0.68	0.68	0.73	0.80

Data Source: Wesley Gray and Tobias Carlisle. *Quantitative Value: A Practitioner's Guide to Automating Intelligent Investment and Eliminating Behavioral Errors.* (Hoboken: Wiley Finance) 2012.

The bigger the value premium, the better a given price-to-value ratio identifies undervalued and overvalued stocks. It's a more robust test than simply measuring the performance of the undervalued stock. Again, both enterprise multiples stand out. The EBIT variation of the enterprise multiple generated the largest average value premium at 7.5 percent annually, while the EBITDA variation earned 6.2 percent. Among the other historical price-to-value ratios, the enterprise value-to-free cash flow ratio generated the smallest spread, indicating that it did the worst job sorting undervalued and overvalued stocks.

The EBIT and EBITDA enterprise multiples still outperform after adjusting for volatility. Both had slightly higher volatility relative to the market, but this was predominantly upside volatility. This lead both variations of the enterprise multiple to have the best volatility-adjusted returns. Empirically, the enterprise multiple—and Greenblatt's EBIT variation in particular—does the best job of identifying undervalued stocks.

Why is the enterprise multiple so good at identifying undervalued stocks? First, the denominator in the enterprise multiple—the enterprise value—provides a more full picture of the price paid than does the market capitalization. The enterprise value is closer to a stock's true cost because, in addition to market capitalization, it includes other information about the contents of the company's balance sheet, including its debt, cash, and preferred stock (and in some variations minority interests and net payables-to-receivables). Such things are significant to acquirers of the business in its entirety, which, after all, is the way that value investors think about each stock. The enterprise value can be viewed as a theoretical takeover price of a company. After a takeover, the acquirer assumes the company's liabilities, including its debt, but gains use of the company's cash and cash equivalents. Including debt is important here. Market capitalization alone can be misleading. Loughran and Wellman, citing Damodaran, give the example of General Motors, which in 2005 had a market cap of $17 billion, but debt of $287 billion. Market capitalization greatly understated the true cost of General Motors, but the enterprise value captured General Motors' huge debt load, and so gave a more full accounting of its impact on General Motors' returns. (The risk of a large debt burden moved from the theoretical to the real when General Motors filed for bankruptcy protection in June 2009.) Often a stock that appears superficially undervalued on a book value basis is recognized as being fully valued, or overvalued once its debt load is factored into the calculation. Other researchers confirm that enterprise value is superior to market capitalization, and especially so when companies carry dissimilar debt loads.[22] It is the ease with which enterprise value makes a comparison of companies with differing capital structures that makes it so effective.

The measure of earnings employed in the enterprise multiple—operating earnings, whether defined as EBIT or EBITDA—also contains more information than net income, and so should give a more full view of the firm's income. Neither EBIT nor EBITDA are impacted by non-operating gains or losses, where net income is impacted by non-operating losses. Non-operating losses are important over a full operating cycle, but muddy the picture in any given year. Loughran and Wellman view operating earnings—EBIT or EBITDA—as a more transparent and less easily manipulated, short-term measure of profitability, making a comparison of companies within and across industries possible. Critics point out that EBIT and EBITDA are measures of accounting profit and not a substitute for cash flow, which is where the rubber really hits the road. It would therefore make sense for any valuation proceeding from an enterprise multiple analysis to include some consideration of a company's operating cash flow, and the extent to which accounting profits translate into cash generation.

Like a careful value investor, the enterprise multiple prefers companies holding cash and abhors companies with high levels of unserviceable debt. In practice, that tendency can be a double-edged sword. Enterprise multiple screens will contain many small "cash boxes"—companies with large net cash holdings relative to their market capitalization—often because the main business has been sold, or the business is a legacy in run-off that lingers like our vestigial appendix. Such stocks tend to have limited upside. On the flip side, they also have happily virtually no downside. In this way they are vastly superior to the highly leveraged companies favored by the price-to-book value ratio, which tends to serve up heavily leveraged slivers of somewhat discounted equity. The enterprise multiple is a more complete measure of relative value than the academic favorite price-to-book value, or any of the other common price-to-value ratios. The enterprise multiple includes debt as well as equity, contains a clearer measure of operating profit, and captures changes in cash from period to period. The empirical returns to portfolios created using the enterprise multiple bear out this rationale. Why does the simple enterprise multiple outperform the Magic Formula, the enterprise multiple and the return on invested capital combined? How can we reconcile the theory behind the deep value strategy—which amounts to fair companies at wonderful prices—with the theory behind Warren Buffett's wonderful companies at fair prices strategy?

Mean Reversion and Return on Invested Capital

Michael J. Mauboussin has conducted extensive research on the properties of return on invested capital and the manner in which investors should incorporate those estimates into valuations. Mauboussin, the head of Global

Financial Strategies at Credit Suisse and an adjunct professor of finance at Columbia Business School since 1993, is the author of four books on value investing and behavioral finance. In 2012, he published a brilliant book called "The Success Equation: Untangling Skill and Luck in Business, Sports and Investing,"[23] which provides a *tour de force* of the data on the tendency of return on invested capital to revert to the mean. His findings are instructive. Mauboussin's research supports Graham's view that, while some businesses do generate persistently high or low returns on invested capital beyond what chance dictates, there exists a strong tendency toward mean reversion in most businesses. For those businesses that do post sustainable high returns, Mauboussin could not prospectively identify the factors behind those sustainable high returns. In other words, they cannot predict which businesses will sustain high returns on capital and which will revert back to the mean, which is the average experience. Recall that Graham warned about constituting notions of "a good business" on the basis of a superior record:[24]

> *Abnormally good or abnormally bad conditions do not last forever. This is true of general business but of particular industries as well. Corrective forces are usually set in motion which tend to restore profits where they have disappeared, or to reduce them where they are excessive in relation to capital.*

Mauboussin observes that reversion to the mean is a powerful force, and it impacts return on invested capital as it does many other data series. The *mean* to which return on capital reverts is the cost of capital. Microeconomic theory dictates that high returns on invested capital attract competition that gradually drives down returns to the cost of capital until the industry participants can no longer earn an economic profit on average. Mauboussin demonstrated the reversion-to-the-mean phenomenon using data from 1,000 non-financial companies from 2000 to 2010. The chart in Figure 4.3 shows a clear trend toward nil economic profit, at which point return on invested capital equals the cost of capital.

Mauboussin counsels that we "should be careful not to over interpret this result because reversion to the mean is evident in any system with a great deal of randomness. We can explain much of the mean reversion series by recognizing the data are noisy." He notes that any system combining skill and luck will exhibit mean reversion over time:[25]

> *The basic idea is outstanding performance combines strong skill and good luck. Abysmal performance, in contrast, reflects weak skill and bad luck. Even if skill persists in subsequent periods, luck evens out across the participants, pushing results closer to average.*

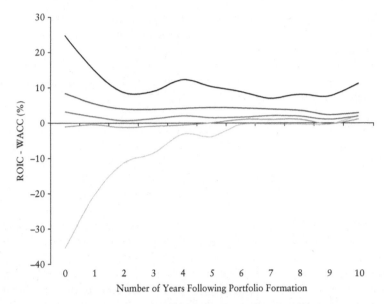

FIGURE 4.3 Change in Median ROIC by Quintile (2000 to 2010)
Source: Michael J. Mauboussin, *The Success Equation: Untangling Skill and Luck in Business, Sports and Investing.* (Boston: Harvard Business Review Press), 2012.

> *So it's not that the standard deviation of the whole sample is shrinking; rather, luck's role diminishes over time.*
>
> *Separating the relative contributions of skill and luck is no easy task. Naturally, sample size is crucial because skill only surfaces with a large number of observations. For example, statistician Jim Albert estimates that a baseball player's batting average over a full season is a fifty-fifty combination between skill and luck. Batting averages for 100 at-bats, in contrast, are 80 percent luck.*

Even so, Mauboussin did find persistence in some businesses' returns on invested capital over the period 2000 to 2010. *Persistence* here is the likelihood a company sustained its return on invested capital over the period examined. He found that a small subset of businesses did generate persistently high returns on invested capital, at levels that could not be attributed solely to chance, but he couldn't identify the underlying causal factors. It's one thing to note *post hoc* that some companies did sustain high or low returns on capital over the period examined, and quite another to do it *ex ante*, or before the fact. The difficulty is that we don't know the factors that *predict* future sustainable high returns on invested capital.

Mauboussin examined three possibilities—historical growth rates, the economics of the business's industry, and the business model—but could not identify factors that helped us to predict persistently high returns on capital. He found some correlation between historical growth and persistence, but noted, "[t]he bad news about growth, especially for modelers, is it is extremely difficult to forecast:"[26]

> *While there is some evidence for sales persistence, the evidence for earnings growth persistence is scant. As some researchers recently summarized, "All in all, the evidence suggests that the odds of an investor successfully uncovering the next stellar growth stock are about the same as correctly calling coin tosses."*

He also noted that two industries were overrepresented in the businesses that sustained high returns on invested capital over the period examined: the pharmaceuticals and biotechnology industry and the software industry, and commented that a good strategic position in a generally favorable industry was associated with sustainable high returns. Of course, this is difficult to determine prospectively, and was Graham's precise complaint:[27]

> *It is natural to assume that industries which have fared worse than the average are "unfavorably situated" and therefore to be avoided. The converse would be assumed, of course, for those with superior records. But this conclusion may often prove quite erroneous.*

Finally, Mouboussin suggested that the business model adopted by a business was correlated with the sustainability of returns. This is perhaps the most useful and interesting variable considered by Mauboussin. He equates strategy expert Michael Porter's two sources of competitive advantage—*differentiation* and *low-cost production*—to return on invested capital by breaking it into its two prime components: *net operating profit after tax (NOPAT) margin* and *invested capital turnover*. (*NOPAT margin* equals NOPAT divided by sales, and *invested capital turnover* equals sales divided by invested capital. Return on invested capital is the product of *NOPAT margin* and *invested capital turnover*.) Mauboussin found that differentiated businesses with a consumer advantage—those that generated high returns via high NOPAT margins, rather than high invested capital turnover—were overrepresented in the businesses that sustained high return on capital over the period examined. He gives as an example of such a business the "successful jewelry store that generates large profits per unit sold (high margins) but doesn't sell in large volume (low turnover)." Another example is See's Candies, which takes commodity inputs—sugar, cocoa, and

milk—and turns them into a branded consumer good that commands a premium price, earning high margins as it does so. The other possible business
model—a low-cost business with a production advantage, which earns low
NOPAT margins on high invested capital turnover—was underrepresented
in the businesses that sustained high return on capital over the 2000 to 2010
period. He gives as an example of this business model the "classic discount
retailer, which doesn't make much money per unit sold (low margins) but
enjoys great inventory velocity (high turnover)."[28]

Mauboussin's research into the drivers of sustainable high returns on
capital was comprehensive, but yielded little that helps us to predict which
businesses will earn persistently high returns on capital in the future. All that
we do know is that while some businesses do generate persistently high or
low returns on invested capital, most businesses exhibit a strong tendency
toward mean reversion. A good industry and a consumer advantage tilt the
odds in favor of sustainability, but it's still not conclusive. Quoting Michael
Porter, Mauboussin observes:[29]

> *It is impossible to infer the cause of persistence in performance
> from the fact that persistence occurs. Persistence may be due to
> fixed resources, consistent industry structure, financial anomalies,
> price controls, or many other factors that endure . . . In sum, reli-
> able inferences about the cause of persistence cannot be generated
> from an analysis that only documents whether or not persistence
> occurred.*

Here is the simple truth: mean reversion is pervasive, and it works on
financial results as it does on stock prices. On average, super-normal returns
on capital revert to the mean. Only special cases avoid mean reversion, and
the factors that separate the also-rans from the special cases are impossible to identify prospectively. Without Buffett's genius for business analysis,
we should be very wary of models that justify an elevated intrinsic value
by a very high return on invested capital or a very high rate of growth.
They are seductive because they allow us to fit a glamour stock into a value
framework. The problem as Graham saw it, is that growth is too difficult
to value:[30]

> *To my mind the so-called growth-stock investor—or the average
> security analyst for that matter—has no idea of how much to pay
> for a growth stock, how many stocks to buy to obtain the desired
> return, or how their prices will behave. Yet these are basic questions.
> That's why I feel the growth-stock philosophy can't be applied with
> reasonably dependable results.*

Intrinsic value models that assume away mean reversion in return on invested capital will systematically render valuations that are too optimistic. In a few instances this will be justified. In the vast majority it will not. Mauboussin concludes with the crucial observation that the investor's objective is to find *mispriced* securities or "situations where the expectations implied by the stock price don't accurately reflect the fundamental outlook:"[31]

> *A company with great fundamental performance may earn a market rate of return if the stock price already reflects the fundamentals. You don't get paid for picking winners; you get paid for unearthing mispricings. Failure to distinguish between fundamentals and expectations is common in the investment business.*

Both business and investment are systems the results of which are determined by a mix of skill and luck, thus we expect them both to exhibit mean reversion over time. Value investors anticipate mean reversion in securities prices, but if we seek only Buffett's "wonderful companies," we are ignoring or underestimating the impact of mean reversion at the business level. Just as expensive, cellared bottles of wine turn out to be vinegar, so too do apparently high-quality stocks disappoint. Anticipation of mean reversion in financial results is the main point of distinction for deep value from Buffett's "wonderful companies" method. At its core, such an investment strategy is a bet that the business will not revert to the average, but will continue to earn superior returns on capital. As Graham theorized, and Mauboussin has demonstrated, it is the rare company that does not return to the pack. In most cases competition and other corrective forces work on the highly profitable business to push its returns back to the mean. The better bet is the counterintuitive one: deep undervaluation *anticipating mean reversion*. It's Warren Buffett in his American Express investment, rather than his See's Candy investment. An appreciation of mean reversion is critical to value investment. In the next chapter we examine a legend about the relationship between luck, skill, and mean reversion and the research into mean reversion in securities.

Notes

1. Steven Friedman. "Joel Greenblatt and Robert Goldstein of Gotham Asset Management, LLC." *Santangel's Review*, March 2011.
2. Benjamin Graham. "A Conversation with Benjamin Graham." *Financial Analysts Journal*, Vol. 32, No. 5 (1976), pp. 20–23.
3. Ibid.
4. Ibid.

5. J. Greenblatt, R. Pzena, and B. Newberg. "How the small investor can beat the market." *The Journal of Portfolio Management*, Summer 1981, 48–52.
6. Ibid.
7. Joel Greenblatt. *You Can Be A Stock Market Genius*. (New York: Fireside) 1997.
8. Warren Buffett. "Chairman's Letter." *Berkshire Hathaway, Inc. Annual Report*, 1977.
9. Joel Greenblatt. *The Little Book that Beats the Market*. (Hoboken: Wiley) 2006.
10. Ibid.
11. Ibid.
12. Wesley Gray and Tobias Carlisle. *Quantitative Value: A Practitioner's Guide to Automating Intelligent Investment and Eliminating Behavioral Errors*. (Hoboken: Wiley Finance) 2012.
13. James Montier. "The Little Note that Beats the Market." *DrKW Macro Research*, March 9, 2006.
14. Ibid.
15. Gray and Carlisle, 2012.
16. Montier.
17. Ibid.
18. Eugene Fama and Kenneth French, "Q&A: Why Use Book Value To Sort Stocks?" *Dimensional Fama/French Forum*, 2011. Available at http://www.dimensional.com/famafrench/2011/06/qa-why-use-book-value-to-sort-stocks.html.
19. Aswath Damodaran. *Damodaran on Valuation: Security Analysis for Investment and Corporate Finance*. (New York: John Wiley & Sons) 2006.
20. Tim Loughran and Jay W. Wellman. "New Evidence on the Relation Between the Enterprise Multiple and Average Stock Returns.(September 5, 2010)." Available at SSRN: http://ssrn.com/abstract=1481279 or http://dx.doi.org/10.2139/ssrn.1481279.
21. Warren Buffett. "Chairman's Letter." *Berkshire Hathaway, Inc. Annual Report*, 1992.
22. S. Bhojraj and C. M. C. Lee. "Who Is My Peer? A Valuation-Based Approach to the Selection of Comparable Firms," *Journal of Accounting Research* 40 (2002), 407–439.
23. Michael J. Mauboussin. *The Success Equation: Untangling Skill and Luck in Business, Sports and Investing*. (Boston: Harvard Business Review Press), 2012.
24. Benjamin Graham and David Dodd. *Security Analysis: The Classic 1934 Edition*. (New York: McGraw Hill) 1934.
25. Mauboussin.
26. Ibid.
27. Graham and Dodd.
28. Mauboussin.
29. Ibid.
30. Janet Lowe. *The Rediscovered Benjamin Graham: Selected Writings of the Wall Street Legend*. (New York: John Wiley & Sons) 1999.
31. Mauboussin, 2007.

CHAPTER 5

A Clockwork Market

Mean Reversion and the Wheel of Fortune

"Even if we grant that analysis can give the speculator a mathematical advantage, it does not assure him a profit. His ventures remain hazardous; in any individual case a loss may be taken; and after the operation is concluded, it is difficult to determine whether the analyst's contribution has been a benefit or a detriment. Hence the latter's position in the speculative field is at best uncertain and somewhat lacking in professional dignity. It is as though the analyst and Dame Fortuna were playing a duet on the speculative piano, with the fickle goddess calling all the tunes."
—Benjamin Graham, *Security Analysis* (1934)

The ancient Romans attributed King Servius Tullius's exceptional good fortune to his consorting with the Goddess Fortuna.[1] Born to a slave, he rose to become the sixth king of ancient Rome, ruling for 44 years from 578 to 535 BCE. The Romans associated good luck with divine favor, and Servius was regarded as the luckiest of the kings. One evening, his mother—a Vestal Virgin responsible for cultivating the sacred flame in the royal household—took the sacrificial offerings from the royal table, and, as usual, cast them into the fire. As the flames died, a phallus arose from the hearth. Frightened, she ran to Tanaquil, the head of the household, and told her what had happened. Believing the apparition to be the *Lar* of the house, a deity that guarded the hearth, or the god *Vulcan*, Tanaquil dressed her in bridal garments, and shut her back in the room. Thus Servius's good fortune started when he was born to a divine sire in the royal household.

The Roman historian Plutarch wrote that of all Rome's ancient kings, Servius was naturally the least suited to monarchy and the least desiring of it. He was made king only through Fortuna's favor. While he was still a child his head shone with a glow like lightning. This was said to be a "token of his birth from fire," and a good omen pointing to his future accession to the throne. When the old king on his deathbed suddenly appointed Servius king, Tanaquil shouted his accession to the throne from a palace window known as the *Porta Fenestella*. He wanted to resign, but Tanaquil prevented him from doing so by making him swear that he would remain in power. Thus, says Plutarch, Servius owed to Fortuna his kingship, which he received unexpectedly, and was compelled to retain against his will. Servius in turn built the first temples and shrines to her, establishing Fortuna's Roman cult. For his devotion, Fortuna is said to have visited his bedchamber through the *Porta Fenestella*, the same palace window from which Tanaquil declared him king. Servius was indeed divinely favored.

Plutarch says that Servius knew "[f]ortune is of great moment, or rather, she is everything in human affairs" because it was through good fortune that he had ascended from slave to king.[2] In Roman mythology Fortuna was the goddess of fate, and the personification of chance. She turned the *Rota Fortunae*—the Wheel of Fortune—which dictated the destiny of man. The wheel had four stages—*Regnabo, Regno, Regnavi, Sum sine regno* (I shall reign, I reign, I reigned, I am without a kingdom)[3]—and turned constantly, moving man from one stage to the next. Fortuna's "wildly spinning wheel" was, according to Shakespeare, "to signify to you, which is the moral of it, that she is turning, and inconstant, and mutability, and variation."[4] Fortuna was also regarded as fickle, and cruel because she didn't make a distinction between the worthy and the unworthy. Seneca warned in the *Agamemnon*[5]:

> O Fortune, who dost bestow the throne's high boon with mocking hand, in dangerous and doubtful state thou settest the too exalted. Never have sceptres obtained calm peace or certain tenure; care on care weighs them down, and ever do fresh storms vex their souls.
>
> . . .
>
> Whatever Fortune has raised on high, she lifts but to bring low. Modest estate has longer life; then happy he whoe'er, content with the common lot, with safe breeze hugs the shore, and, fearing to trust his skiff to the wider sea, with unambitious oar keeps close to land.

Servius should have taken heed of Seneca's warning. The coda to his story is that Fortuna eventually abandoned him in brutal fashion. His daughter, Tullia, and his son-in-law, Tarquin the Arrogant, had him murdered in the street by a gang of thugs. Tullia then drove her chariot to the senate house where she hailed Tarquin as the new king. As she returned home along the street where Servius had been killed, she encountered her father's body lying prostrate where the thugs had left it. She steered her chariot toward him, and then drove her chariot wheel over his body. Thus did Fortuna lift up Servius from slave to king, only to forsake him, and have him crushed symbolically under her wheel. Fortuna is a cruel mistress.

Fortuna and her wheel of fortune are fitting motifs for deep value investment. Fortuna, as the personification of luck, is a pervasive influence on the stock market. It pushes the outcomes we observe away from the outcomes we expect, and in so doing obscures the presence, or absence, of skill. We can see the impact of luck in the financial results of businesses and the performance of investment strategies. It is chance, randomness, and dispersion, but its influence only extends to the short term. Over the longer term, the role of luck diminishes and the impact of skill becomes more pronounced. Where early good luck gives way to average skill, the leader returns to the pack. Where average skill overcomes early bad luck, the laggard catches up to the pack. Thus Fortuna's wheel turns, *Regno* (I reign) becomes *Regnavi* (I reigned), and *Sum sine regno* (I am without a kingdom) becomes *Regnabo* (I shall reign). This is mean reversion.

By putting the words, "Many shall be restored that now are fallen and many shall fall that now are in honor" on the facing page of *Security Analysis*, Graham gave the most prominent position in his seminal text to the idea that Fortuna's wheel turns too for securities, lowering those that have risen and lifting those that have fallen. The line, from Horace's *Ars Poetica*, echoes the phrase spoken by the wise men of legend who boiled down the history of mortal affairs into the four words, "This too will pass." This is *regression toward the mean*, an expression coined by Sir Francis Galton (1822 to 1911) with the 1886 publication of his paper "Regression Towards Mediocrity in Hereditary Stature."[6] In the paper, Galton proposed that the children of unusually tall or unusually short parents tended to be closer to the average height than their parents. Galton had observed in his research that the children of taller parents tend to be taller than average, but not as tall as their parents, and the children of shorter parents tended to be shorter than average, but not as short as their parents. He described the change in the children's heights relative to their parents' heights as a "regression towards mediocrity," now known as regression toward the mean.

In statistics the term is typically used to describe a phenomenon quite distinct from that identified by Galton. Mean reversion in statistics is the process by which an initial sampling error diminishes as repeated or larger samples show values closer to the expected value. For example, we expect on the toss of a fair coin that heads or tails is equally likely, and so the chance that we see heads is 50 percent. If we flip a fair coin 10 times, we expect to see 5 heads and 5 tails, but it's possible that we will see 8 out of 10 heads, or 80 percent heads. The law of large numbers holds that if we perform the same experiment a large number of times, the average of the results should be closer to the expected value—50 percent heads—and will become closer still as more trials are performed. So, if we flip the coin 100 times more, the average number of heads for the whole 110 flips will be closer to 50 percent simply because the most likely outcome from 100 additional flips is 50 heads. If we add the 50 heads from the second trial to the eight heads from the first trial, the proportion of heads for the whole series declines from 8 ÷ 10 or 80 percent, to 8 ÷ 10 + 50 ÷ 100 = 58 ÷ 110 or 52.7 percent. If we flipped the coin 1,000 times more, we expect to observe 500 heads and 500 tails, and the proportion of heads for the whole series would decline from 58 ÷ 110 to 558 ÷ 1110 or 50.5 percent. The law of large numbers holds that as we continue to flip the coin, it is highly likely that the proportion of heads we observe will converge toward 50 percent.

It is important to note that the observed proportion of heads does not converge toward the expected 50 percent because a run of tails follows the run of heads. It occurs because the subsequent ratio of heads and tails conforms to the underlying probability (50 percent heads, 50 percent tails), and the absolute error (8 heads) becomes proportionately smaller relative to the number of trials. The belief in a run of tails following a series of heads is known as the *gambler's fallacy*. This is the mistaken idea that deviations from the expected probabilities in independent trials of a random process make future deviations in the opposite direction more likely. In other words, this is the belief that a tail is due following a run of heads. Coin flips are independent trials of a random process, which means that the likelihood of a head or tail is independent of any earlier appearance of a head or a tail. Even after the run of eight heads, given a fair coin, the chance of a head remains at 50 percent.

BEWARE THE FICKLE GODDESS

Mean reversion pervades finance, but it's not the purely statistical mean reversion of the coin flip. Mean reversion in the markets looks a lot more like the gambler's fallacy made real—movements in security prices, individually and in aggregate, tend to be followed by subsequent price movements in the opposite direction. The more extreme the initial price movement, the greater will be the subsequent adjustment in the opposite direction. This phenomenon is observable in the financial results of businesses, in the market prices of securities, in the movements of indices, and in the results of investment managers. The reasons are manifold, but the most obvious is that the trials aren't independent—our own trading decisions are affected by the buying or selling preceding our trade. English economist John Maynard Keynes observed in *The General Theory of Employment, Interest, And Money* (1936) that "[d]ay-to-day fluctuations in the profits of existing investments, which are obviously of an ephemeral and nonsignificant character, tend to have an altogether excessive, and even an absurd, influence on the market."[7] Two economists known for research into both market behavior and individual decision-making, Werner De Bondt and Richard Thaler, theorized that it is this overreaction to meaningless price movements that creates the conditions for mean reversion. De Bondt and Thaler speculated that investors overreact to short-term, random fluctuations in market prices, and this overreaction causes the stock prices to temporarily depart from intrinsic value. Stock prices subsequently mean revert over time toward intrinsic value. If this is in fact the case, the stock prices that have moved the most—up or down—are candidates for a big move in the opposite direction. De Bondt and Thaler tested this idea in 1985.[8] Using data for the period 1926 to 1982, they formed portfolios of the 35 most extreme winners (those that had risen the most), and the 35 most extreme losers (those that had fallen the most) measured over the 3 years before the selection date. They then tracked the subsequent 3-year performance of the portfolios. Figure 5.1, from De Bondt and Thaler's paper, shows the performance of the portfolios of Losers (those that had fallen the most over the prior three years), and the Winners (those that had risen the most over the prior three years).

Figure 5.1 shows that the Loser portfolios comprehensively outperformed the Winner portfolios, suggesting that big stock price movements in one direction tend to be followed by big price movements in the opposite direction. De Bondt and Thaler proposed that the cause of the backtracking was investors overreacting to high-profile news events and becoming either overly optimistic or pessimistic about the stock in the short term. The stock price subsequently reverted toward its intrinsic value as the impact of that news event receded from memory.

In a second study published in 1987, De Bondt and Thaler revisited the research from a new perspective.[9] They hypothesized that the mean reversion they observed in stock prices in the first study might have been caused by investors focusing too much on the short term. This fixation on the recent past and failure to look beyond the immediate future would cause investors to miscalculate future earnings by failing to account for mean reversion. If earnings were also mean reverting, then extreme stock price increases and decreases might, paradoxically, be predictive of mean reversion not just in stock *prices*, but in *earnings* too (*paradoxically* because we would ordinarily expect earnings to lead prices, and not the other way around). In other

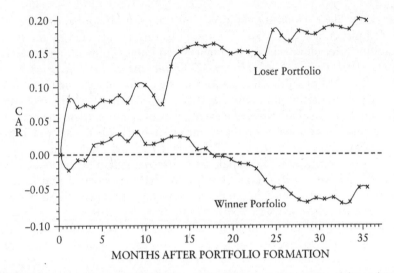

FIGURE 5.1 Cumulative Average Returns for Winner and Loser Portfolios of 35 Stocks over 36 months (1933 to 1982)
Source: Werner F.M. De Bondt and Richard H. Thaler. "Does the Stock Market Overreact?" *Journal of Finance* 40 (3) (1985): 793–805.

words, a stock *price* that has fallen a great deal becomes a good candidate for subsequent *earnings* growth, and a stock that has gone up a lot is likely to see *earnings* contract.

Using data for the period 1966 to 1983, De Bondt and Thaler replicated the original experiment, forming portfolios of extreme winners and losers measured by the increase or decrease in stock prices over the three-year period prior to the selection date. They then tracked the *earnings* performance of the stocks in each portfolio for the preceding three years and for the subsequent four years. The earnings for each were indexed to 100 at the selection date. Figure 5.2 uses data extracted from De Bondt and Thaler's paper to show the change in average earnings per share for stocks in the Winner and Loser portfolios.

Astonishingly, and as De Bondt and Thaler had anticipated, the earnings of stocks in the Loser portfolio grew at a faster rate after the selection date than the earnings of stocks in the Winner portfolio. The stocks in the Loser portfolio—which had seen earnings fall 72 percent over three years—saw earnings increase 234.5 percent over the next four years. By contrast, the stocks in the Winner portfolio—which had seen earnings growing rapidly at 50 percent over three years—saw earnings *decrease* after selection by 12.3 percent over the next four years. As they had theorized, the Loser

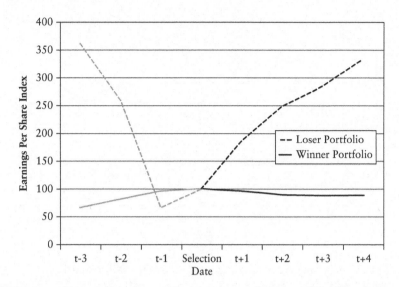

FIGURE 5.2 Change in Average Earnings Per Share for Stocks in Winner and Loser Portfolios (1966 to 1983)
Source: Eyquem Investment Management LLC using data from Werner F.M. De Bondt and Richard H. Thaler. "Further Evidence on Investor Overreaction and Stock Market Seasonality?" *Journal of Finance* 42 (3) (1987): 557–581.

portfolio—the stocks with the largest market price declines—saw far superior earnings performance in comparison to the Winner portfolio—the stocks with the largest increases in market price. The Loser portfolio also delivered superior stock price performance in the four years after the selection date, gaining a cumulative 24.6 percent over the market. Over the same period the stocks in the Winner portfolio returned 11.7 percent *less* than the market.

De Bondt and Thaler noted in the second paper that the winner-loser effect they had observed in the first paper was likely an overvalued-undervalued effect because Loser firms tended to have lower price-to-book value ratios while the Winner firms tended to have higher price-to-book value ratios. To examine precisely this point, they conducted another examination of the data, categorizing the portfolios not on the basis of how much the stock price had gone up or down, but by how under- or overvalued each was. They ranked the stocks by market price-to-book value, and then characterized the cheapest fifth of stocks as the Undervalued portfolio, and the most expensive fifth of stocks as the Overvalued portfolio. Figure 5.3 shows the change in average earnings per share for the Undervalued and Overvalued

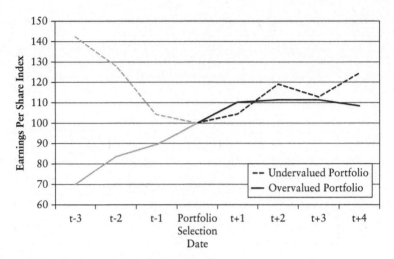

FIGURE 5.3 Change in Average Earnings Per Share for Undervalued and Overvalued Portfolios (1926 to 1983)
Source: Eyquem Investment Management LLC using data from Werner F.M. DeBondt and Richard H. Thaler. "Further Evidence on Investor Overreaction and Stock Market Seasonality?" *Journal of Finance* 42 (3) (1987): 557–581.

portfolios in the three years leading up to the selection date and in the four years following the selection date.

Figure 5.3 demonstrates that earnings grew faster for the Undervalued portfolio after the selection date than they did for the Overvalued portfolio. The stocks in the Undervalued portfolio, which had seen earnings fall 30 percent in the preceding three years, saw earnings increase 24.4 percent in the following four years. Again and by contrast, the stocks in the Overvalued portfolio, which had seen earnings growing rapidly—up 43 percent in the preceding three years—saw earnings growth continue over the following four years, but at a much lower rate, an anemic 8.2 percent cumulative gain. Like the stocks in the Winner portfolio, the Overvalued portfolio failed to deliver on its promise of a high rate of earnings growth, which had been implied by the growth in earnings in the three years leading up to the selection date. The Undervalued portfolio delivered the better *earnings* performance. The differential in growth was also reflected in the performance of each portfolio. The Undervalued portfolio delivered a cumulative average return over the four years following the selection date of 40.7 percent *in excess of the market.* Meanwhile, the stocks in the Overvalued portfolio returned 1.3 percent *less* than the market over the same four years. These are striking results.

De Bondt and Thaler's findings stand the conventional wisdom on its head and show compelling evidence for mean reversion in stocks in a variety of forms. Big gains and drops don't persist. Rather, extreme drops in stock prices tend to be followed by big gains and big drops follow extreme gains. Big drops in stock prices also tend to be followed by significant *earnings* increases and significant stock price increases are followed by slower rates of increase or declines in *earnings*. If we rank stocks on the basis of market price in relation to book value, the undervalued, low price-to-book value stocks grow earnings faster than the overvalued, high price-to-book value stocks, and, consequently, enjoy faster stock price appreciation. It seems that, if we want rapid earnings growth and accompanying stock price appreciation, the place to look for it is counterintuitive. Overpriced, high earnings growth, rapidly appreciating stocks will disappoint. Rather, it will be found in undervalued stocks enduring significant earnings compression and plunging market prices. This is not a phenomenon limited to individual businesses and securities. As we'll see next, De Bondt and Thaler's unexpected findings extend to the performance of stock markets and economies.

UNDERVALUED MARKETS

Warren Buffett wrote an extraordinary article that appeared in *Fortune* in late 1999 called "Mr. Buffett on the Stock Market."[10] It was extraordinary because Buffett rarely comments on the level of the market, preferring instead to focus on the individual companies that make up the market. In a typical statement on his view of the market, made in 1987, Buffett commented, "When investing, we view ourselves as business analysts—not as market analysts, not as macroeconomic analysts, and not even as security analysts."[11] In the 1999 article, published about five months before the peak of the dot-com bubble, Buffett was at pains to explain that he only looked to the market to a "very limited extent:"[12]

> At Berkshire we focus almost exclusively on the valuations of individual companies, looking only to a very limited extent at the valuation of the overall market. Even then, valuing the market has nothing to do with where it's going to go next week or next month or next year, a line of thought we never get into. The fact is that markets behave in ways, sometimes for a very long stretch, that are not linked to value. Sooner or later, though, value counts.

In making his case, Buffett compared two adjacent 17-year periods: 1964 to 1981 and 1981 to 1998. In the 1964 to 1981 period, Buffett wrote,

U.S. gross national product (GNP) almost quintupled, rising 373 percent. The market, by contrast, went nowhere. The Dow Jones Industrial Average stood at 874.12 on December 31, 1964. Seventeen years later, on December 31, 1981, it stood at 875.00. In the following 17-year period, from 1981 to 1998, U.S. gross national product grew only 177 percent—less than half its growth over the preceding 17 years—but the Dow Jones Industrial Average advanced from 875.00 on December 31, 1981, to 9,181.43 on December 31, 1998, a tenfold increase.

Buffett attributed the apparently unusual behavior of the stock market to the relationship between two important variables: interest rates and valuation. "Interest rates," wrote Buffett, ". . . act on financial valuations the way gravity acts on matter: The higher the rate, the greater the downward pull."[13]

> *That's because the rates of return that investors need from any kind of investment are directly tied to the risk-free rate that they can earn from government securities. So if the government rate rises, the prices of all other investments must adjust downward, to a level that brings their expected rates of return into line. Conversely, if government interest rates fall, the move pushes the prices of all other investments upward. The basic proposition is this: What an investor should pay today for a dollar to be received tomorrow can only be determined by first looking at the risk-free interest rate.*

Over the period from 1964 to 1981, the rates on long-term government bonds moved from just over 4.20 percent at the end of 1964 to more than 13.65 percent by late 1981. The more-than-threefold increase in rates depressed the value of the stock market such that the country's extraordinary underlying business growth counted for naught. In the second 17-year period, interest rates fell from 13.65 percent in 1981 to 5.09 percent in 1998, and the stock market advanced more than tenfold.

Many professional investors, economists, and finance journalists assume that the economy—measured by the rate of growth in GNP or gross domestic product (GDP)—drives the rate of gain in the stock market. The quicker the pace of growth, the more favorable is the investment climate, and hence the bigger are the gains that investors should expect. Strong economic growth, goes the received wisdom, equates to strong returns; weak growth leads to low returns; and recessions lead to market crashes. To most people, this observation is so obvious as to be trite: The performance of the stock market is tethered to the performance of the underlying economy. But if this is in fact the case, how was it that, in the first 17-year period identified by Buffett, the stock market performed so poorly while the stock market's underlying businesses performed so well, and in the second 17-year period, the underlying business growth slowed while the stock market exploded? How did the market and the economy diverge so much over the periods from 1964 to 1998?

The evidence is that valuation, rather than economic growth, determines investment returns at the market and country level. Research undertaken by Elroy Dimson, Paul Marsh, and Mike Staunton from the London Business School suggests that chasing growth economies is akin to chasing overvalued stocks, and generates similarly disappointing results.[14] In one study of 17 countries' stock markets going back to 1900, Dimson, Marsh, and Staunton found that there was a *negative* relationship between investment returns and growth in GDP per capita; in other words, higher GDP growth led to lower stock market returns. In a second test, they took the five-year growth rates of the economies and divided them into quintiles, or fifths. The stock markets in the economies with the highest growth rate produced average returns over the following year of 6 percent. Those in the lowest-growth quintile produced returns of 12 percent, double the returns of the high-growth economies. In a third test, Dimson, Marsh, and Staunton could find no statistical link between one year's GDP growth rate and the next year's investment returns. In each country, returns were either unrelated to short-term growth of GDP, or *inversely related*, which means that high growth predicted low returns, and vice versa.

Perhaps this is a phenomenon limited to developed economies and their stock markets, where growth rates have plateaued relative to emerging markets. Perhaps, but no. Other research extending Dimson, Marsh, and Staunton's findings to emerging markets, where presumably GDP growth rates are at their highest, finds the same relationship. Paul Marson, the chief investment officer of Lombard Odier, one of the largest independent Swiss private banks, examined the drivers of returns in developing countries over the period 1976 to 2005, and could find no correlation between GDP growth and stock market returns.[15] Commenting on Marson's research in its *Buttonwood* column, *The Economist* identified China as the classic example of this phenomenon; average nominal GDP growth between 1993 and 2009 was 15.6 percent, the compound stock market return over the same period was *negative* 3.3 percent. Buttonwood contrasted China's performance with "stodgy old Britain," which saw average nominal GDP growth of just 4.9 percent, but annual market returns of 6.1 percent—better than nine percentage points ahead of booming China. On his *Efficient Frontier* web site, author and American financial theorist William J. Bernstein observed that "[y]ou don't have to go cross-eyed with regression analyses to convince yourself; a few anecdotes tell the story:"[16]

During the twentieth century, England went from being the world's number one economic and military power to an overgrown outdoor theme park, and yet it still sported some of the world's highest equity returns between 1900 and 2000. On the other hand, during the past quarter century Malaysia, Korea, Thailand and, of course, China have simultaneously had some of the world's highest economic growth rates and lowest stock returns.

Just as De Bondt and Thaler's Winner and Overvalued portfolios had lower returns than the Loser and Undervalued portfolios, so do high-growth nations have lower returns than low-growth nations. Why does high growth seem to depress stock market returns and low growth seem to generate high stock market returns? It is not that growth destroys returns, but that the market already recognizes the high-growth nation's potential, and bids the price of its equities too high. Market participants become overly optimistic during periods of high growth, driving up the prices of stocks and lowering long-term returns, and become too pessimistic during busts, selling down stocks and creating the conditions for high long-term returns. The effects of recession on the stock market, according to Jay Ritter, "are partly due to higher risk aversion . . . but also due partly to an irrational overreaction."[17] De Bondt and Thaler would be proud. Ritter adds that this "irrationality" generates volatility "and mean-reversion over multi-year horizons."[18] Graham, too, would agree.

The implications for mean reversion in stocks are counterintuitive. Stocks with big market price gains and historically high rates of earnings growth tend to grow earnings more slowly in the future, and underperform the market. Stocks with big market price losses and historically declining earnings tend to see their earnings grow faster, and outperform the market. Undervalued stocks with historically declining earnings grow earnings faster than overvalued stocks with rapidly increasing earnings. This is mean reversion, and, as Benjamin Graham first identified, it's the phenomenon that leads value strategies to beat the market. Buffett's version of Graham's explanation for it as it applies to stocks is as lucid as it gets (there's no record of Graham using precisely this analogy):[19]

> *In the short-run, the market is a voting machine—reflecting a voter-registration test that requires only money, not intelligence or emotional stability—but in the long-run, the market is a weighing machine.*

BLIND TO THE TURN OF FORTUNA'S WHEEL

Sebastian Brant's *Ship of Fools* (1494) is a collection of stories about a ship laden with corrupt, foolish, or oblivious passengers setting sail for a "fool's paradise," and seemingly ignorant of their direction. Albrecht Dürer created a woodcut for each of the follies undertaken by the various fools. Figure 5.4 shows one such Dürer woodcut. It depicts men wearing ass-eared head-dresses clinging to Fortuna's wheel, which Fortuna's hand "puppets." As they ascend up the wheel, the men turn into asses; at the apex, the ass reaches for the sun; and, as they descend, they turn back into men. The woodcut seems to be a commentary on our ignorance of the role of luck and randomness in life, and the inevitable end to *Regno* (I reign). At Regno, instead of preparing for *Sum sine regno* (I am without a kingdom), we reach for the sun, imagining that we'll continue to ascend or remain at the pinacle forever.

FIGURE 5.4   Albrecht Dürer's *The Wheel of Fortune* from Sebastian Brant's *Ship of Fools* (1494)
Source: Sebastien Brant. *The Ship of* Fools. Translated by Alexander Barclay. (Edinburgh: William Paterson) 1874.[20]

Like the ass reaching for the sun at the apex of Dürer's woodcut, we tend to be unwitting to the consequences of mean reversion. Behavioral psychologist Daniel Kahneman, winner of the 2002 Nobel Prize in economics, recounts in his autobiography that his first observation of this unawareness was "the most satisfying Eureka experience" of his career.[21] While attempting to lecture a group of Israeli air force flight instructors that praise is more effective than punishment for promoting learning, Kahneman was interrupted by one of the most experienced instructors in the audience. He began by conceding that positive reinforcement might work in the wider community, but denied that it was ideal for flight cadets. He said, "On many occasions I have praised flight cadets for clean execution of some aerobatic maneuver, and in general when they try it again, they do worse. On the other hand, I have often screamed at cadets for bad execution, and in general they do better the next time. So please don't tell us that reinforcement works, and punishment does not, because the opposite is the case." Kahneman says that he then understood an important truth about the world: Because we tend to reward others when they do well, and punish them when they do badly, and because there is regression to the mean, it is part of the human condition that we are statistically punished for rewarding others and rewarded for punishing them. He immediately arranged a demonstration in which each participant tossed two coins at a target behind his back, without any feedback. They measured the distances from the target and could see that those who had done best the first time had mostly deteriorated on their second try, and vice versa. Kahneman knew that this demonstration would not undo the effects of "lifelong exposure to a perverse contingency," but it set him on a path that would eventually lead to the Nobel Memorial Prize in economics. The evidence is that our attitude to mean reversion in stock prices is informed by the same perverse contingency.

Behavioral finance researchers Joseph Lakonishok, Andrei Shleifer, and Robert Vishny conducted a landmark study in 1994 into the reasons why value strategies beat the market. Lakonishok et al. concluded that they do so because value strategies are contrarian to the "naïve" strategies followed by other investors who, like the asses clinging to the wheel in Dürer's woodcut, fail to fully appreciate the implications of mean reversion.[22] These naive strategies might range from extrapolating past earnings growth too far into the future; to assuming a trend in stock prices; to overreacting to good or bad news; or to simply equating a good investment with a well-run company irrespective of price. Some investors get overly excited about stocks that have done well in the past and bid them up, so that these so-called glamour stocks become overvalued. Similarly, they overreact to stocks that have performed poorly, oversell them, and these out-of-favor so-called value stocks become undervalued. As De Bondt and Thaler demonstrated, the "naïve extrapolation" investment strategies identify stocks that under-perform the market. Value investors take positions contrarian to these naïve extrapolation strategies, overinvesting in value stocks with poor historical and expected growth, and underinvesting in, or outright shorting, the glamour stocks with good historical and expected performance.

Using data from 1968 to 1990, Lakonishok et al. tested whether a simple contrarian value investment strategy—one that bet against stocks with high expectations (the glamour stocks), and bet for the stocks with poor expectations (the value stocks)—produced superior returns. By examining the returns for stocks globally from 1980 to 2013 we can replicate and extend Lakonishok et al.'s research.[23] We examined returns in the following 23 developed-market countries: Australia, Austria, Belgium, Canada, Denmark, Finland, France, Germany, Greece, Hong Kong, Ireland, Italy, Japan, Netherlands, New Zealand, Norway, Portugal, Singapore, Spain, Sweden, Switzerland, the United Kingdom, and the United States. We excluded the smallest 50 percent of stocks by market capitalization in each country to remove micro capitalization stocks. Each stock in the universe was sorted according to its ratio of market price-to-book value, cash flow, and earnings. The sorted stocks were then divided into five quintile portfolios (each portfolio containing 20 percent of the stocks by number). We then tracked quintile-by-quintile annualized performance, calculated in U.S. dollars, for the five years after the selection date. Figure 5.5 shows the average annualized five-year returns to each quintile portfolio for each price ratio.

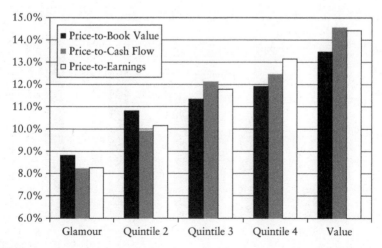

FIGURE 5.5 Global Markets Average Annualized Five-Year Returns for All Price Ratios (1980 to 2013)
Source: Eyquem Investment Management LLC.

Figure 5.5 demonstrates that no matter which price ratio we choose to examine, over the 33-year period under consideration, the quintile containing the stocks with the lowest ratio of price to a fundamental measure (the value quintile, on the far right of the chart) outperformed the quintile containing the stocks with the highest ratio of price to a fundamental measure (the glamour quintile, on the far left of the chart). The quintiles also perform in rank order: the value quintile outperforms the next cheapest quintile (quintile 2), and so on until we reach the glamour quintile, which underperforms. We found similar evidence when we further divided the universe of stocks remaining into large capitalization (the largest third) and small capitalization (the smallest two thirds). Figure 5.6 shows the average annualized five-year returns for stocks ranked by price-to-book value and divided into small and large capitalization portfolios.

Figure 5.6 demonstrates that the value quintile's outperformance over the glamour quintile is not only a small capitalization phenomenon. The large capitalization value stocks also outperform large capitalization glamour stocks. The extent to which the value quintile outperforms the glamour quintile is known as the *value premium*. Table 5.1 shows the returns and other performance statistics, including the value premium, for stocks of all market capitalizations greater than the 50 percent cut-off, and for the two subsets, small capitalization and large capitalization.

There is a lot of information in Table 5.1, so let's examine what it means. The table shows that the glamour quintile (in column 1) earns the

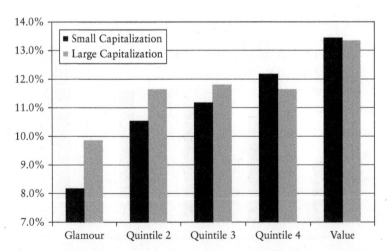

FIGURE 5.6   Global Markets Annualized Average Five-Year Returns for Price-to-Book Value Quintiles (1980 to 2013)
Source: Eyquem Investment Management LLC.

TABLE 5.1 Average Annualized Five-Year Performance Statistics by Capitalization for Price-to-Book Value Quintiles (1980 to 2013)

		Glamour				Value	Value Premium
		1	2	3	4	5	(5-1)
All	Annual Return	8.80%	10.82%	11.32%	11.89%	13.48%	4.68%
	Standard Deviation	19.03%	18.24%	17.45%	16.08%	16.44%	
	Sharpe Ratio	0.21	0.33	0.37	0.43	0.52	
Large Cap	Annual Return	9.85%	11.62%	11.78%	11.65%	13.36%	3.51%
	Standard Deviation	19.77%	18.90%	17.27%	16.12%	16.45%	
	Sharpe Ratio	0.25	0.36	0.40	0.42	0.52	
Small Cap	Annual Return	8.23%	10.46%	11.22%	12.14%	13.41%	5.18%
	Standard Deviation	19.21%	18.61%	17.88%	16.67%	16.96%	
	Sharpe Ratio	0.17	0.30	0.35	0.43	0.50	

lowest returns with the worst Sharpe ratio, and the value quintile earns the highest returns with the best Sharpe ratio. The quintiles also perform in almost perfect inverse rank order from glamour to value (column 5 outperforms column 4 and so on). Value not only beats glamour in terms of annual returns, it also does so on a risk-adjusted basis.

These are the average returns over the entire period. There's no guarantee that the value premium is positive over shorter periods of time. The value premium winks in and out of existence, and value sometimes underperforms glamour. In Figure 5.7, we examine the value premium (or discount) on a rolling five-year basis for large and small capitalization stocks.

Figure 5.7 shows that the value premium varies from period to period and is occasionally negative, during which times glamour has outperformed value. The worst period of extended underperformance has been the most recent period from 2010 to 2013. Over the short period of data available, this level of underperformance is unusually long. This may be related to the huge outperformance over the period from 2000 to 2005, when value generated its largest sustained premium over glamour. This period of outperformance might, however, also be attributable to the earlier underperformance of value stocks through the dot-com bubble in the late 1990s. The value premium, it seems, also mean reverts. If so, we are likely to again see

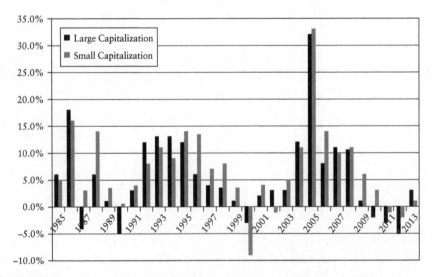

FIGURE 5.7   Rolling Five-Year Annualized Value Premium (Discount) for Price-to-Book Value Quintiles (1985 to 2013)
Source: Eyquem Investment Management LLC.

sustained outperformance from the value quintile following this latest brief period of underperformance.

The update to Lakonishok et al.'s research demonstrates that, aside from short periods of underperformance, value stocks generate a consistent value premium, and beat both the market and glamour stocks over the long haul. The reasons why are a source of some controversy. Behavioral finance economists like De Bondt and Thaler and Lakonishok, Shleifer, and Vishny believe that they do so because they are contrarian to overreaction and naïve extrapolation. The alternative explanation for the superior returns to value strategies, argued by influential efficient market economists Eugene Fama and Ken French, is that they are *fundamentally riskier*. Value strategies seem to outperform, claim Fama and French, as compensation for this additional risk. The same argument was used to criticize De Bondt and Thaler's research into overreaction. To be fundamentally riskier, value stocks must underperform glamour stocks with some frequency, and particularly in what Lakonishok et al. describe as "bad" states of the world, such as extreme down markets or recessions. Lakonishok et al. found that while the value strategy does disproportionately well in good times, its performance in bad times is also impressive. In fact, over longer horizons value strategies almost always outperform glamour strategies, and they do particularly well in those bad states of the world. They could not find any measure of risk that explained the huge difference in average returns to the value strategy. They were able to find, however, evidence that investors appear to be extrapolating past performance, even though the future does not warrant such extrapolation.

Lakonishok et al. describe the essence of naïve extrapolation as the idea that investors are excessively optimistic about glamour stocks because they tie their expectations of future growth to past growth, and excessively pessimistic about value stocks for the same reason. They tested the validity of this assertion by comparing the actual growth rates of fundamental measures like sales, earnings, and operating income to past and expected rates of growth of the same fundamental measures. Lakonishok et al. calculated expected growth rates from each security's price ratios. If the market puts a high price on a security relative to its fundamentals, it is implicitly expecting high growth in those fundamentals. In other words, for example, the higher the price-to-earnings ratio, the faster the market expects earnings to grow. We can show this with Gordon's constant growth model, which is a model for determining the intrinsic value of a stock given a series of dividends that grow at a constant rate.[24] The equation is as follows:

$$P = \frac{D_1}{r - g}$$

where

P_1 is the current stock price;

D_1 is the value of next year's dividends;

g is the constant growth rate in perpetuity expected for the dividends; and

r is the discount rate.

If we apply the Gordon model, holding constant the dividend (D_1) and discount rate (r), a high price (P) implies a high growth rate (g). The same intuition applies if we substitute for dividends, sales, earnings, cash flow, or operating income.

When Lakonishok et al. compared the growth rates implied by the market price to the actual growth rates appearing after the selection date, they found a remarkable result—one that supports De Bondt and Thaler's research, and Graham's intuition—*value stocks grow fundamentals faster than glamour stocks*. The high prices paid for glamour stocks imply that the market expects them to generate high rates of growth. Contrary to this expectation, however, the growth rates do not persist. The evidence shows quite clearly that growth rates of glamour stocks either fall to the growth rates of value stocks or even overshoot them and become lower. In other words, growth stocks' fundamentals mean revert as De Bondt and Thaler suggested. Rather than anticipate this mean reversion, however, the market tends to tie forecasts to past growth rates, pricing glamour stocks far too optimistically relative to value stocks. Given these expectations, glamour stocks' growth reliably disappoints investors, and out-of-favor value stocks reliably supply positive surprises.

Lakonishok et al's landmark research established three propositions central to value investment. First, many different investment strategies that involve buying out-of-favor value stocks outperform glamour strategies and beat the market. Second, the likely reason that these value strategies work so well relative to the glamour strategies is due to the fact that the actual growth rates of fundamentals (earnings, sales etc.) of glamour stocks relative to value stocks after selection are much lower than they were in the past, or as the multiples on those stocks indicate the market expects them to be. That is, market participants appear to consistently overestimate future growth rates of glamour stocks relative to value stocks, failing to appreciate that mean reversion is the more likely outcome. Third, value strategies appear to be less risky than glamour strategies.

This conclusion raises an obvious question: if we are aware that value stocks outperform glamour stocks, why is it that investors continue to favor glamour stocks over value stocks? One possible explanation suggested by Lakonishok et al. is that investors simply do not know about the phenomenon. Benjamin Graham's advocacy of value investment strategies, beginning at least 80 years ago with the publication of *Security Analysis*, and the wild success of his most famous pupil, Buffett, makes this highly unlikely. Buffett has written at length about value investment in his letters to the shareholders of Berkshire Hathaway since the 1960s, describing his process and his influences. A more plausible explanation is that investors prefer glamour strategies to value strategies for behavioral reasons. As we'll see, this is not a phenomenon unique to lay investors. De Bondt and Thaler found "considerable evidence" that professional security analysts and economic forecasters tended to display the same so-called "overreaction bias." Lakonishok et al. also argued that both individual and institutional investors engage in suboptimal behavior, for cognitive reasons or because of so-called principal-agency problems. We'll examine those reasons next.

Notes

1. Frank C. Babbitt (trans). *Plutarch: De Fortuna Romanorum. Moralia.* (Cambridge: Vol. IV of the Loeb Classical Library edition) 1936.
2. Ibid.
3. Carmina Burana.
4. William Shakespeare. *Henry V Act 3, Scene VI.* Available at http://www.online-literature.com/shakespeare/henryV/16.
5. Frank J. Miller (trans). *Seneca's Tragedies With an English Translation by Frank Justus Miller in Two Volumes II: Agamemnon, Thyestes, Hercules Octaeus, Phoenissae, Octavia.* (New York: G.P. Puttnam's Sons) 1917. Available at http://archive.org/details/tragedieswitheng02seneuoft.
6. F. Galton. "Regression Towards Mediocrity in Hereditary Stature." *The Journal of the Anthropological Institute of Great Britain and Ireland.*15: 246–263, 1886.
7. J. M. Keynes. *The General Theory of Employment, Interest and Money* (New York: Palgrave Macmillan. 1936.
8. Werner F.M. De Bondt and Richard H. Thaler. "Does the Stock Market Overreact?" *Journal of Finance* 40 (3) (1985): 793–805.
9. W. De Bondt and R. Thaler. "Further Evidence on Investor Overreaction and Stock Market Seasonality," *Journal of Finance*, July, 42 (3) (1987), pp. 557–581.
10. Warren Buffett and Carol Loomis, "Mr. Buffett on the Stock Market." *Fortune Magazine*, November 1999. Available at http://money.cnn.com/magazines/fortune/fortune_archive/1999/11/22/269071.
11. Warren Buffett, "Chairman's Letter." *Berkshire Hathaway, Inc. Annual Report,* 1987.
12. Buffett and Loomis, 1999.
13. Ibid.
14. Elroy Dimson, Paul Marsh, and Mike Staunton. *The Triumph of the Optimists: 101 Years of Global Investment Returns.* (Princeton: Princeton University Press) 2002.

15. Buttonwood. "Buttonwood's Notebook: The Growth Illusion." *The Economist*. August 28, 2009. Available at http://www.economist.com/blogs/buttonwood/2009/08/the_growth_illusion.
16. William J. Bernstein. "Thick as a BRIC." *Efficient Frontier*, 2006. Available at http://www.efficientfrontier.com/ef/0adhoc/bric.htm.
17. Jay Ritter. "Economic Growth and Equity Returns." Working Paper, University of Florida, November 2004.
18. Ibid.
19. Warren Buffett. "Chairman's Letter." *Berkshire Hathaway, Inc. Annual Report*, 1985.
20. Sebastien Brant. *The Ship of Fools*. Translated by Alexander Barclay. (Edinburgh: William Paterson) 1874. Available at http://www.gutenberg.org/files/20179/20179-h/images/t311.png.
21. Daniel Kahneman. "Daniel Kahneman—Autobiographical." *The Nobel Prizes 2002*, Editor Tore Frängsmyr, Nobel Foundation, Stockholm, 2003. Available at http://www.nobelprize.org/nobel_prizes/economic-sciences/laureates/2002/kahneman-bio.html.
22. J. Lakonishok, A. Shleifer, and R.W. Vishny. "Contrarian Investments, Extrapolation, and Risk." *Journal of Finance*, Vol. XLIX, No. 5, (1994) pp. 1541–1578.
23. Suggested by *Value vs. Glamour: A Global Phenomenon (December 2012)*. The Brandes Institute, 2012. Available at http://www.brandes.com/Institute/Documents/White%20Paper-Value%20Vs.%20Glamour%202012.pdf.
24. Lakonishok et al., 1994.

CHAPTER 6

Trading in Glamour: The Conglomerate Era

Speculation, Investment, and Behavioral Finance

"Do you," said I, looking at the shore, "call it 'unsound method?'"
"Without doubt," he exclaimed hotly. "Don't you?"
"No method at all," I murmured after a while.
— Joseph Conrad, *Heart of Darkness* (1899)

ergot \ *(ûrgt)* \, *noun:*
A fungus (Claviceps purpurea) that infects rye and other cereal grasses fed to livestock. Ingestion produces convulsions and hallucinations. May have been responsible for outbreaks of mass hysteria in medieval Europe.
— Comes from French, from Old French *argot*, a rooster's spur, suggested by the fungus's shape.[1]

Tex Thornton needed $750,000. He'd borrowed $300,000 from Wells Fargo Bank to make the down payment on Litton Industries, a San Carlos, California, manufacturer of magnetrons sold to military-oriented businesses, and had to provide a personal note as collateral to secure even that amount.[2] Now he needed another $750,000 to buy the company from its founder, Charles V. Litton, or the deposit would be lost. At a meeting with investment bankers from Lehman Brothers in New York, Thornton sketched out his plan for little Litton Industries, then earning just $3 million a year in revenues. Thornton believed Litton could become a $100 million-a-year corporation in five years by acquiring other businesses for paper—stock in Litton. Most small military electronics companies were outcompeted or taken over by larger competitors. Litton's only chance was to rapidly expand, Thornton told the bankers. "There's no other way to succeed in military electronics."[3] Such an approach would be possible, Thornton argued, provided he could get Litton's stock price up. The buoyant stock market in 1953 would help, but the key to getting and keeping a high price-to-earnings ratio on Litton's stock would be making sure it was regarded as a glamorous, high-growth technology business. Thornton told them, "I want to start a company that will become a strong blue chip in the scientific and technological environment of the future. It would be a balanced company—not just engineering, not just manufacturing, not just financial. You can't win a ball game with only a pitcher and catcher, and you can't have a strong company unless it's balanced."[4]

The investment bankers must have been skeptical. Thornton was operating a company he had just formed called Electro Dynamics Corporation.[5] Despite its impressive name, Electro Dynamics Corporation had no business and no assets. What it did have was a core of refugees from Hughes Aircraft with expertise in research and development and procuring contracts for government business.[6] After World War II ended Thornton had landed at Hughes Aircraft, a newly formed subsidiary of Hughes Tool, which was owned by the eccentric Howard Hughes. Like its eponymous founder, Hughes Aircraft was a basket case. Its most notable achievement was the "Spruce Goose," the huge wooden flying boat that never flew. It had few government contracts, and its track record of failing to deliver on those few contracts it did have gave it a bleak future. Hughes was an absentee landlord. The business was actually run by Noah Dietrich, Hughes's chief aide, and Dietrich wanted to dissolve it. Although Thornton was unaware of it, Dietrich had him installed to assist in its dismantling. Instead, Thornton turned the business around, transforming Hughes Aircraft into a highly profitable military electronics business with a research and development division the envy of the industry. Despite the company's success, Dietrich and Thornton clashed constantly. Hughes either refused to intervene or was incapable of doing so. When Dietrich fired one of Thornton's top lieutenants without consulting Thornton, he and a group of top executives resigned in protest. In his five years at Hughes Aircraft, Thornton had grown the business from revenues of just $8.5 million and a loss, to $600 million and an $8 million profit.[7] Thornton believed he could replicate his success at Hughes Aircraft, but this time he'd be working for himself. Rather than start from scratch, he'd find a small technology business with an established customer base that could be purchased cheaply. After a short search, he settled on Litton Industries because it was still owned by its founder Charles Litton, who was an engineer and inventor. Charles Litton recognized that he had taken Litton Industries as far as he could—he wanted to start businesses, not manage them—and Litton Industries could use professional management. Thornton thought he and the Hughes Aircraft refugees were just what Litton Industries needed—professional managers with expertise in a high-technology business. He knew he could transform Litton Industries, but first he needed $750,000 to buy it.

Despite the flimsiness of Electro Dynamics Corporation, Thornton's presentation persuaded the investment bankers at Lehman Brothers, and they agreed to raise the money to buy Litton Industries. It was purely a bet on Thornton. They did so by creating 50 units, comprising 20 bonds, 50 shares of convertible preferred stock, and 2,000 shares of common stock.[8] Each unit was offered for $29,200 for a total of $1,460,000 before commissions.[9] Thornton used the capital raised to pay Charles Litton the remainder of the purchase price and to pay off the notes from Wells Fargo, leaving around $400,000 for working capital. In 1954 Electro Dynamics Corporation became Litton Industries, and Thornton got to work implementing the strategy he'd described to the investment bankers from Lehman Brothers. As he had with Litton Industries, Thornton scoured the United States for potential takeover targets. His most difficult task was to persuade the owners that an exchange of stock was preferable to cash. He had a compelling pitch: Thornton argued that it was better to own a part share of a publicly listed company with several lines of business rather than all of a private company in a single line of business. A portfolio of diverse, centrally managed businesses with access to capital on the public markets was better able to ride out the vagaries of the business cycle than a single, private business. If the sale was completed through an exchange of shares, the event wasn't taxable, and the shares in the public company would continue to appreciate. Should they ever decide to sell, the shares were as liquid as cash. Many business owners bought Thornton's pitch, and Litton Industries grew rapidly.

By 1958, it had revenues of $83 million, earned $3.7 million in profit, and was regarded as a rapidly growing specialist in military electronics.[10] Earnings per share had grown from $0.28 to $2.13 as shares outstanding had ballooned from 525,000 to almost 1.7 million. Thornton made sure that the media knew all about Litton. Rare for the time, he engaged in publicity campaigns that touted Litton's successes, burnishing its image as a glamorous, high-technology company. He took every opportunity to discuss his *free-form management* style—really just cover for Litton's somewhat ad hoc acquisition policy. Thornton knew that the company's success turned on his ability to maintain the appearance of success. A growing share price made stock an attractive currency to the vendors of the businesses he wanted to buy, and a high share price made it an attractive currency to Thornton. Every spring the company sent its shareholders a thick, high-gloss annual report, printed on heavy weight stock, and filled with a brightly optimistic, slightly breathless commentary more at home in the pages of *Vanity Fair* than wrapped around financial statements.[11] The tone set by the report was not to distract from the financials—far from it, they were the centerpiece, like a Thanksgiving turkey nestled with pride amongst the trimmings—but to add a patina of glamour appropriate to such a high growth, high-tech-nology enterprise. The balance sheet was clean and the income statement showed earnings per share growing at a rapid clip. Nothing was hidden. If the return on equity was a little anemic, and more of the gains came from mergers and acquisitions than operations, then such was the nature of the conglomerate business. The shareholders didn't seem to care, as long as this new man of high-technology engineered revenues and earnings that climbed straight up. The report heaved with graphs, charts, and statistics highlight-ing the company's outstanding performance, *de rigueur* for a scientifically directed organization. Thornton knew his audience well.

While Thornton may have sold Litton as a high-technology business, there was nothing particularly bleeding edge about his management style. Like the other *conglomerateurs* bolting on smaller firms to the larger hodge-podge, Litton used its shares—which traded at a high price-to-earnings ratio because of its apparent high rate of growth and the general fad for conglomerates—to acquire the stock of other companies with lower price-to-earnings ratios, but often at a significant premium. The objective was to transform the earnings of the target, acquired at a lower price-to-earnings ratio, into earnings of the conglomerate, which traded at a higher price-to-earnings ratio, and create the illusion of rapid growth at the conglomerate. A conglomerate with a market capitalization of $20 million, and trading on a price-to-earnings ratio of 20, for example, could target a company with the same level of earnings, $1 million, but trading on a price-to-earnings ratio of 8. The conglomerate could offer a 25 percent premium over the market price, and still only pay $10 million, or 10 times earnings, for the target. Once the acquisition was completed, the conglomerate doubled its earn-ings to $2 million, but only increased its share count by 50 percent. Thus the earnings of the target, now transmogrified into conglomerate earnings, boosted the earnings per share of the acquirer by 33 percent. The conglom-erate appeared to show a high rate of growth in earnings per share, and the stock followed suit, shooting up to maintain the same multiple on markedly higher earnings.

By 1959 Litton hit $120 million in sales, and Thornton exceeded the five-year target he had set in the presentation to Lehman Brothers by $20 million. In 1958 Litton had completed several large transactions, but the one that contributed the most to pushing Litton past the $100 million-in-sales mark—Monroe Calculating Machine Company—was characteristic of Thornton's acquisition policy. Monroe was neither military, nor electronics—it made outdated mechanical tabulating machines—but Thornton was attracted to it because the controlling family was willing to sell cheaply, and for stock in Litton. In 1957 Monroe had sales of $44 million, earnings of $1.8 million, earnings per share of $6.00, and a book value per share of $42.71.[12] Litton, by contrast, had revenues of $28 million, the same earnings of $1.8 million, earnings per share of $1.51, and a book value per share of $6.71.[13] Monroe had more cash and better financial ratios, but Litton was growing faster, and was the more glamorous of the two companies. Monroe was prepared to accept one-and-a-half shares in Litton for every Monroe share, which meant that Litton shareholders would own three-quarters of the combination, and Monroe shareholders one quarter. Litton shareholders received almost three times the earnings per share and more than four times the book value per share in Monroe for each share given up in Litton. By contrast, Monroe shareholders received a little over one-third the earnings, and less than one-quarter the book value per share in Litton for each share given up in Monroe. Such was the price of joining the conglomerate. Thus, the high-growth, high-technology stock swallowed the much bigger, but declining business. Even though it had strayed a long way from its original military electronics business, the market continued to treat the combination as if it was a much larger version of that original business. This was Thornton's real skill: He could acquire a low-quality business in an industry only tenuously and tangentially connected to electronics or the military, and then persuade the market that the *synergies* from the combination warranted a higher valuation still.

By 1966, Litton had sales of $1 billion, and sold more than 5,000 products, including such high-technology exotica as oil drilling rigs, submarines, credit cards, trading stamps, and, of course, mechanical tabulating machines.[14] The torrid pace of acquisitions since Thornton had taken over in 1954 had burned out a number of the top executives. Those that left were called *LIDOs*—Litton Industries Drop Outs—and Litton became known as a "school for conglomerateurs."[15] One notable LIDO was Henry Singleton, who, along with another Litton alumnus, left to form Teledyne. Buffett has described Singleton as a "managerial superstar,"[16] with "the best operating and capital deployment record in American business."[17] The LIDOs and others aped Litton, but none had Thornton's zeal for publicity and deft touch in investor relations. Even after it extended well beyond the high-technology businesses upon which much of its allure rested and started buying more run-of-the-mill companies, Thornton managed to maintain Litton's air of glamour and growth. That year Litton traded on an average price-to-earnings ratio of 33, while other conglomerates traded on much lower multiples.[18] Textron, for example, traded on an average price-to-earnings ratio of 11, Ling-Temco-Vought traded on 13 times earnings, and ITT traded for 17 times earnings. All were valued at half or less than Litton.[19] It was a testament to Thornton's ability to woo Wall Street analysts, acquire companies, and produce attractive annual reports. Cracks, however, were beginning to appear. While Thornton could keep Litton perceived as a high-technology military electronics conglomerate the price paid for Litton stock would stay high, but this relied upon ever-increasing earnings per share. The actual businesses owned by Litton were becoming "bland, flabby, starved for capital, and mismanaged"[20] as the exodus of LIDOs took its toll on the managerial talent pool. Part of Thornton's "free-form management" philosophy was the belief that a good manager could operate in any industry.[21] It was an elaborate illusion—more self-deception, and hubris than intentionally misleading—and in 1968 it was shown to be what it was.

In January 1968, after 57 quarters of continued growth, Litton announced for the first time that earnings would decline by $11 million from the peak of $58.4 million earned in the previous year. The stock was savaged. Though the conglomerates themselves continued on, this, more than any other event, ended investor ardor for conglomerates. The market seemed to wake from its reverie, recognizing for the first time that earnings-per-share-growth-through-acquisition wasn't sustainable, and that, in any case, earnings per share growth wasn't necessarily a worthwhile end in itself. A satirical article appeared in *Barron's* in 1968 describing the gimmick employed by the conglomerateurs:[22]

> *Get hold of the speeches and annual report of the really savvy swingers, who know the lingo and make it sing. . . . You have to project the right image to the analysts so that they realize you're the new breed of entrepreneur. Talk about the synergy of the free-form company and its interface with change and technology. Tell them about your windowless room full of researchers . . . scrutinizing the future so your corporation will be opportunity technology oriented. . . . Analysts and investors want conceptually oriented (as opposed to opportunist) conglomerates, preferably in high technology areas. That's what they pay the high price-earnings ratios for, and life is a lot less sweaty with a high multiple.*

Critics charged that Litton's true skill rested not in high technology, but in publicity and investor relations.[23] They also noted that Litton was adept at the use of unusual—although not illegal—accounting techniques that obfuscated the true state of the businesses and exaggerate its growth.[24] Refusing to let the dream die, one of Litton's executives said in 1968, "There is no question in anybody's mind that Litton is going to be a successful large company, but our objective is to be a successful large *growth* company."[25] It was too late. The market had seen the man behind the curtain.

It is remarkable that it took so long for the investment community—financial analysts, investment bankers, the business-owner vendors, and professional investors—to understand the simple game performed by the conglomerateurs: Use overpriced stock to buy businesses at a price that allows for growth in earnings per share; promote the growth as a manifestation of managerial skill, and the result of high technology; rinse and repeat. The metric missing from the discussion was the intrinsic value given up and received in each merger. In his shareholder letters, Warren Buffett counselled that managers should consider whether they would complete a sale of their company in its entirety on the same terms as they proposed to complete the sale of a portion of the company, which was the economic reality of a merger.[26] If the transaction amounted to the sale of $2 of the acquirer's intrinsic value in exchange for $1 of the target's intrinsic value, even if it was accretive to earnings per share, they should ask themselves if it was a worthwhile transaction.[27] Part of the confusion arose from the language used to describe the *dilution* of earnings per share in such mergers, which tended to obfuscate rather than clarify the exchange of intrinsic values:[28]

> *The attention given this form of dilution is overdone: current earnings per share (or even earnings per share of the next few years) are an important variable in most business valuations, but far from all powerful. There have been plenty of mergers, non-dilutive in this limited sense, that were instantly value destroying for the acquirer. And some mergers that have diluted current and near-term earnings per share have in fact been value-enhancing. What really counts is whether a merger is dilutive or anti-dilutive in terms of intrinsic business value (a judgment involving consideration of many variables). We believe calculation of dilution from this viewpoint to be all-important (and too seldom made).*

Though they ended up owning the majority of the combination, the dilution of intrinsic value in the merger with Monroe was considerable for Litton's shareholders. Had they fully understood the economic consequences of the transaction, they may have grieved for the quarter of the thriving military electronics business given up for a three-quarter share in a dying mechanical tabulating machine business.

From 1968 onward, the veneer of growth, glamour, and high technology smeared over the conglomerates failed to conceal the increasingly bloated and sluggish businesses underneath. Until then, the booming stock market, low interest rates, and generally bountiful conditions for business had hidden many of the manager's sins, and allowed them to "build [the] house from the roof down," as one humorist described it.[29] As the market turned and interest rates climbed, the heavily cyclical businesses owned by the con-glomerates returned to earth, putting the lie to the claim that diversification allowed them to ride out a downturn. Though they promoted themselves as new men with a "free-form" vision for the organization, the reality was that most were little more than paper-shuffling financial engineers riding a market boom. "The most damaging result of the conglomerate merger era," wrote *Fortune's* Lewis Berman, "was the false legitimacy it seemed to confer on the pursuit of profits from financial manipulation rather than by produc-ing something of genuine economic value."[30]

In the introduction to *Security Analysis*, Graham had written that it was "striking" how the financial scene in the 1920s—the boom that preceded the bust in 1929—was dominated by what he described as "purely psycho-logical elements."[31] "In previous bull markets," Graham wrote, "the rise in stock prices remained in fairly close relationship with the improvement in the business during the greater part of the cycle; it was only in its invariably short-lived culminating phase that quotations were forced to disproportion-ate heights by the unbridled optimism of the speculative contingent."[32]

> *The "new-era" doctrine-that "good" stocks (or "blue chips") were sound investments regardless of how high the price paid for them was at bottom only a means of rationalizing under the title of "invest-ment" the well-nigh universal capitulation to the gambling fever. We suggest that the psychological phenomenon is closely related to the dominant importance assumed in recent years by intangible factors value, viz., good-will, management, expected earning power, etc. Such value factors, while undoubtedly real, are not subject to mathematical calculation; hence the standards by which they are measured are to a great extent arbitrary and can suffer the widest variations in accordance with the prevalent psychology.*

Graham could just as easily have been describing the conglomerate era. It wasn't a recent phenomenon in 1969, or even 1929 for that matter, that purely psychological elements dominated the market. In 1720 an anony-mous pamphleteer had decried the speculation in the shares of the South Sea Company, warning that, "The additional rise of this stock above the true capital will be only imaginary; one added to one, by any rules of vulgar arithmetic, will never make three and a half; consequently, all fictitious value must be a loss to some persons or other, first or last."[33] But neither was 1720 the birth of speculation.

As Edward Chancellor chronicled in his brilliant book *Devil Take The Hindmost: A History of Financial Speculation*, the "purely psychological element" has been associated with markets as long as markets have existed, beginning in the second century B.C. with the Roman financial system, which had many of the characteristics of the modern financial system, including stock and bond markets in the Forum, near the Temple of Castor. There "crowds of men bought and sold shares and bonds of tax-farming companies, various goods for cash and on credit, farms and estates in Italy and in the provinces, houses and shops in Rome and elsewhere, ships and storehouses, slaves and cattle."[34] Described as being comparable to the speculative fever that swept over Britain in the 1720s South Sea bubble, there was said to be "scarcely a soul one might say, who does not have some interest in these [tax-farming] contracts and profits which are derived from them."[35] Petronius Arbiter, a Roman courtier during the reign of Nero believed to be the author of the satirical novel the *Satirycon*, wrote later that, "filthy usury and the handling of money had caught the common people in a double whirlpool, and destroyed them."[36] The conglomerate fad was just one more speculative mania in a long line of speculative manias. It wouldn't be the last.

GLITZ AND GLAMOUR'D

The most vexing question from the conglomerate era is why the professional investment community—institutional investors, mutual funds, and research analysts—were so mesmerized by Thornton and the other conglomerateurs. Litton might have been a mirage, but it wasn't a fraud. It hid nothing in its heavily footnoted annual reports, or in its 10-Ks submitted to the SEC.[37] Reading those documents would have revealed that it was a collection of fair-to-middling businesses helmed by a charismatic salesman adroit at applying organizational gloss.[38] From its inception, the stock had performed very well as earnings exploded, and the multiple expanded. Already heady at 33 times earnings in 1965, it had swollen to 40 times earnings by the January 1968 announcement of its first drop in earnings. Note that Litton didn't announce a *loss* in 1968—just a *decline* in earnings of about 19 percent—and neither was it involved in a corporate scandal, yet the stock was crushed, plummeting from $90 to $53. It was unnecessary to be a securities analyst to see that at such a high price any small glitch in the story would lead to carnage in the stock, so how did so many professionals miss it?

We imagine that professional investors understand the drivers of investment success, carefully review documents filed with the SEC, calculate the odds that a given business will survive and prosper, weigh intrinsic value, and then cleverly bet to maximize the gain. If this is in fact the case, it is not reflected in the data. The most famous demonstration of the paucity of professional investors to differentiate between good stocks and bad and to beat the market is Alfred Cowles III's presentation to the Econometric Society of Cincinnati on the last day of 1932. Cowles, who subscribed to many different stock market services, decided that he'd be better off subscribing to only one—the best, naturally—but no data existed tracking the performance of the stock market analysts. Starting in 1928, Cowles collected the track records of the most widely circulated financial services and, with the aid of a punch card calculating machine, he studied their records. Of the 16 statistical services, 25 insurance companies, 24 forecasting letters, and the *Dow Theory* editorials of William Peter Hamilton over the period from December 1903 to December 1929, Cowles found only a handful had beaten the market. Worse, Cowles concluded of the performances of those few who had beaten the market that their results were "little, if any, better than what might be expected to result from pure chance."[39] He made the last claim after he assembled random market analyses from shuffled decks containing hundreds of cards, and found that the cards tended to beat the professional analysts. More recently John C. Bogle, legendary founder of The Vanguard Group, appeared before the Senate Subcommittee on Financial Management, the Budget, and International Security on November 3, 2003, to demonstrate the paucity of the returns generated by professional investors. Bogle's argument was that the competitive nature of the investment industry meant that the return of the average mutual fund should equal the return of the market less the fees charged by the mutual fund industry. Bogle testified:[40]

> *During the period 1984–2002, the U.S. stock market, as measured by the S&P 500 Index, provided an annual rate of return of 12.2 percent. The return on average mutual fund was 9.3 percent. The reason for that lag is not very complicated: As the trained, experienced investment professionals employed by the industry's managers compete with one another to pick the best stocks, their results average out. Thus, the average mutual fund should earn the market's return—before costs. Since all-in fund costs can be estimated at something like 3 percent per year, the annual lag of 2.9 percent in after-cost return seems simply to confirm that eminently reasonable hypothesis.*

While Bogle's thesis that professional investors can't beat the market because they *are* the market is "eminently reasonable," as he says, the data actually show that professional investors underperform the market by over 1 percent per year *before accounting for costs and management fees*.[41] Why might this be so? It seems that professional investors prefer glamour stocks and, as we have seen, glamour stocks lead, on average, to inferior performance.

Why would professional investors, often paid on the basis of the returns they generate, seek out stocks likely to lead to returns that are lower than the averages? Perhaps they are doing so unknowingly. Lakonishok et al. examine this point, finding that professional investors also make errors in judgment, extrapolating past growth rates of glamour stocks even when such growth rates are highly unlikely to persist. Like the lay investor, they too commit the investment sin of putting too much weight on the recent past for the particular stock under examination, rather than a *rational prior*, which is the probability of returns to glamorous, high-growth *story* stocks. This is a common judgment error not just in the stock market, but also in many situations requiring predictions about uncertain future states. It is known as "neglect of the base rate," and it was first examined by two pioneers in behavioral finance research, Daniel Kahneman and Amos Tversky, who gave it a prominent place in their groundbreaking paper, "Judgment under Uncertainty: Heuristics and Biases" (1974).[42] Kahneman and Tversky found that we make decisions about uncertain future events based on three *heuristics*—short cuts or simple rules of thumb—that help us break down complex cognitive tasks into simpler operations. Each leads us to make poor decisions about uncertain events because it leads us to consider irrelevant evidence, and in so doing diverts us from considering the underlying probabilities about the events.

The three heuristics are representativeness, availability, and anchoring and adjusting. *Representativeness* leads us to consider only how well something matches our stereotype of that group of things. So, for example, Kahneman and Tversky asked a group of subjects to determine whether an individual was a lawyer or engineer. The subjects were told that the individual had been randomly selected from a sample of professionals consisting of 70 engineers and 30 lawyers. When given a description of the individual's personality, the subjects assessed the likelihood that the individual was an engineer or lawyer by the extent to which the personality description matched the stereotype of an engineer or a lawyer, rather than using the underlying probabilities. The question was then altered such that no information was conveyed about the individual's personality, and the subjects used the underlying probabilities properly. The example illustrates that when no specific, representative evidence is given, we use the prior probabilities correctly, but when *worthless* representative evidence is given, we tend to ignore the prior probabilities and become distracted by the representative evidence. The *availability* heuristic leads us to consider only those things that can be brought to mind with ease, often because we have personal experience with them. For example, we assess the risk of heart attack among middle-aged people by recalling such occurrences among our acquaintances, rather than by considering the underlying probabilities. The *anchoring and adjusting heuristic* causes us to stick with our first impression, even in the face of additional evidence that should cause us to change our view.

Each heuristic manifests in a variety of different ways. Most of the time they are very useful and efficient but, in assessing probabilities and predicting uncertain future states, they can lead us into systematic and predictable errors. The problem, writes Leonard Mlodinow in his wonderful book *The Drunkard's Walk*, is that the mechanisms by which we analyze uncertain, probabilistic conditions are an "intricate product of evolutionary factors, brain structure, personal experience, knowledge and emotion" so complex that "different structures within the brain come to different conclusions."[43] The confusion is often that the logical left hemisphere of our brains looks for a pattern, while the right hemisphere behaves more intuitively. Mlodinow gives the following example of the tension between our pattern-seeking behavior and our more intuitive impulses: The game is called *probability guessing*. Subjects are shown lights that have two colors, say red and green. The lights flash so that one color appears more frequently than the other, but without any pattern. So, for example, red might appear twice as often as green in a sequence like red-red-green-green-red-red-green-red-red-red-red-green and so on. After watching for a period of time, the subject must guess which color will appear next. Mlodinow tells us that there are two basic strategies. The first is to always guess the color that appears most frequently. This is the strategy favored by rats and other animals, and our intuitive hemisphere. If we employ this strategy, we are guaranteeing a certain level of success, but can do no better. If red appears twice as often as green, two-thirds of our guesses will be correct, and one-third will be incorrect. The other strategy is to figure out the pattern. This is the strategy favored by MBA students and our logical hemisphere. If the lights flash in a pattern, and we can figure out that pattern, we can guess correctly every single time. If the lights flash randomly we can guess correctly only to the extent that we favor the color that flashes more regularly. We make an intuitive tradeoff when we try to guess correctly—we forgo the guaranteed, but known, error rate for the possibility that we get all correct. This is the reason that rats tend to outperform MBA students in these types of experiments. Our native intuition is wrong, and our reasoning apparatus poor under conditions of uncertainty.

There are few arenas that allow us to demonstrate the full range of our heuristic pathologies quite like the stock market. The research is clear that value stocks—defined as a low price in relation to some fundamental measure like earnings, book value, or cash flow—outperform glamour stocks, which have a high price in relation to those fundamental measures. Yet we are intuitively attracted to glamour stocks. We like them because they have done well in the recent past, either in terms of stock price performance or growth in earnings; they have received some good news; or we confuse a well-run company with a good investment. The same impulse leads us to avoid value stocks because the earnings or stock price has fallen, they have problems, or we think a poorly run company must be a bad investment. When we do so, we are ignoring the base case, and instead focusing on factors that are not predictive of performance. For example, Kahneman and Tversky write that a favorable view of a company's products leads us to draw favorable conclusions about its stock. If we invest in a company's stock based on our view of its products, we ignore the reliability of this type of evidence, which is low, and the accuracy of a prediction based on it, which is also low. For example, in August 2012 Apple, Inc. was regarded as an innovative company, with fantastic products, and stellar earnings growth, and it became the most valuable stock by market capitalization in history. Figure 6.1 shows a chart of Apple, Inc.'s stock price over the year following its coronation as most valuable company in history.

While it continued selling popular products, growing both revenue and income, and paying dividends, Apple, Inc.'s stock fell 45 percent from its $700 peak to well below $400. This illustrates the problem with assessments based on the favorability of our view of the company, which is not predictive, rather than basing it on measures that we know have in the past predicted returns. Had we done so, we might have observed that above $700, Apple, Inc. stock was overvalued on some measures, and overvaluation is a condition that leads to lower future returns. We might also have

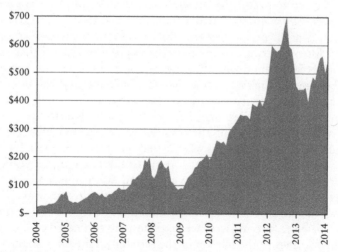

FIGURE 6.1 Apple, Inc. 10-Year Stock Price Chart
Source: Eyquem Investment Management LLC.

observed that below $400 it was one of the most undervalued large capitalization stock in the United States, and, as we know, undervaluation is a condition for future market-beating returns.

Shortly after Graham published *Security Analysis* in 1934, John Burr Williams published his 1938 masterpiece *The Theory of Investment Value*.[44] Williams's *discounted cash flow* theory of intrinsic value is the bedrock of modern valuation and forms the intellectual basis for a variety of valuation models, including, for example, Gordon's growth model, which we saw earlier. The models all require an estimate for future cash flows, earnings, or dividends, making allowance for any growth, and out to perpetuity. Money has a time value—a dollar today is worth more than a dollar in a year—so we must then discount back to today those future cash flows at the appropriate discount rate. While the theory is sound, the slip 'twixt cup and lip is in its practical application. The three variables—future cash flows, the growth rate, and the discount rate—are all sources of potential forecast error. Discounted cash flow models are extremely sensitive to discount rates, which can lead to large errors, but the real problem is that the model assumes we have some way of forecasting future cash flows and the growth rates embedded in them. Time and again, we have been shown to be poor forecasters, preferring to extrapolate the current trend, rather than assume mean reversion. Kahneman and Tversky call this the "misconception of regression," and it rears its head time and again in investment.

Studies of financial analysts' earnings forecasts, for example, have found them to fail to incorporate into the forecast an expectation of mean reversion when it is bound to occur, and therefore to deliver results that are *no better than random chance*. In 2007 Roy Batchelor examined the records of financial analysts over the period 1990 to 2005, and found them to be consistently wrong, persistently erring on the side of over-optimism because they extrapolated up an existing trend without allowing for mean reversion. Figure 6.2 is a chart showing Batchelor's finding that analysts tend to be too optimistic.[45]

The chart shows that forward earnings forecasts are rarely correct and tend to overshoot actual earnings. Batchelor finds this bias to over-optimism to be systematic. The size of the forecast error declines when economic growth accelerates and increases when economic growth slows. In Batchelor's research, actual earnings beat the forecasts only twice in 25 years—both times during recoveries following a recession. When the forecasts did hit the target it was because the underlying economic growth was unusually strong, which is to say the forecast turned out to be right because the usual assumptions in the forecast were wrong. The analysts missed completely any turn in the fortunes of the market or the economy. Like naïve extrapolation investors, they failed to account for any possibility of mean reversion when mean reversion is the *probable* outcome.

FIGURE 6.2   Analysts Are Systematically Overoptimistic
Source: Roy Batchelor. 2007 "Bias in Macroeconomic Forecasts," *International Journal of Forecasting* 23 2, pp. 189–203, April–June 2007.

This failure to account for mean reversion is endemic in forecasting. In *The Fortune Sellers: The Big Business of Buying and Selling Predictions,*[46] William Sherden examined research about the accuracy of short-term macro-economic forecasts (fewer than three years into the future) conducted since the 1970s. Sherden found that economists, like the financial analysts in Batchelor's research, also missed turning points in the economy. Their fore-casting was no better than a "naïve forecast" that the near future would look like the recent past, and their ability to forecast accurately was, on average, no better than flipping a coin. The economists were engaged in naïve extrap-olation, just like the naïve investors of Lakonishok et al.'s research. Sherden also found that the economists' predictions tended to be too optimistic. Tellingly, increased sophistication—more powerful computers, more arcane models, and mountains of historical data—had not improved the accuracy of their forecasts. There is no evidence that their ability has increased since the 1970s (if anything, the evidence is that it has deteriorated over time).[47] In their analysis of forecasts published in *The Wall Street Journal* between 1985 and 2001, the U.S. Federal Reserve also found that economists tended to miss turning points.[48] The forecasts were most accurate in the middle of an economic expansion, when the near future most closely resembles the recent past, and naïve extrapolation would be the method most likely to yield an accurate answer. The forecasts were least accurate at turning points, completely missing, for example, the start of the 1990s recession in July 1990, and the popping of the dot-com bubble in January 2001. It's clear that financial analysts, economists, and forecasters of all kinds behave like Lakonishok et al.'s naïve extrapolation investors, ignoring mean reversion, remaining too optimistic, and missing turning points in the markets and the economy as a result. When those turning points manifest, as they are bound to do, it is easy to claim that it was unforeseeable.

It should come as no surprise that professional investors make cognitive errors. They are, after all, human. Kahneman and Tversky, in their research, found that even clinical psychologists specialized in cognition—and aware of the research into heuristics—and other statistically sophisticated research psychologists made the same errors when they thought intuitively. In an experimental setting they were able to avoid elementary errors like the *gambler's fallacy* that we discussed in an earlier chapter, but were prone to the same errors when the problems were disguised, made more intricate, or manifest in another setting. Kahneman and Tversky show, for example, that clinical psychologists who conduct selection interviews for staff are confident in their predictions even though there is a "vast literature that shows selection interviews to be highly fallible."[49] Similarly, a study of statistical research psychologists found that they put too much faith in the results of small-sample studies—leading them to grossly overestimate the likelihood that the results could be replicated and were representative of the population—when small-sample studies are known to have high rates of error. If psychologists expert in cognition and statistics make cognitive errors, it's wholly plausible that professional investors also make cognitive errors.

It's not difficult to understand why professional investors buy glamour stocks. One implication of DeBondt and Thaler's research, for example, is that we should favor stocks with earnings that have declined over the last three years, to stocks that have grown earnings over the last three years. This is not a difficult concept to understand, but remarkably difficult to implement in practice. Our intuition is that stocks that have seen their earnings decline for three straight years will see earnings continue to decline. The stock with earnings that have grown feels much safer. It's intuitive to extrapolate out a trend in earnings, and it's uncomfortable to invest on the expectation that they will mean revert. Similarly, we find it frightening to buy companies with plummeting stock prices, and much easier to buy stocks with advancing prices. Lakonishok et al.'s research shows that the lower a stock price is relative to some fundamental measure, the more likely it is to outperform, but stocks rarely get cheap without problems. It's difficult to ignore those problems, which aren't predictive, and focus on the undervaluation, which is. This is how cognitive errors occur. The prior probability is simple to understand, but the practical implementation of that understanding isn't easy.

Even if professional investors can overcome their own cognitive errors, there are other reasons that may lead them to prefer glamour stocks to value stocks. As is often the case, during Apple, Inc.'s rise and fall, it was the most popular stock among professional investors.[50] The reason is that there is a principal-agency problem in professional investment too: a professional investor might not act in the best interests of the investors in her fund. Lakonishok et al. observe, for example, that professional investors might prefer glamour stocks because they appear to be "prudent" investments, and hence easy to justify to investors in the fund. Here, though the professional investor is immune from cognitive error, the sponsors of the professional investor's fund are not. It is they who commit the judgment error, regarding glamour stocks as "safer" than value stocks, even though, as we have seen, they are riskier. Thus the professional investor knows that the strategy of investing in glamour stocks is not prudent at all, but does so because potential and existing sponsors in the fund regard it as prudent. Another possibility, which De Bondt and Thaler demonstrated in their research, is that professional investors are forced to be oriented to the short term because they are judged on short-term performance, and value strategies require longer time horizons to consistently pay off. Lakonishok et al. posit that professional investors will rationally look for stocks that appear likely to earn them immediate returns, rather than a small annual premium over the market over the next five years. They cannot afford to underperform the index or their peers for any period of time, for if they do, their sponsors will withdraw the funds. A value strategy that takes three to five years to pay off, but may underperform the market in the meantime, might simply be too risky for professional investors from a career perspective. The problem, of course, is that by attempting to avoid short-term underperformance, they are captured by it. The sum of these errors leads even professional investors to invest as if they prefer glamour stocks, and, consequently to underperform the market. The likely reason, given the experience of clinical and research psychologists, is that they make cognitive errors. They are easy to make because the incorrect decision feels intuitive, while the correct decision feels counterintuitive. Extrapolation is instinctive, while mean reversion is not. The lesson is that, if we understand both the characteristics that lead stocks to outperform and the physiognomies that lead investors to underperform, the difference between the two is behavioral.

Notes

1. Adapted from *The American Heritage Science Dictionary*. (Boston: Houghton Mifflin Company) 2008.

2. Robert Sobel. *The Rise and Fall of the Conglomerate Kings.* (New York: Stein and Day) 1984.
3. Ibid.
4. David Bird. "Charles B. Thornton Dead at 68; Was a Litton Industries Founder." *The New York Times*, November 26, 1981.
5. Sobel, 1984.
6. Ibid.
7. Ibid.
8. Ibid.
9. Ibid.
10. Ibid.
11. Ibid.
12. Ibid.
13. Ibid.
14. Bird, 1981.
15. Sobel, 1984.
16. Warren Buffett. "Shareholder Letter," *Berkshire Hathaway, Inc. Annual Report,* 1982.
17. John Train. *The Money Masters.* (New York: Harper & Row) 1980.
18. Sobel, 1984.
19. Ibid.
20. Ibid.
21. Ibid.
22. Ibid.
23. Anonymous. "Lehman Brothers Collection: Litton Industries, Inc. Company History". *Harvard Business School Baker Library Historical Collection*, 1960. Available at http://www.library.hbs.edu/hc/lehman/company.html?company=litton_industries_inc.
24. Sobel, 1984.
25. Ibid.
26. Buffett, 1982.
27. Ibid.
28. Ibid.
29. Sobel, 1984.
30. Ibid.
31. Benjamin Graham and David Dodd. *Security Analysis: The Classic 1934 Edition.* (New York: McGraw-Hill) 1996.
32. Ibid.
33. Edward Chancellor. *Devil Take the Hindmost: A History of Financial Speculation* (New York: Penguin Group) 2000.
34. Ibid.
35. Ibid.
36. Ibid.
37. Sobel, 1984.
38. Ibid.

39. Justin Fox. *The Myth of the Rational Market: A History of Risk, Reward, and Delusion on Wall Street.* (New York: HarperCollins) 2009.
40. John. C. Bogle. "Statement of John C. Bogle to the United States Senate Governmental Affairs Subcommittee," November 3, 2003. Available at http://www.vanguard.com/bogle_site/sp20031103.html.
41. J. Lakonishok, A. Shleifer, and R. W. Vishny. "Contrarian Investments, Extrapolation, and Risk." *Journal of Finance*, Vol. XLIX, No. 5, (1994) pp. 1541–1578.
42. Amos Tversky and Daniel Kahneman. "Judgment under Uncertainty: Heuristics and Biases." *Science*, New Series, Vol. 185, No. 4157. (Sep. 27, 1974), pp. 1124–1131. http://www.jstor.org/pss/1738360.
43. Leonard Mlodinow. *The Drunkard's Walk: How Randomness Rules Our Lives.* (New York: Pantheon Books) Reprint edition, 2009.
44. John B. Williams. *The Theory of Investment Value.* (Fraser Publishing Co.) 1997.
45. Roy Batchelor. "Bias in Macroeconomic Forecasts," *International Journal of Forecasting 23* 2, 189–203, April–June 2007.
46. William A. Sherden. *The Fortune Sellers: The Big Business of Buying and Selling Predictions.* (New York: John Wiley & Sons) 1999.
47. Chris Leithner. *Leithner Letter No. 163–166 26, July–26 October 2013.* Leithner & Company Pty. Ltd. Brisbane, 2013. I am grateful to Chris for highlighting these articles in his letter.
48. Jon E. Hilsenrath. "Economists' Forecasts Are Worst When They Might Be Most Useful." *The Wall Street Journal*, July 1, 2002.
49. Kahneman and Tversky, 1974.
50. Meena Krishnamsetty and Jake Mann. "Apple is the hedge fund king once again." *The Wall Street Journal MarketWatch.* May 16, 2013. Available at http://www.marketwatch.com/story/apple-is-the-hedge-fund-king-once-again-2013-05-16.

CHAPTER 7

Catch a Falling Knife
The Anatomy of a Contrarian Value Strategy

"There is no a priori probability about it. A strange enigma is man!"
"Someone calls him a soul concealed in an animal," I suggested.
"Winwood Reade is good upon the subject," said Holmes. "He remarks that, while the individual man is an insoluble puzzle, in the aggregate he becomes a mathematical certainty. You can, for example, never foretell what any one man will do, but you can say with precision what an average number will be up to. Individuals vary, but percentages remain constant. So says the statistician."
— Arthur Conan Doyle, *The Sign of Four* (1890)

Ronald Alfred Brierley launched *New Zealand Stocks and Shares*—"The Leading Investment Journal," as it described itself—in 1956 at the age of 19.[1] He had decided to run a tiny classified advertisement selling the newsletter. If no one subscribed he'd abandon the project and be out of pocket only the cost of the advertisement. At the time the market capitalization of the entire New Zealand stock market was just NZ£300 million[2]—about $12 billion in 2014 U.S. dollars[3]—and the newspaper relegated financial news to a half page squashed between the golf and horse racing results, so he can't have expected much of a response. To his delight, five checks for NZ£1 10s came in, for a grand total of NZ£7 10s (about $400), which was enough to produce the first edition. Brierley authored every one of its six pages of "expert reports," folding and stuffing the finished product into envelopes, each of which he personally licked closed. The first edition advised under the heading "Buying Below Par Can Be Profitable"—*par* being a somewhat archaic per share value below which a company promised not to issue shares—that, "When share values drop, the prices for some shares fall more than the circumstances really warrant and in these instances there may exist a good chance to make a profitable investment."[4] It provided a list of 33 issues below par, and recommended the "Hauraki Whaling Company."[5] While *New Zealand Stocks and Shares* had only five subscribers, Brierley decided to print 1,000 copies. He reasoned that every listed company in New Zealand would want a copy, and, after six months when no doubt they would have grown attached to the newsletter he could invoice them for the back copies. Brierley found that about one in four paid up. He wrote back to those who didn't pay, noting that "National Investments"—the grandiose name under which he published the newsletter—was "disappointed" that they had decided not to pay, and sought the full amount for the back issues. Those who refused again received a further letter from the 19-year-old Brierley that began, "We are disappointed in view of the fact that we are writing an article on your organization."[6] Very few resisted further.

By the 1960s *New Zealand Stocks and Shares* was no longer an amateurish, six-page newsletter with five subscribers, but a well known, if slightly outré, publication in New Zealand.[7] Brierley was unrestrained by any sense of propriety, and often harshly criticized management, employing a sarcastic tone to goad them into returning capital to shareholders. Brierley said, "I was conscious of the fact that if one wrote offensive untruths it would be possible to be sued for large sums of money, so one tried to write offensive truths. Really, what seemed offensive in those days is now innocuous." Still, it was unheard of in New Zealand's establishment business circles at the time. Some wit declared the publication was less *Stocks and Shares*, and more "Shocks and Stares."[8] As he had researched listed companies in New Zealand, Brierley had been struck by the number dominated by elderly, entrenched board members who sat on underperforming assets and retained earnings with a death grip, refusing to pay dividends. Many of the businesses had outlived their useful lives, but the companies that owned them were overcapitalized, with passive shareholders who allowed the business to drift along. Brierley imagined "aging directors, dozy and distant in the wood-paneled dimness of their boardrooms, recovering from a heavy luncheon at the club. Goodness knows, there was no need for them to be on full alert. It was their game and generally they found everyone played fair."[9] He decided to shake it up.

Brierley had some experience agitating at companies. He had published in *Stocks and Shares* a series of articles written in his usual sardonic manner about an offer for Wellington Loan and Investment Company Limited. When a second offer emerged that pushed up the price, a local newspaper credited Brierley with the increase. He used the publicity to launch R. A.

Brierley Investments Limited, and took out a number of advertisements in local newspapers promising "real adventure in the stock market:"[10]

> *R. A. Brierley Investments Limited is modeled on the successful techniques of the new overseas school of enterprising financiers— the takeover men—the merger experts—the "corporate raiders". You've read the amazing stories of these millionaires. . .the same opportunities are here in New Zealand.*
>
> *Now—even if you've never owned a share in your life—you can join in the secret and dramatic planned assaults on sleepy public companies. Mail the coupon below—today—for a free copy of the prospectus.*

Those who did mail in the coupon received a thin, blue-bound document that set out the company's objectives: It would "take over other companies and reorganize their finances, selling off surplus assets and reinvesting the funds for the more useful development of an existing business."[11] It would also "invest in industries where mergers were inevitable."[12] He offered newspaper quotes and analysis of the takeover technique employed by Charles Clore, a British financier. Though R. A. Brierley Investments had no earnings or assets, the capital raising was successful. In 1961, at 23, Brierley was running a public company with 200 shareholders holding 144,000 five-shilling shares for a total capitalization of about NZ£30,000 after costs (about $1,000,000).

R. A. Brierley Investments' first bid was for the Otago Farmers Co-operative Association of New Zealand Limited in July 1961.[13] Otago Farmers had been moved to the unofficial list of the New Zealand Stock Exchange for failing to comply with official listing requirements. It was a typical Brierley target: an unusual legal structure, a slight taint provided by the removal from the official list, generating lackluster earnings, but with hidden and valuable assets. As he had with *Stocks and Shares*, Brierley personally folded and stuffed the offer documents, and licked each envelope. He hoped that the provocative bid would attract shareholders to R. A. Brierley Investments, but believed the chances of actually getting control of Otago Farmers were remote. He was right. The offer was not well received. Many of the shareholders returned the offer documents scrawled with obscenities in the reply-paid envelopes Brierley had included.[14] The bid wasn't a total loss, however. Shortly after Brierley's offer, the company announced a change in its policy on shareholder discounts, and the market price of the stock leapt.[15]

Brierley launched his second bid for Southern Cross Building and Banking Society Limited in December 1961 for 20 shillings per share paid over three years.[16] Like Otago Farmers, Southern Cross's earnings were lackluster, but its balance sheet was liquid, and contained land and buildings held at cost, and therefore likely very undervalued. The chairman declared it a "damn nuisance" that Brierley had launched just before Christmas—a classic Brierley tactic—believing that he was trying to catch them asleep at the wheel—he was.[17] He had also sent his offer under the heading "Memorandum to the Members of Southern Cross" with his name and address at the bottom, which, by coincidence, was in the same building as Southern Cross, giving the impression that Southern Cross had itself issued the memorandum. Management fired off an open letter to Brierley charging him with acting in bad faith, pointing to the low-ball bid, which was to be paid over three years, and was also conditional on acceptance by 51 percent of shareholders. Brierley responded with his own open letter, noting, "If their statement is meant to imply that the shares are worth more than 20 shillings each, this seems strange in view of the fact that the society has itself arranged a number of sales over the past few years around the 12-shilling mark, and the directors themselves have purchased shares at this level without previously having felt compelled to advise the members that they were worth more."[18] In March 1962 management announced a one-for-one bonus issue "to demonstrate the strength of [Southern Cross's] structure by bringing its balance sheet more in line with its assets position."[19] The company also revalued its land and buildings at almost double the 1961 book value. The share price responded. Though it was another unsuccessful bid, local newspapers again recognized Brierley's role in pushing up the stock price. Brierley said, "It was a vintage example of an organization selling at vastly less than its value which all of a sudden discovers it can reward its shareholders like never before in its history."[20]

After a third bitterly fought and failed takeover bid, Brierley found some success in 1963 when he got control of the Finance Corporation of New Zealand.[21] He wanted the impressive name, which obscured the fact that the company been formed in 1952 to finance the hire purchase of radios. It had been orphaned when its parent, the Radio Corporation of New Zealand Limited, was taken over, and in the rest of its 11-year existence had earned just NZ£19,000 (about $630,000). He immediately issued a prospectus under the name Finance Corporation of New Zealand to raise NZ£100,000 in 10 percent unsecured notes. Brierley was right about the power of the name. The issue was massively oversubscribed, raising NZ£266,000 (about $8.6 million), and made Brierley a force to be reckoned with.

Brierley used the capital to harass the detritus of the stock market—unlisted public companies for which there was no active market, and in which many of the shareholders could not be found. In the 1930s, forestry companies had used *share-hawkers* to sell stock door-to-door, promising that the shares would be valuable when the forests were felled 30 years hence.

Many of the shareholders simply forgot they held the shares. In some companies these lost or missing shareholders—known as "Gone, No Address" or "GNAs"—comprised 30 percent of the share register.[22] The obvious attraction to Brierley of companies with many GNAs was that control could be had without buying 50 percent of the shares. In 1964 Brierley found one, Mamaku Forests, that he valued at 25 shillings per share, but could be bought for 7 shillings. One director discovered that Brierley was buying, and informed him that if he bid for the whole company at 17 shillings, the board would support him.[23] Brierley did so, and, although another bidder emerged with a higher bid, the board supported Brierley. As he had suspected, only 70 percent of the shares were tendered—the rest were GNAs—and Brierley had control of a substantial public company with shareholder funds of NZ£20,000 (about $650,000) for an outlay of about NZ£11,000 (about $350,000) or a little over half price.[24]

Brierley started examining companies in Australia. In 1964 he placed an advertisement in the *Australian Financial Review* seeking what he described as "special situations."[25] One letter in response described a holding in Citizens and Graziers Life Assurance Company Limited. It provided the history of the company, noted that it was unlisted, mentioned that it hadn't paid a dividend in 30 years, and included the detail that the company had just sold its life assurance business. Brierley immediately grasped that its assets would consist primarily of cash, and would likely be undervalued. He started buying the stock. The board had intended to turn the company into an investment operation, but needed approval by 75 percent of the shareholders. Brierley raced to acquire 25 percent so that he could block the conversion, launching a "first come, first served" bid for Citizens and Graziers in 1966.[26] The directors capitulated when Brierley reached the 25 percent threshold, recommending to shareholders that they accept his bid. Brierley then used Citizens and Graziers to bid for Industrial Equity Limited, a non-operating company formed in 1964 to operate a "buy-write" business, a trading strategy that generates income by selling call options on acquired shares.[27] The buy-write business hadn't generated much income, and the stock traded at a significant discount to its asset backing, which consisted entirely of listed stocks. The directors had decided to wind up the company and liquidate it, so Brierley's bid was welcomed with open arms. In Industrial Equity, Brierley had his vehicle for investing in Australia. He immediately started searching for other Australian companies to acquire.

He found fertile soil in Australia's food and agricultural sector. The industry was dominated by a number of small family controlled companies. Subsidies and long relationships with large multinational companies like Heinz, Cadbury, and Nabisco, had made them fat, inefficient, and torpid. Each was a classic Brierley target: deeply undervalued, with complacent management, low returns, and even lower payout ratios, highly liquid balance sheets, and surplus assets. Brierley was convinced that the industry would consolidate, and in the early 1970s took positions in a number of companies at what was the industry's trough. The largest was Southern Farmers Cooperative Limited, which possessed two attributes Brierley sought. It had been a cooperative, but had converted to a limited liability company, and, in the process had uncovered 1,600 GNAs who had gone missing in the conversion.[28] The formerly unusual legal structure meant that it flew under the investment radar, and the large number of GNAs meant that Brierley would not require 50 percent of the stock to control the company. Brierley estimated the intrinsic value of Southern Farmers' shares, which traded in the market for $1.30, at almost $8 per share, making it at the time one of the most undervalued companies on the Australian stock market.[29] He saw that Southern Farmers was so overcapitalized, and with so many fallow assets that could be sold, that he could get control of it for practically nothing once the capital was returned.

In 1974 Brierley put a third of Industrial Equity's capital into Southern Farmers before the directors even realized he was preparing a bid. Believing Brierley wanted to strip the cash, the directors caused the company to return almost 7 percent of its capital to shareholders as a 50-cent-per-share cash dividend. As a substantial shareholder, Industrial Equity was one of the main beneficiaries of the return of capital, which just served to reduce its holding costs by almost 40 percent. Realizing their tactical error, Southern Farmers then merged with a consortium of agricultural companies, which had the effect of reducing the proportionate size of Brierley's shareholding, but also delivered to him another large cash payment. Industrial Equity put the cash to good use, acquiring Noske Limited, a company that Southern Farmers wanted. In 1976, Southern Farmers bought Noske from Industrial Equity in an exchange of shares, boosting Industrial Equity's holding in Southern Farmers again. Brierley was also appointed to the board of Southern Farmers, delivering him effective control of it. The company became his platform for consolidating the food and agricultural industry. By 1978, it was the third-largest company in the industry by assets.

Shareholders hailed him in 1986 at the twenty-fifth annual meeting of Brierley Investments—the "R. A." had been dropped in 1971. In the 25 years since its founding, Brierley Investments had grown to 160,000 shareholders, sported a NZ$4.5 billion market capitalization (about $9.2 billion), and controlled 300 companies around the world with NZ$11.8 billion (almost $20 billion) in assets. NZ£500 invested in 1961—New Zealand converted from pounds to dollars in July 1967 at a rate of two dollars to one pound—was worth an extraordinary NZ$3 million by 1986, a compound annual growth rate of approximately 38 percent. It was a full validation of Brierley's investment strategy, which, at one stage, had led him to be described as the "bag-lady of business" for his attraction to stocks that were "down-at-heel and dispossessed."[30] It was an unfair portrayal. Sounding remarkably like Warren Buffett, Brierley told his biographer in 1990 that he "preferred what he calls 'bricks and mortar' companies, with easily identifiable assets, producing a relatively simple product," and "deliberately steered away from companies involved in technology because he does not understand them."[31] There were two significant differences, however. Where Buffett sought wonderful companies, Brierley sought only deeply undervalued companies in which he could reveal their "true value for all the world to see."[32] As he explained in 1990:[33]

> *If you own the value, the unlocking is secondary. Once you own something, if the value is there, you might have to rack your brains to find a solution, but it is better than finding there is no value to unlock.*

Where Buffett wanted high-quality, autonomous managers, Brierley viewed Brierley Investments as a "monitoring organization that continually evaluated the performance of various companies and acted as a catalyst to promote the most effective ownership of a company."[34] His biographer, Yvonne van Dongen noted that his "achievement as a spur to management was not just limited to the firms he took over, but extended to all the firms threatened by his presence. There were many companies . . . who set in motion a plan of action that Brierley himself had intended to instigate."[35]

His 1987 bid for the 143-year old British life insurance company Equity and Law Life Assurance Society PLC was Brierley's defining bid. Equity and Law presented an unwieldy target, with formidable protection, and a recherché value. The company was protected by a variety of regulations peculiar to the insurance industry a board heaving with knights, lords, and other blue-bloods; and cross-shareholdings from other insurers, with the risk that a threat to one would likely be perceived as a threat to all. The value proposition too was abstruse. Equity and Law had a market capitalization of £350 million, but earned £8 million on just £2.8 million in equity. What it did have was substantial float from the life insurance policyholders' funds. Other Brierley Investments executives were uneasy about the bid. One asked, "How do you make a profit out of it," to which Brierley replied enigmatically, "If you can't see that by now, perhaps you shouldn't be in this business."[36] Brierley had judged the intrinsic value to be found in significantly improving the performance of Equity and Law's considerable, and underexploited float, on which Equity and Law had been generating only a meager return. He also saw that there was a good chance that a bid might force into the open a competing bid from another insurer. It was an asymmetric value proposition—limited downside, substantial upside—and too good to pass on.

Brierley had been soaking up shares of Equity and Law for two years when in September 1987 the Insurance Companies Act of 1982 forced his hand. The Act required approval of the United Kingdom's Department of Trade and Industry for a shareholding exceeding 33.3 percent of the voting power, and Brierley had pushed to 29.6 percent. Approval by the Department of Trade and Industry took six weeks, which left only one week to complete the takeover under UK law.[37] On September 4, 1987, Brierley bid 363p cash per share for Equity and Law, valuing the company at £374 million (about $1.2 billion).[38] The board immediately rejected the bid as "unwelcome and undervalued."[39] In the Bangkok airport lounge en route back to Australia, Brierley learned of a new 400p bid from French insurer Compagnie du Midi, which had previously discussed with Brierley acquiring his stake in Equity and Law.[40] Equity and Law's board also rejected Compagnie du Midi's bid. Within the month, however, it had accepted a revised 446p bid from Compagnie du Midi. The media and other Brierley Investments executives expected him to accept the bid too, and so they were shocked when he bid again at 450p. Why bluff and risk losing Compagnie du Midi's offer for 4p, less than 1 percent more? Brierley's assessment was the correct one, however, and Compagnie du Midi responded with a revised 450p bid, the absolute limit of Equity and Law's value, which Brierley accepted.[41] The revised offer delivered to Brierley Investments a profit of £42.9 million (about $140 million) or 42 percent on its position.[42] Brierley had rolled the dice and won handsomely, but had used up his political capital at Brierley Investments at the time he would need it most.

Equity and Law was the last takeover for Ron Brierley at Brierley Investments. The October 19, 1987 stock market crash occurred two weeks after Compagnie du Midi's bid closed. The New Zealand stock market fell more than any market in the world. From its peak of 3,968.89, it fell 32 percent to 2,000 over the following three months.[43] Brierley Investments fared even worse, dropping 40 percent from $4.43 to $2.70.[44] Brierley Investments' executives believed that had Compagnie du Midi withdrawn, Brierley Investments might have been sunk.[45] Worse, he had gambled the company on a 1 percent increase on Compagnie du Midi's bid. Brierley had predominantly used cash in takeovers to avoid diluting his own shareholding, but Brierley Investments was an investment company, and Brierley had never held a controlling shareholding in it. In 1961 he had subscribed shares along with the other shareholders and ended up with just 15 percent. By 1987 that shareholding had dwindled to 3.7 percent of the shares outstanding as stock had been issued for acquisitions. In 1989 Brierley was pushed out of the company he had founded. He moved on in 1990 to Guinness Peat Group, a listed corporate shell he salvaged from the crash of another corporate raider. He was chairman of Guinness Peat until he stepped down in late 2010, although he remains on the board as a non-executive director. At 76 he continues to dig for hidden value and agitate through Australian Stock Exchange-listed Mercantile Investment Company.

CONTRARIAN VALUE

Brierley's *modus operandi* was to find stocks with a business at a trough, with a valuation to match. From his investment in Otago Farmers, to his bet on Southern Cross, to his entry into the Australian food and agricultural industry and his run at Equity and Law, each was an investment in an undervalued stock at a fundamental nadir, made with the expectation that business conditions would improve and the valuation would mean revert as well. Benjamin Graham taught that value investing is investing on the anticipation that the market price can depart from intrinsic value in the short term, but will revert to it over the long term. Graham's deeper lesson was that value oscillates, too. We err when we examine a stock's financial statements to analyze its fundamental performance and assume that the trend will persist. Graham's view, rediscovered by behavioral finance researchers De Bondt and Thaler, and confirmed by Lakonishok, Shleifer, and Vishny, is that this impulse to naïvely extrapolate leads us to systematically overpay for glamour stocks—*good* companies at expensive valuations—and avoid value stocks—*poor* companies at low valuations. The so-called *contrarian investor* approaches the problem anticipating mean reversion in both fundamentals and valuation. Does such a strategy lead to outperformance over a simple value investment strategy that examines only valuation?

Lakonishok, Shleifer, and Vishny have examined this contrarian value strategy, analyzing the returns to stocks purchased on the basis that they have both poor historical fundamentals and a low valuation, implying an expectation for continued poor performance. They find that the contrarian value strategy does in fact outperform the simpler value strategy we examined earlier that invests only on the basis of an analysis that examines whether the security is undervalued without consideration given to the business's historical performance. Lakonishok, Shleifer, and Vishny tested the *contrarian value investment* strategy by examining the universe of stocks according to two variables—historical performance and expected future performance—and then dividing the universe into three portfolios—the bottom 30 percent, the middle 40 percent, and top 30 percent. The *Glamour* portfolios contained stocks with the highest historical growth—which Lakonishok defined

TABLE 7.1 Average Five-Year Cumulative Return to Contrarian Value Portfolios and Glamour Portfolios (1963 to 1990)

	Glamour Portfolio Average Five-Year Cumulative Return (%)	Contrarian Value Portfolio Average Five-Year Cumulative Return (%)	Difference (Contrarian Value—Glamour) (%)
Price-to-Book Value and Sales Growth	84.2	161.8	77.6
Price-to-Cash Flow and Sales Growth	71.2	171.1	99.9
Price-to-Earnings and Sales Growth	67.4	171.6	104.2

as the highest sales growth because earnings and cash flow can turn negative and sales cannot except in very unusual circumstances—and the highest valuation determined on the basis of price-to-book value, cash flow, and earnings multiples. The *Contrarian Value* portfolios contained stocks with the lowest sales growth and the lowest price-to-book value, cash flow, and earnings multiples. This means, for example, that a stock in the Contrarian Value portfolio must have had poor historical business performance and a low valuation, manifesting as both low or negative sales growth and a low multiple. This helps to distinguish the value stock from a stock the market treats as a "temporary loser," which has had high growth in the recent past, but the market expects to slow down and hence has applied to it a low multiple. Conversely, a glamour stock should also be distinguished from a "temporary winner," which has had low growth in the recent past, but which the market expects to recover and hence has applied to it a high multiple. Lakonishok et al. tested the performance of each portfolio over the five years following formation. Table 7.1 shows the results of the study.

The Contrarian Value portfolios in Table 7.1 comprehensively outperformed the Glamour portfolios, and by a significant margin over five years. The average five-year cumulative difference in returns is between 77.6 and 104.2 percent, which is substantial. This is an intriguing finding. The Contrarian Value portfolios were all cheaper than the Glamour portfolios, but they were also much less attractive on a fundamental basis. We can examine each portfolio on the historical performance of its component stocks before selection. Prior to selection, the Glamour portfolios had grown their businesses at significantly higher rates than the Contrarian Value portfolios. Table 7.2 shows the growth in earnings, cash flow, sales,

TABLE 7.2 Average Five-Year Cumulative Growth of Fundamentals of Stocks Prior to Selection for Contrarian Value and Glamour Portfolios (1963 to 1990)

Pre-Selection Characteristics of Price-to-Earnings and Sales Growth Portfolios

	Glamour	Contrarian Value
Growth in Earnings (%)	18.7	9.7
Growth in Cash Flow (%)	18.1	7.4
Growth in Sales (%)	15.2	2.5
Growth in Operating Earnings (%)	18.2	5.9

Pre-Selection Characteristics of Price-to-Book Value and Sales Growth Portfolios

	Glamour	Contrarian Value
Growth in Earnings (%)	15.9	−6.7
Growth in Cash Flow (%)	18.0	1.3
Growth in Sales (%)	62.3	10.7
Growth in Operating Earnings (%)	14.3	0.2

Pre-Selection Characteristics of Price-to-Cash Flow and Sales Growth Portfolios

	Glamour	Contrarian Value
Growth in Earnings (%)	14.2	8.2
Growth in Cash Flow (%)	20.5	4.7
Growth in Sales (%)	11.2	1.3
Growth in Operating Earnings (%)	15.9	−6.7

and operating earnings for each of the Glamour and Contrarian Value portfolios in the years leading up to the formation of each portfolio.

Table 7.2 shows that the Glamour stocks were considerably more attractive on a fundamental basis at the time of acquisition than the stocks in the Contrarian Value portfolios. In every instance, the Glamour portfolios were growing sales, earnings, operating earnings, and cash flow at a considerably faster rate than the comparable Contrarian Value portfolios. Table 7.3 shows that the Glamour portfolios were also considerably more expensive than the Contrarian Value portfolios.

The stocks in the Contrarian Value portfolios were comprehensively cheaper than the comparable Glamour portfolios on every metric but one; the stocks in the Contrarian Value portfolios formed using price-to-book value and sales growth were more expensive on a price-to-earnings basis than the stocks in the comparable Glamour portfolio, possibly because the earnings

TABLE 7.3   Valuation Characteristics of Contrarian Value and Glamour
Portfolios (1963 to 1990)

Characteristics of Portfolios Formed Using Price-to-Earnings and Sales Growth

	Glamour	Contrarian Value
Price-to-Earnings Ratio	19.6×	6.5×
Price-to-Cash Flow Ratio	10.8×	3.7×
Price-to-Sales Ratio	0.7×	0.2×
Price-to-Operating Earnings Ratio	6.3×	2.3×

Characteristics of Portfolios Formed Using Price-to-Book Value and Sales Growth

	Glamour	Contrarian Value
Price-to-Earnings Ratio	17.2×	38.5×
Price-to-Cash Flow Ratio	9.5×	6.3×
Price-to-Sales Ratio	0.7×	0.2×
Price-to-Operating Earnings Ratio	5.7×	3.2×

Characteristics of Portfolios Formed Using Price-to-Cash Flow and Sales Growth

	Glamour	Contrarian Value
Price-to-Earnings Ratio	18.5×	8.8×
Price-to-Cash Flow Ratio	12.5×	3.6×
Price-to-Sales Ratio	0.9×	0.2×
Price-to-Operating Earnings Ratio	7.2×	2.2×

in those portfolios were so weak. These results support the earlier findings
of De Bondt and Thaler, who found that the Loser portfolios—those with
three years of falling earnings—outperformed the Winner portfolios—those
with the greatest gains in earnings over three years. Lakonishok, Shleifer, and
Vishny's findings suggest that a contrarian strategy—one that actively seeks
out undervalued companies with poor historical performance—will outperform overvalued companies with excellent historical performance. The natural question is whether poorly performing value stocks in the Contrarian
Value portfolios outperform value stocks with good historical performance,
described here as High-Growth Value. Table 7.4 sets out the results.

Table 7.4 shows that the Contrarian Value portfolios comprehensively
outperformed the comparable High-Growth Value portfolios, although note
that the High-Growth Value portfolios also outperformed the comparable
Glamour portfolios in Table 7.1. Table 7.5 shows that the High-Growth
Value portfolios contained stocks that were considerably more attractive

TABLE 7.4 Average Five-Year Cumulative Return of "High Growth" Value Portfolios and Contrarian Value Portfolios (1963 to 1990)

	High Growth Value Average Five-Year Cumulative Return (%)	Contrarian Value Average Five-Year Cumulative Return (%)	Difference (Contrarian Value—High Growth Value) (%)
Price-to-Book Value and Sales Growth	117.1	161.8	44.7
Price-to-Cash Flow and Sales Growth	116.3	171.1	54.8
Price-to-Earnings and Sales Growth	136.5	171.6	35.1

TABLE 7.5 Five-Year Average Growth of Contrarian Value and "High Growth" Value Portfolios (1963 to 1990)

Pre-Selection Characteristics of Price-to-Earnings and Sales Growth Portfolios

	High-Growth Value	Contrarian Value
Growth in Earnings (%)	16.9	9.7
Growth in Cash Flow (%)	16.3	7.4
Growth in Sales (%)	13.9	2.5
Growth in Operating Earnings (%)	16.0	5.9

Pre-Selection Characteristics of Price-to-Book Value and Sales Growth Portfolios

	High-Growth Value	Contrarian Value
Growth in Earnings (%)	6.8	−6.7
Growth in Cash Flow (%)	4.0	1.3
Growth in Sales (%)	60.3	10.7
Growth in Operating Earnings (%)	0.4	0.2

Pre-Selection Characteristics of Price-to-Cash Flow and Sales Growth Portfolios

	High-Growth Value	Contrarian Value
Growth in Earnings (%)	14.3	8.2
Growth in Cash Flow (%)	14.0	4.7
Growth in Sales (%)	10.6	1.3
Growth in Operating Earnings (%)	11.8	−6.7

on a fundamental basis at the time of acquisition than the comparable Contrarian Value portfolios.

In every category, the High-Growth Value portfolios look more attractive than the Contrarian Value portfolios. Table 7.6 shows the multiples of earnings, cash flow, sales, and operating earnings paid for each of the High Growth and Contrarian portfolios. Note that the multiples are comparable.

What is stunning in these results is that, while the High-Growth Value and Contrarian Value portfolios contained stocks trading on approximately the same price-to-value ratios, the stocks in the High-Growth Value portfolios were in some instances cheaper than the stocks in the Contrarian Value portfolios and yet the Contrarian Value portfolios delivered comprehensively better returns.

These results establish two propositions. First, valuation is more important than growth in constructing portfolios. Cheap, low-growth portfolios

TABLE 7.6 Valuation Characteristics of Contrarian Value and "High Growth" Value Portfolios (1963 to 1990)

Characteristics of Portfolios Formed Using Price-to-Earnings and Sales Growth

	High-Growth Value	Contrarian Value
Price-to-Earnings Ratio	6.3×	6.5×
Price-to-Cash Flow Ratio	3.9×	3.7×
Price-to-Sales Ratio	0.3×	0.2×
Price-to-Operating Earnings Ratio	2.2×	2.3×

Characteristics of Portfolios Formed Using Price-to-Book Value and Sales Growth

	High-Growth Value	Contrarian Value
Price-to-Earnings Ratio	8.7×	38.5×
Price-to-Cash Flow Ratio	4.0×	6.3×
Price-to-Sales Ratio	0.2×	0.2×
Price-to-Operating Earnings Ratio	2.1×	3.2×

Characteristics of Portfolios Formed Using Price-to-Cash Flow and Sales Growth

	High-Growth Value	Contrarian Value
Price-to-Earnings Ratio	7.0×	8.8×
Price-to-Cash Flow Ratio	3.5×	3.6×
Price-to-Sales Ratio	0.2×	0.2×
Price-to-Operating Earnings Ratio	2.1×	2.2×

systematically outperform expensive, high-growth portfolios, and by wide margins. The second, more counterintuitive finding is that, even in the value portfolios, high growth leads to underperformance and low or no growth leads to outperformance. This is a fascinating finding. Intuitively, we are attracted to high growth and would assume that high-growth value stocks are high-quality stocks available at a bargain price. The data show, however, that the low- or no-growth value stocks are the better bet. It seems that the uglier the stock, the better the return, even when the valuations are comparable.

This counterintuitive behavior can be found in sub-liquidation stocks too. Recall that Henry Oppenheimer tested the performance of two portfolios of net current asset value stocks, one containing only stocks that had been profitable over the preceding year, and another containing only stocks that had been operating at a loss.[46] He found that the portfolio containing stocks operating at a loss tended to outperform the portfolio of profitable stocks. Table 7.7 shows the results of Oppenheimer's research on profitable and loss-making net nets to 1983, and our update to 2010.[47]

Oppenheimer also found that profitable, dividend-paying stocks generated a lower return than profitable stocks that did not pay a dividend. Table 7.8 shows the results of Oppenheimer's research to 1983, and our update to 2010.

TABLE 7.7 Average Yearly Returns to Profitable and Loss-Making Net Current Asset Value Portfolios (1970 to 2010)

	Profitable Net Nets Average Annual Return (%)	Loss-Making Net Nets Average Annual Return (%)	Difference (Loss-Making—Profitable) (%)
1970 to 1983	33.1	36.2	3.1
1983 to 2010	26.2	49.0	12.8

TABLE 7.8 Average Yearly Return to Profitable Dividend Paying and Non-Dividend Paying Net Current Asset Value Portfolios (1970 to 2010)

	Average Annual Return to Dividend-Paying Net Nets (%)	Average Annual Return to Non Dividend-Paying Net Nets (%)	Difference (Non Dividend—Dividend) (%)
1970 to 1983	27.0	40.6	13.6
1983 to 2010	19.3	33.2	13.9

As Tables 7.7 and 7.8 demonstrate, our results support Oppenheimer's conclusion that profitable net net stocks significantly underperformed the loss-makers, and profitable dividend payers significantly underperformed the profitable stocks that did not pay dividends. These findings led Oppenheimer to conclude that choosing only profitable stocks, or profitable dividend-paying stocks, would "not help" an investor, but he may have been understating the case. With the caveat that the volatility-adjusted returns are lower for the loss makers and the non-dividend payers, it's clear that the ugliest of the ugly generate the best returns.[48]

As counterintuitive as these findings appear to be, it is a phenomenon repeated throughout the value investment literature. One famous example is Tom Peters' bestseller published in 1982 called *In Search of Excellence*.[49] Described as "the greatest business book of all time,"[50] Peters profiled companies that had been identified as "excellent" on the basis of outstanding financial performance determined on the basis of profitability and growth, and suggested that the companies' attributes could be used as a "blueprint for corporate excellence in general."[51] Those financial performance characteristics included such metrics as asset growth, return on capital, and return on sales. In 1987, five years after the publication of Peters' book, Michelle Clayman conducted a study of the companies identified by Peters, examining 29 of the 36 that were still in existence as independent, publicly listed stocks.[52] She found that in the five years after Peters had identified these stocks as "excellent," most had experienced declines in growth rates and returns on equity and capital. Eighty-six percent had experienced declines in asset growth rates, 83 percent had lower returns on capital, and 83 percent had lower returns on sales. Only 4 of the 29 companies showed increases on 3 or more attributes. Most were no longer "excellent" companies by Peters' measures. Clayman attributed the declines to "a phenomenon in nature called 'reversion to the mean,' which asserts that, over time, properties of members of groups tend to converge to the average value for the group as a whole [because] economic forces tend to move things towards equilibrium."[53]

> *In the world or finance, researchers have shown that returns on equity tend to revert to the mean. Economic theory suggests that markets that offer high returns will attract new entrants, who will gradually drive returns down to general market levels.*

Eighteen of Peters' 29 "Excellent" companies—almost two-thirds—underperformed the S&P 500 index, and 11 outperformed. Sixty-nine percent had a drop in price-to-book value ratios. As a portfolio, however, Peters' excellent companies did beat the S&P 500 by 1 percent a year, which

TABLE 7.9   Average Five-Year Financial Characteristics of Peters' "Excellent" and Clayman's "Unexcellent" Companies (1976 to 1980)

	Excellent	Unexcellent
Asset Growth (%)	21.78	5.93
Equity Growth (%)	18.43	3.76
Price-to-Book Value (%)	2.46	0.62
Average Return on Capital (%)	16.04	4.88
Average Return on Equity (%)	19.05	7.09
Average Return on Sales (%)	8.62	2.49

is impressive. Clayman wrote that she believed "the majority of the excellent companies underperformed because the market overestimated their future growth and future return on equity and, as a result, their [price-to-book value] ratios were overvalued."[54] Using the same variables as Peters, Clayman went "in search of disaster." She constructed a portfolio of "Unexcellent" companies drawn from the S&P 500 Index, and ranked in the bottom third on every variable. Table 7.9 contains a comparison of the financial characteristics of both Peters' excellent companies, and Clayman's unexcellent companies. Peters' companies appear much more attractive on every measure but valuation.

One might intuitively expect a portfolio of Peters' excellent companies to outperform a portfolio of Clayman's unexcellent companies, but that wasn't the case. Twenty-five of the 39 unexcellent companies outperformed the S&P 500, and 14 underperformed. As a portfolio, however, the unexcellent companies outperformed the market by an astonishing 12.4 percent annually.

It wasn't an improvement in the fundamental performance of these unexcellent companies that led to the market price outperformance. Like Peters' excellent companies, the operating performance of the unexcellent companies *declined* on average, although not to the same degree as the excellent companies. In the unexcellent companies, 67 percent experienced a decline in asset growth rates, 51 percent had lower average returns on capital, 51 percent had lower average returns on equity, and 56 percent had lower average returns on sales. Strikingly, examined at the end of the five-year period, Peters' excellent companies were still more attractive on a fundamental basis than Clayman's unexcellent companies. What stands out, however, is that only three of the unexcellent companies had a decline in the ratio of price-to-book value, which means that the market revalued up 36 of 39 companies. This amounted to an average revaluation across the portfolio of 58 percent, a clear example of reversion to the mean. Clayman concludes that the "evidence suggests that companies with low [price-to-book value] ratios are likely to see those ratios drift upward over time. The financial analyst must, instead, look beyond current and historical financial and behavioral attributes to estimate investment returns."[55]

> *Over time, company results have a tendency to regress to the mean as underlying economic forces attract new entrants to attractive markets and encourage participants to leave low-return businesses. Because of this tendency, companies that have been "good" performers in the past may prove to be inferior investments, while "poor" companies frequently provide superior investment returns in the future. The "good" companies underperform because the market overestimates their future growth and future return on equity and, as a result, accords the stocks overvalued price-to-book ratios; the converse is true of the "poor" companies.*

There is a caveat to this study. In 1994 Clayman revisited the original study, screening on the same financial characteristics, and then dividing the S&P 500 universe into deciles, a more systematic approach than the ad hoc selection drawn from Peters' list.[56] The best companies in the top decile were labeled as "Good," and the worst companies in the bottom decile labeled "Poor." Measured over the five-year period from 1988 to 1992, the Good portfolio generated an annual return of 17 percent, outperforming the Poor portfolio, which could only manage a return of 11.2 percent, annualized. Clayman attributes the difference in results to the fact that the later period was more favorable to glamour stocks than to value stocks, which is unusual. Examining the universe divided into deciles on the basis of price-to-book value alone, the more expensive, high price-to-book value decile generated an average return of 14.3 percent, outperforming the cheaper, low price-to-book value decile, which generated an average return of 12.6 percent annually. She also notes that, ". . . even though the average price-to-book ratio of the good companies fell between the two periods, the faster growth of equity (book value) meant that price performance was not impaired," which, too, is unusual.[57] It's worth noting that the outperformance occurred during a period where glamour outperformed value, which does occur periodically, but not consistently or over the long term, and also that the outperformance relied on book value growing faster than the rate at which the price-to-book value ratio fell, which is an unusual and risky assumption. The more conventional position would be to assume value would continue to outperform glamour, and book value would not grow faster than the price-to-book value ratio falls. The first paper fit into existing microeconomic theory, where the second paper did not, suggesting that the first paper was more likely describing the phenomenon correctly and the second was an outlier.

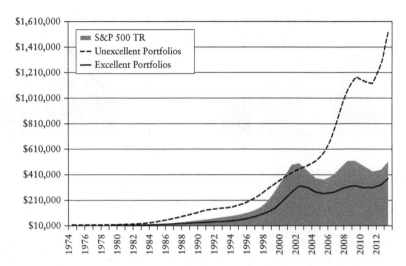

FIGURE 7.1 Comparison of Unexcellent and Excellent Stock Portfolios (1972 to 2013)
Source: Stifel Financial Corp. and Eyquem Investment Management LLC.

The issue was resolved in 2013 when Barry B. Bannister of Stifel Financial Corp., a brokerage and investment bank based in St. Louis, Missouri, tested Peters' excellent companies and Clayman's unexcellent companies from June 1972 to June 2013.[58] Bannister found that the unexcellent stock portfolios returned 13.74 percent on average over the full period versus 9.77 percent for the excellent portfolios. Not only did the excellent portfolios underperform the unexcellent portfolios, they underperformed the market, which returned 10.59 percent annualized over the full period. Figure 7.1 shows the value of $1,000 invested in the unexcellent company portfolios compared to the same amount invested in excellent company portfolios on the last day of June 1972 as of June 30, 2013, and includes the S&P 500 for reference.

Bannister found that the unexcellent portfolios outperformed the excellent portfolios in the majority (67 percent) of years in the four-decade experiment. The advantage of the unexcellent portfolios persisted even after adjusting for volatility. Further, though we might assume that excellent stock portfolios offer "defensive" characteristics, excellent stock portfolios only outperformed the unexcellent portfolios in 11 of 22, or 50 percent of periods featuring "global economic difficulty," which Bannister defined as global real GDP growth less than the average of the full period. This compares to the unexcellent portfolios outperforming the excellent counterparts in 15 of 17 (or 88 percent) of periods that did not feature global economic difficulty.

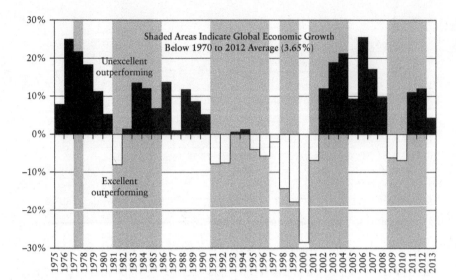

FIGURE 7.2   Relative Performance of Unexcellent and Excellent Stock Portfolios
(Trailing Three-Year Annualized Returns 1972 to 2013)
Source: Stifel Financial Corp. and Eyquem Investment Management LLC.

Figure 7.2 shows the relative performance of the unexcellent and excellent
portfolios during periods of lower-than-average global economic growth.

Bannister wrote that the consistent outperformance of the unexcellent portfolios over the S&P 500 and the excellent portfolios was "easily
defensible:"[59]

> In theory, high returns invite new entrants that drive down profit-
> ability, while poor returns cause competitors to exit, as well as lead
> to potential new management or acquisition by a competitor or
> financial buyer.
>   Investment analysts must weigh whether excellence in financial
> metrics is discounted in the stock price with potential downside
> risk. We conclude that what constitutes "excellence" for managers
> is most often not the case for investors.

Bannister concluded that exceptional long-term equity returns were
available from unexcellent portfolios of "past financial metric laggards provided that they were supported by a disciplined value investment process."
The stocks outperformed as the businesses of the unexcellent companies
reverted to the mean.

What about a more nebulous concept like "admiration"? Deniz Anginer and Meir Statman examined the performance of companies on *Fortune Magazine's* annual survey of "America's Most Admired Companies" over the period 1983 to 2007.[60] *Fortune* has been publishing the results of annual surveys of company reputations since 1983. The survey published in March 2007 included 587 companies in 62 industries. Fortune asked more than 3,000 senior executives, directors, and securities analysts to rate the 10 largest companies in their own industries on 8 "attributes of reputation:" quality of management; quality of products or services; innovativeness; long-term investment value; financial soundness; ability to attract, develop, and keep talented people; responsibility to the community and the environment; and wise use of corporate assets. *Fortune's* rating of a company is the average rating given on the eight attributes. Anginer and Statman constructed two portfolios using the *Fortune* ratings, each consisting of one half of the *Fortune* stocks. The "Admired" portfolio contained the stocks with the highest *Fortune* ratings and the "Spurned" portfolio contained stocks with the lowest ratings. Anginer and Statman found that spurned stocks outperformed admired stocks. Over the entire sample period, the spurned portfolio returned 18.3 percent each year on average, while the admired portfolio could manage only 16.3 percent per year. Not only was admiration associated with underperformance, but, strikingly, increases in admiration resulted in lower returns. For example, stocks in the most spurned quartile for which reputation decreased returned 18.8 percent per year on average, while those whose reputation increased returned only 13.2 percent per year. Why might this be so? As we saw in an earlier chapter, Kahneman and Tversky found that a favorable view of a company's products leads us to draw favorable conclusions about its stock. It's possible that admiration is another proxy for a favorable view of a company, and Anginer and Statman have simply identified another aspect of this phenomenon. Whatever the cause, it seems admired companies tend to be bid up like glamour stocks, and spurned companies ignored like value stocks, creating the opportunity for a contrarian bet.

Another study examined the performance of stocks assigned ratings by *Standard and Poor's Ratings Services*, the 150-year old indexer and ratings agency.[61] Standard and Poor's examines financial metrics like profitability and financial leverage to rank stocks from A+ to D, where A+ is the best ranking a stock can receive and D the worst. Figure 7.3 shows the annual returns earned by each rating "bucket" over the period 1986 to 1994.

As you'd likely expect by now, Figure 7.3 demonstrates that the lowest-rated stocks earned the highest returns, and the highest-rated stocks had the lowest returns. Aswath Damodaran, a professor of finance at New York University Stern School of Business and an expert in valuation, notes in

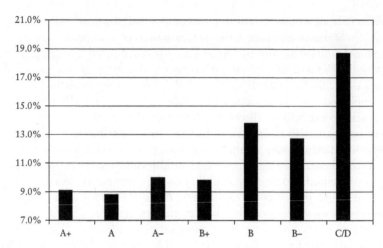

FIGURE 7.3 Comparison of Standard and Poor's Stock Ratings and Returns
(1986 to 1994)
Source: Eyquem Investment Management LLC and Aswath Damodaran, *Value
Investing: Investing for Grown Ups?* (April 14, 2012).

relation to the chart that "the higher returns for lower rated companies may
well reflect the higher perceived risk in these companies, but it indicates that
investors who bought the highest ranked stocks, expecting to earn higher
returns, would have been sorely disappointed."[62]

What these studies demonstrate is that mean reversion is a pervasive
phenomenon, and one that we don't intuitively recognize. Our untrained
instinct is to pursue the *glamorous* stock, the *high-growth* stock, the *story*
stock, the excellent stock, the admired stock, the A+ stock, or even the
profitable net net, but study after study shows that this instinct leads us to
underperform. Buying well-run companies with good businesses seems to
make so much sense. Buying well-run companies with good businesses at
bargain prices seems to make even more sense. The research shows, however,
that the better investment—rather than the better company—is the *value*
stock, the scorned, the unexcellent, the Ds, the loss-making net nets. And the
better value stock, according to Lakonishok, Shleifer, and Vishny's research,
is the *low-* or *no-growth* value stock, what they describe as "contrarian
value," and what I regard as deep value; the ugliest of the ugly. What is clear
is that value investing in general, and deep value investing in particular, is
exceedingly behaviorally difficult. It is counterintuitive and against instinct,
which is why many investors shy away from it. To succeed as deep value
investors, we need to overcome our behavioral biases. If we are subject to

the same behavioral biases as other investors, how can we exploit that irrationality without falling victim to it ourselves?

THE BROKEN-LEG PROBLEM

Most deeply undervalued, fundamentally weak stocks are that way because their futures appear uncertain—they are losing money or marginally profitable—and, on an individual basis, don't appear to be good candidates for purchase. We know, however, that in aggregate they provide excellent returns, outperforming the market in the long run and suffering fewer down years than the market. This is an area in which our native intuition fails us. As we have seen, no matter how well trained we are, humans tend to have difficulty with probabilistic, uncertain, and random processes. Confronted with problems requiring an intuitive grasp of the odds in an unfamiliar context, even the best investors and behavioral finance experts flounder. If mere awareness that our judgment is clouded by our nature does little to correct the errors we make, how then can we protect against them? Since the 1950s, social scientists have been comparing the predictive abilities of traditional experts and what are known as statistical prediction rules. The studies have found almost uniformly that statistical prediction rules are more consistently accurate than the very best experts. Paul Meehl—one of the founding fathers of research in the field—said in 1986:[63]

> *There is no controversy in social science which shows such a large body of qualitatively diverse studies coming out so uniformly in the same direction as this one . . . predicting everything from the outcomes of football games to the diagnosis of liver disease and when you can hardly come up with a half a dozen studies showing even a weak tendency in favour of the clinician, it is time to draw a practical conclusion.*

Meehl's practical conclusion is this: For a very wide range of prediction problems, statistical prediction rules—often very simple models—make predictions that are at least as reliable as, and typically more reliable than, human experts. This observation is now so well-accepted as to be known as *The Golden Rule of Predictive Modeling*.[64]

Rory Sutherland, the vice-chairman of Ogilvy Group UK—the advertising agency founded by David Ogilvy, who was an early advocate of quantification and research in advertising—is a self-described champion of the application of behavioral economics in advertising. Sutherland believes that we are more likely to follow simple, absolute rules—"if X, then Y"—that work with our nature than others that are subtle, and require a "continuous exercise of self-restraint:"[65]

> *Let's consider the old rule of restricting yourself to a maximum number of units of alcohol a week. It demands constant vigilance. It often requires you to stop drinking while drunk. And it is fiendishly easy to cheat: you simply convince yourself that a 25cl glass of 14.7 percent Chilean Merlot is one unit when it is really three. Better men than us have deceived themselves this way: Immanuel Kant rationed himself to one pipe of tobacco after breakfast; he stuck to his rule, but friends noticed that by the end of his life, all his pipes were enormous.*

Sutherland's observation applies equally to investing. Value investors follow a simple algorithm that states something like the following: *Buy if market price is equal to or less than some fixed discount from intrinsic value. Sell if market price is equal to or exceeds intrinsic value.* Graham's net current asset value rule for acquiring sub-liquidation stocks is an example of such a simple, unambiguous investment strategy; simple to calculate, with concrete rules for its application. Graham recommended it as a "foolproof method of systematic investment—once again, not on the basis of individual results but in terms of the expectable group outcome."[66] The net current asset value calculation couldn't be simpler: *Net current asset value equals current assets less all liabilities.* And the rules couldn't be more concrete: *Buy if market price is two-thirds of net current asset value or less. Sell if market price has risen 50 percent, or two years have elapsed since acquisition, whichever occurs first.* As we've seen, the returns to the net current asset value rule are astronomical. The problem with it is that it is very limited in its application. Few stocks pass its "buy" criteria in an ordinary market. It is possible, however, to apply the underlying *philosophy* without employing the actual rule. We can calculate intrinsic value in any number of ways, and apply the same directive. This is all that is meant by a statistical prediction rule. At root, it is simply an exhortation to adhere strictly to the philosophy of value investment: Buy only if market price is some fixed discount from intrinsic value or less, pass otherwise. Sell only if market price is equal to or greater than intrinsic value, or a better opportunity can be found, hold otherwise.

Resistance to the application of statistical prediction rules in value investment runs deep. Many investors recoil at the thought of ceding control of investment decisions to a statistical model, believing that it would be better to use the output from the statistical prediction rule and retain the discretion to follow the rule's output or not. There is some evidence to support this possibility. Traditional experts are shown to make better decisions when they are provided with the results of statistical prediction. The issue is that they continue to underperform the statistical prediction rule alone. The reason is known as the "broken leg" problem:[67]

> *Suppose an actuarial formula accurately predicts an individual's weekly movie attendance. If we know that the subject has a broken leg, it would be wise to discard the actuarial formula.*

Statistical prediction rules get broken-leg problems incorrect because the particular case is so different from the base rate. If that is the case, goes the argument, then surely these anomalous cases could benefit from an expert overriding the rule? The studies find that they do not. In fact, experts predict less reliably than they would have if they had just used the statistical prediction rule.[68] The statistical prediction rule tends to be a ceiling from which the expert detracts, rather than a floor to which the expert adds. The reason is that when experts are given statistical prediction rules along with permission to override them, the experts find more broken legs than there really are. Our resistance to the statistical-prediction rule findings is due to our tendency to be overconfident in our ability to reason subjectively and hence the reliability of our predictions. It is self-reflexive: Our confidence in our reasoning abilities reinforces our confidence in our judgments, and our overconfident judgments encourage our belief in the reliability of our faculties.

In the original edition of *Security Analysis*, Graham warned against blindly buying a basket of securities trading at a low ratio of some of fundamental measure like price-to-earnings without considering other "unknown factors" necessarily excluded from such an analysis. Graham reasoned:[69]

> *Theoretically these unknown factors should have an equal chance of being favorable or unfavorable, and thus they should neutralize each other in the long run. For example, it might be thought that a simple way to make money could be found by purchasing a number of common stocks currently earning the largest percentage on the market price and simultaneously selling those earning the smallest percentage, the idea being that helpful or harmful future changes should be about equally distributed over both groups, so that the group purchased should maintain its better aggregate showing and therefore do better in the market. But it may well be that the low price for the apparently attractive issues is due to certain important unfavorable factors which, though not disclosed, are known to those identified with the company—and vice versa for the issues seemingly selling above their relative value. In speculative*

situations, those "on the inside" often have an advantage of this kind which nullifies the premise that good and bad changes in the picture should offset each other, and which loads the dice against the analyst working with some of the facts concealed from him.

Thus sound analysis required that more factors be considered. What else should be considered? "Such a study could be carried to an unlimited degree of detail," warned Graham, "hence practical judgment must be exercised to determine how far the process should go."[70] We should now recognize Graham's "unknown factors" as examples of broken-leg problems. The great challenge for modern value investors is the ease with which we can access information. The temptation is to use it all, when all we need is the right information. Seth Klarman has observed that some investors insist on "trying to obtain perfect knowledge about their impending investments, researching companies until they think they know everything there is to know about them:"[71]

They study the industry and the competition, contact former employees, industry consultants, and analysts, and become personally acquainted with top management. They analyze financial statements for the past decade and stock price trends for even longer.

This diligence is admirable, but it has two shortcomings. First, no matter how much research is performed, some information always remains elusive; investors have to learn to live with less than complete information. Second, even if an investor could know all the facts about an investment, he or she would not necessarily profit.

Klarman continued that this did not mean that fundamental analysis was not useful. "It certainly is," he continued:[72]

But information generally follows the well-known 80/20 rule: the first 80 percent of the available information is gathered in the first 20 percent of the time spent. The value of in-depth fundamental analysis is subject to diminishing marginal returns.

Most investors strive fruitlessly for certainty and precision, avoiding situations in which information is difficult to obtain. Yet high uncertainty is frequently accompanied by low prices. By the time the uncertainty is resolved, prices are likely to have risen.

Investors frequently benefit from making investment decisions with less than perfect knowledge and are well rewarded for bearing the risk of uncertainty.

The time other investors spend delving into the last unanswered detail may cost them the chance to buy in at prices so low that they offer a margin of safety despite the incomplete information.

The contrarian value investment strategy is well suited to the application of statistical-prediction rules. All of these stocks have what appear to be broken legs. The intrinsic value is uncertain because its discovery requires the anticipation of an event not obvious in the historical financial data—mean reversion. Rather we must rely on the statistical base case for undervalued, money-losing securities—that they will spontaneously mean revert toward a state of earning power commensurate with their assets. Graham—referring to net nets, but the broader point applies to all deep value stocks—observed that "[t]he objection to buying these issues lies in the probability, or at least the possibility, that earnings will decline or losses continue, and that the resources will dissipated and the intrinsic value ultimately become less than the price paid."[73] As we have seen, there is some validity to this concern on an individual company level. In his study, Montier found that an individual stock selected by the net current asset value strategy was two-and-and-a-half times more likely to suffer a permanent loss of capital than the average stock (Montier found that about 5 percent of net current asset value stocks declined 90 percent or more in a single year, while only 2 percent of all stocks suffered a similar decline).[74] Recall that what was true at the individual company level, however, was not true at an aggregate level. The net net portfolios had fewer down years than the market (the net nets only suffered losses at the portfolio level in 3 years in the 23-year sample, while the overall market saw 6 years of negative returns).[75] Not only did the strategy outperform over the full period, it had fewer losing years, even though the average net net was two-and-a-half times more likely than the average stock to suffer a terminal decline. Montier's findings in relation to net nets are emblematic of our attitude to deep value stocks generally. Confronted with a choice to invest in one of two undervalued stocks—one with a high rate of growth in its sales, earnings, and cash flow, with good asset growth, and a high return on equity and capital; the other with drooping earnings, anemic sales growth, lagging cash flow generation, no asset growth, and feeble returns on equity—we choose the first one. It's a no-brainer. The high-growth value stock is a diamond in the rough, and the other is a clear value trap; undervalued, yes, but probably undervalued for all the right reasons. As we already know, our intuition here is wrong. We've ignored the base case for these undervalued stocks and not properly accounted for the likelihood of mean reversion in both stocks.

These biases—ignorance of the base case and ignorance of mean reversion—are key contributors to the ongoing returns to deep value investment. We know that a portfolio of deep value stocks will, on average, generate better returns and suffer fewer down years, than the market, but we fixate on the fact that any individual deep value stock is more likely to suffer a permanent loss of capital. The reason is that even those of us who identify as value investors suffer from cognitive biases and make behavioral errors. We prefer high-growth value stocks when the research is clear that high-growth value stocks underperform their low or no growth brethren. As Damodaran has observed:[76]

> *Any investment strategy that is based upon buying well-run, good companies and expecting the growth in earnings in these companies to carry prices higher is dangerous, since it ignores the possibility that the current price of the company already reflects the quality of the management and the firm. If the current price is right (and the market is paying a premium for quality), the biggest danger is that the firm loses its luster over time, and that the premium paid will dissipate. If the market is exaggerating the value of the firm, this strategy can lead to poor returns even if the firm delivers its expected growth. It is only when markets under estimate the value of firm quality that this strategy stands a chance of making excess returns.*

In 1976, more than 40 years after the publication of the first edition of *Security Analysis* in 1934, Graham gave an interview to the *Financial Analysts Journal* where he reversed his earlier position, telling the interviewer that he was "no longer an advocate of elaborate techniques of security analysis in order to find superior value opportunities."[77] Instead, Graham advocated a "highly simplified [approach] that applies a single criteria or perhaps two criteria to the price to assure that full value is present and that relies for its results on the performance of the portfolio as a whole—that is, on the group results—rather than on the expectations for individual issues." He counseled:[78]

> *What's needed is, first, a definite rule for purchasing which indicates* a priori *that you're acquiring stocks for less than they're worth. Second, you have to operate with a large enough number of stocks to make the approach effective. And finally you need a very definite guideline for selling.*

As he was in many things, Graham was ahead of his time in advocating for what sounds remarkably like a statistical-prediction rule.

Investors who embrace a deep value strategy do so as much for its returns as for its ability to identify undervalued stocks at a fundamental nadir with a poor outlook. They prize these apparently unappetizing stocks because shareholders are always more likely to cede control of a holding they apprehend to be a loser, even though the research is clear that they outperform. Our intuition for the extrapolation of trends makes the impact of mean reversion on business results a mystery to most investors. It is this unusual contrast between the statistical likelihood of mean reversion—it's the probable outcome—and the fact that the market prices securities as if it's a remote possibility, that keeps deep value investing so profitable, and interesting. The nuances of mean reversion can make deep value seem a little "inside baseball" for most investors. In the following chapters we explore several examples of practitioners recognizing the conditions for mean reversion, and employing deep value strategies to capitalize on it.

Notes

1. Yvonne van Dongen. *Brierley: The Man Behind The Corporate Legend.* (Auckland: Penguin Books (NZL) Ltd) 1990.
2. Ibid.
3. All conversions are from data on the *Reserve Bank of New Zealand* "Inflation Calculator" Extracted November 2013. Available at http://www.rbnz.govt.nz/monetary_policy/inflation_calculator.
4. van Dongen, 1990.
5. Ibid.
6. Ibid.
7. Ibid.
8. Ibid.
9. Ibid.
10. Ibid.
11. Ibid.
12. Ibid.
13. Ibid.
14. Ibid.
15. Ibid.
16. Ibid.
17. Ibid.
18. Ibid.
19. Ibid.
20. Ibid.
21. Ibid.
22. Ibid.
23. Ibid.
24. Ibid.
25. Ibid.
26. Ibid.
27. Ibid.
28. Ibid.
29. Ibid.
30. Ibid.

31. Ibid.
32. Ibid.
33. Ibid.
34. Ibid.
35. Ibid.
36. Ibid.
37. Ibid.
38. Ibid.
39. Ibid.
40. Ibid.
41. Ibid.
42. Ibid.
43. Ibid.
44. Ibid.
45. Ibid.
46. Henry R. Oppenheimer. "Ben Graham's Net Current Asset Values: A Performance Update." *Financial Analysts Journal*, Vol. 42, No. 6 (1986), pp. 40–47.
47. Jeffrey Oxman, Sunil K. Mohanty, and Tobias Eric Carlisle. *Deep Value Investing and Unexplained Returns*. Midwest Finance Association 2012 Annual Meetings Paper. Available at SSRN: http://ssrn.com/abstract=1928694 or http://dx.doi.org/10.2139/ssrn.1928694.
48. Ibid.
49. Thomas J. Peters and Robert H. Waterman. *In Search of Excellence: Lessons from America's Best-Run Companies*. (New York: Harper and Row) 1982.
50. Ibid.
51. Ibid.
52. Michelle Clayman. "In Search of Excellence: The Investor's Veiwpoint." *Financial Analysts Journal*, May–June 1987, 54. Suggested by Damodaran, 2012.
53. Ibid.
54. Ibid.
55. Ibid.
56. Michelle Clayman, "Excellence Revisited." *Financial Analysts Journal*, May–June 1994, 61. Suggested by Damodaran, 2012.
57. Ibid.
58. Barry B. Bannister and Jesse Cantor. "In Search of "Un-Excellence"—An Endorsement of Value-style Investing" *Stifel Financial Corp*. July 16, 2013.
59. Ibid.
60. Meir Statman and Deniz Anginer. "Stocks of Admired Companies and Spurned Ones." SCU Leavey School of Business Research Paper No. 10-02. Available at SSRN: http://ssrn.com/abstract=1540757 or http://dx.doi.org/10.2139/ssrn.1540757 via Damodaran, 2012.
61. Aswath Damodaran. "Value Investing: Investing for Grown Ups?" (April 14, 2012). Available at SSRN: http://ssrn.com/abstract=2042657 or http://dx.doi.org/10.2139/ssrn.2042657.
62. Ibid.

63. Michael A. Bishop and J. D. Trout. "50 years of successful predictive modeling should be enough: Lessons for philosophy of science." *Philosophy of Science* 69.S3 (2002): S197–S208.
64. Ibid.
65. Rory Sutherland. "The Wiki Man: If you want to diet, I'm afraid you really do need one weird rule." *The Spectator*, April 13, 2013.
66. Benjamin Graham. "A Conversation with Benjamin Graham." *Financial Analysts Journal*, Vol. 32, No. 5 (1976), pp. 20–23.
67. Bishop and Trout, 2002.
68. Ibid.
69. Benjamin Graham and David Dodd. *Security Analysis: The Classic 1934 Edition.* (New York: McGraw-Hill) 1996.
70. Ibid.
71. Seth A. Klarman. *Margin of Safety: Risk-Averse Value Investing Strategies for the Thoughtful Investor*, (New York: HarperCollins) 1991.
72. Ibid.
73. Graham and Dodd, 1996.
74. James Montier. "Graham's Net Nets: Outdated or Outstanding." *SG Equity Research*. Societe Generale, 2008.
75. Montier, 2008.
76. Damodaran, 2012.
77. Graham, 1976.
78. Ibid.

CHAPTER 8

The Art of the Corporate Raid

A History of Corporate Violence

If a man creates in another man's mind an immediate sense of danger which causes such person to try to escape, and in so doing he injures himself, the person who creates such a state of mind is responsible for the injuries which result.
—Lord Coleridge C.J. in Reg. v. Halliday (1889) 61 LT 701

defenestration \dee-fen-*uh*-STREY-sh*uh*n\, noun:
To forcibly throw a person from a window.
—Comes from Latin *de* + *fenestra*, "window".

T. Boone Pickens described Cities Service as a "case study in what was wrong with Big Oil's management."[1] Despite holding an incredible 10 million acres of exploration leases, after years of mismanagement it had depleted its huge oil and gas reserves. These problems were hidden by its enormous cash flow, which for nearly 10 years had climbed along with the price of oil. Its market price, however, reflected its future, and it was deeply undervalued as a result. Other companies in the oil and gas industry traded below the value of their proven reserves—many had made the joke that it was cheaper to drill for oil on Wall Street than it was in the oil patch[2]—but few were as undervalued as Cities in 1982, which traded for one-third the value of those underlying assets.[3] Cities' primary defense to a hostile take-over was its sheer size. In 1982 it was the nineteenth largest oil company in the United States and ranked thirty-eighth on the *Fortune 500*.[4] Pickens wanted to go after Cities, but with assets worth $6 billion, it was six times bigger than Pickens' own company, Mesa Petroleum.

Mesa's stock-in-trade was taking positions in bigger oil companies and telling them how to increase the value of the company and close the market price discount in the stock. Management usually responded that, if Mesa was unhappy with the way the company was managed, it could sell its stock. Pickens likened it to saying, "If you don't like the way the gardener mows your lawn, sell your house."[5] When he surveyed the oil and gas industry in the late 1970s, Pickens saw that it didn't lack for poor managements and undervalued companies. Sounding a little like Benjamin Graham, Pickens wrote in his autobiography:[6]

> *I was intrigued by the relationship of a company's market price to the underlying value of its assets. Many people, including some managements, like to view the stock market as an irrational mechanism. My analysis was the opposite. Over the long haul, the market reflects management's ability to make the most out of its assets. So the price of a company's stock is like a report card. Mesa's stock has almost always traded near or above the appraised value of the assets. A going concern should sell for at least the value of its assets, and something more if it has good management. If a company has poor management, the price of the stock will suffer, usually selling substantially below the appraised value.*

He recognized that the oil and gas industry was overcapitalized and generating more cash flow than it could put to good use. Many oil and gas companies were running down their reserves and not replacing them. From the early to late 1970s, oil prices had increased tenfold and the industry swelled.[7] Then, in the late 1970s, oil consumption fell just as interest rates and drilling costs spiked, leaving excess crude oil reserves. The high oil prices and reduction in exploration and development expenditure turned oil and gas companies into cash cows releasing torrents of free cash flow. The managers tended to squander the free cash flow acquiring businesses in unrelated industries. Oil and gas companies expanded into retailing, manufacturing, office equipment, and mining,[8] and those acquisitions were typically disastrous.[9] The massive misallocation of capital in the industry naturally led the market to value oil and gas stocks on the expectation that the capital destruction would persist, which, in the early 1980s, seemed likely. It also created the perfect combination of conditions for large hostile takeovers. Mesa's bid for Cities would be the first shot in what would become a white-hot market for control of corporations, first in the oil and gas industry and then beyond.

THE TERROR OF THE OIL PATCH

Thomas Boone Pickens, Jr., grew up in the oil business. His father was a *landman*—a businessman who negotiates mineral rights from landowners and then *turns* or sells the rights to third-party mineral prospectors. He studied geology at college. When he graduated 1951, he started working as a geologist for Phillips Petroleum. Founded in 1917 by Frank Phillips, one of the original *wildcatters*—prospectors who drill for oil away from known oil and gas fields—Phillips Petroleum was one of the 20 largest corporations in America when Pickens arrived, and heavily bureaucratic. He started as a field geologist, but was rapidly promoted to well-site exploration work. Chafed by the bureaucracy of such a large corporation, Pickens struck out on his own in late 1954. Acting as his own landman, he sought a *farmout*, where a leaseholder sublets his acreage to a third party willing to drill a well. Pickens approached his old employer Phillips to drill acreage on which it owned leases about to expire, but wasn't interested in drilling. Phillips agreed, and Pickens took the deal to an independent oilman who paid him $2,500 for putting it together.

After cutting his teeth with his first deal, he continued doing work typical for a small oil business—geological consulting, lease exploration and development, farmout structuring, and well-site work—until he struck on the idea of raising external funds to drill his own wells through limited partnerships. The oil partnerships took Pickens' little consulting business to a new level. By early 1964, he was able to roll up the limited partnerships into a public company called Mesa Petroleum, sold to the investors on the basis that shares in a public company with an interest in each well provided more diversification and liquidity than a limited partnership interest in an individual well. Mesa Petroleum started life on April 30, 1964, as a tiny public company; too small, in fact, to be traded on the over-the-counter market, where the smallest public companies trade. With just 239 shareholders, Pickens as chief executive officer and president was also responsible for providing the brokerage service, matching buyers and sellers with each other. The shares changed hands for $6 on average. It generated just $1.5 million in revenue in its first year as a public company. By 1968 Mesa earned $1.5 million on revenues of $6.8 million, and the stock, then traded on the American Stock Exchange, sold for $35. Pickens decided to use Mesa's now-attractive stock for its first acquisition.

In early 1968 he started analyzing the Hugoton Production Company, which was brought to his attention because it had aborted several merger attempts with other companies. What attracted Pickens to Hugoton was its huge gas reserves—it had 1.7 trillion cubic feet versus Mesa's 62 billion—which Hugoton management seemed to be slowly depleting at a below-market price for its gas. The problem was that Hugoton was managed by an investment firm—The Clarke Estates—which was more interested in liquidating the company than maximizing its potential. Pickens believed that more aggressive management could sweat the underexploited assets harder than Hugoton's management. Pickens invited Hugoton's president, Mike Nicolais, for lunch, where he broached the merger. Nicolais played coy at lunch, and called back a week later to squash Mesa's offer. Pickens wasn't so easily dissuaded. Even though Hugoton was much bigger than Mesa and Mesa lacked the resources to take over Hugoton for cash, Pickens saw that Mesa's stock might be attractive to Hugoton shareholders. Mesa offered one share of a newly created preferred stock for each share of Hugoton common. The Mesa preferred stock would convert to 1.8 shares of Mesa after five years, and in the meantime would pay a $2.50 dividend, 50 cents higher than Hugoton's $2 dividend. Pickens planned to use the Hugoton dividend to fund most of the dividend paid by the Mesa preferred stock, with Mesa making up the difference. Pickens gambled that improved gas contracts and sales would mean that Mesa wouldn't have to pay the preferred dividend for long because most preferred stockholders would convert into Mesa common when the stock price went up. Mesa filed the complicated exchange offer in late September, and by mid-October had accumulated 17 percent of Hugoton's common, not enough to exercise control, but enough to be "nettlesome," as Pickens described it. Hugoton management got the message, and in late October announced a merger with a white knight from Los Angeles, Reserve Oil & Gas.

The Hugoton bylaws had a provision that required two-thirds of stockholders to approve a merger. With 17 percent of the stock, Mesa needed another 17 percent to get to the 34 percent threshold at which it could be assured that it could block Reserve's merger plans. Pickens hit the road, making Mesa's case to Hugoton's shareholders that it was the better merger partner. By the time the tender offer ended, Mesa controlled 28 percent of Hugoton. Pickens had a problem. Mesa could borrow to buy more Hugoton stock, but couldn't afford to carry the debt for very long. He contacted Nicolais and told him that he was thinking about reopening the tender offer. Nicolais responded, "I wish you would do that."[10] He asked Pickens for time to think, and then called him back, saying, "Come to New York. We're ready to talk terms."[11] Nicolais pushed Pickens to raise the offer—from 1.8 shares of Mesa common to 1.875—and Pickens "horse-traded" the preferred dividend down to $2.20 from $2.50 per share. In April 1969, Mesa and Hugoton merged, and Mesa survived. The deal was a watershed for Pickens. It vaulted Mesa into the big league, giving it the assets and balance sheet to expand and giving Pickens much-needed deal experience. It was a harbinger of things to come, as Pickens resolved to make acquisitions a key part of Mesa's growth strategy.

Just eight months after the Hugoton merger, Pickens had found his second target, the Southland Royalty Company. Southland owned a majority interest in the mineral rights on the Waddell Ranch in West Texas, a major oil field. Gulf Oil had bought a 50-year lease to produce oil on the Waddell Ranch in 1925. Southland collected the royalties and didn't do much exploration. It invested the royalties instead by diversifying into some odd ventures, including a candy business, which earned its president, Bob Cain, the nickname "Candy" Cain. In the late 1960s the Gulf lease was approaching expiration. The Waddell Ranch wells were still producing and, with more than 100 million barrels of recoverable oil in the field, would likely continue to do so well beyond the end of the lease. At expiration, the mineral rights would revert to Southland, transforming it into one of the largest independent oil companies in the industry.

Gulf's strategy had been to fight Southland in the courts. While Southland had the stronger legal position, it was a much smaller enterprise, and Gulf was applying intense pressure to bring it to the negotiating table. Gulf had picked up 12 percent of Southland's stock on the same day it filed its lawsuit to send the message that if Southland didn't negotiate, Gulf would take it over. Pickens saw that Southland was an "undervalued situation," and a "good deal even if it lost to Gulf,"[12] and so approached Gulf to discuss Southland. Since buying its 12 percent block of Southland, Gulf had realized that holding Southland stock might prejudice its lawsuit, and so was now eager to sell. It was so eager, in fact, that it offered the stock to Pickens on credit, which he promptly snapped up. With its foot now firmly in the door, Mesa filed with the SEC on the day after Christmas in 1969. The bid—an exchange offer like the Hugoton bid—ran into immediate problems. Pickens had ignored the large block of stock controlled by Southland insiders—the board owned more than 30 percent of Southland's common stock—and they were ready for a legal fight. They engaged famed takeover defense lawyer Joe Flom, who targeted the disclosures in Mesa's exchange offer in court. Flom beat Mesa on the disclosure issues in a Delaware court, which delayed the offering with the SEC. Pickens realized that Mesa's bid was unlikely to succeed and so terminated it just four months after launch. He sold the stock on the market, making a small profit and learning several valuable lessons—first, there were practical difficulties with exchange offers, and second, even failed bids could generate a return.

CITIES SERVICE

In May 1982 Mesa held $1 billion worth of Cities' stock. Pickens planned to use it as collateral against a loan for an additional $1.3 billion, which he would use to finance a bid for 51 percent of Cities' common stock at $45 per share, representing a 25 percent premium to the prevailing $36 market price. He saw that, even after paying a sizeable premium, Cities was still cheap at $45.[13] Mesa would be paying less than $5 per barrel for Cities' oil reserves at a time when oil traded north of $30 per barrel. Pickens was putting the finishing touches to Mesa's financing package when Cities, tipped off about Mesa's bid for it, announced a preemptive bid for Mesa. Pickens described the offer as "in some respects . . . a joke."[14] Cities had offered just $17 per share for Mesa stock then trading in the market for $16.75, a miniscule 1.5 percent premium. Still, Cities' bid put Pickens at a substantial timing disadvantage. The tender offer laws required a 20-day standstill before the bidder could pay for the tendered stock. By filing first, Cities would have the opportunity to start buying Mesa stock before Mesa could buy Cities stock.

Pickens' solution was a *bear hug*, a "friendly" offer made to a company's board, rather than directly to the shareholders, and intended to put pressure on the board to respond. The beauty of it, in Pickens' mind, was that it would generate coverage in the media, alerting the stockholders to Mesa's interest in the company, and give Pickens more time to stitch together the finance for a tender offer. Pickens placed a call to Cities' chairman Charles Waidelich, and told him that Mesa was offering $50 per share for Cities. Waidelich explained to Pickens that Cities wasn't interested, and he didn't even intend to let the rest of his board know about the offer. It didn't matter. The call had accomplished Pickens' purpose, which was to put an offer to Cities' board that could be used to let Cities' shareholders know that Mesa was still in the game.

Pickens and his team scrambled to line up equity partners and debt financing. His pitch was that Mesa and its partners would be buying oil in the ground for $5 per barrel when the industry's "finding costs" alone ran to $15 a barrel. No money was required up front. All that potential partners needed to do was agree to buy the stock once it was tendered, by which time the success of the takeover would be assured. It was a compelling pitch, but, with Cities' bid hanging over their heads, Pickens found the going tough. He found plenty of parties interested in Mesa's offer, but not one that wanted to commit. Then, on Thursday, June 17, Gulf Oil announced a $63 per share bid for all of Cities' common stock, almost $20 per share more than Mesa's bid, and close to double the pre-bid market price. The announcement also included the important detail that Cities' board had agreed to accept the offer. Pickens was ecstatic. Mesa couldn't get control of Cities because Gulf's offer was simply too good, but they would crystalize a quick $70 million profit on their huge position in Cities' stock. His mood soured, however, when he realized that Cities' bid for Mesa was still alive. Mesa's lawyer contacted Cities' attorney to get the bad news: Cities proposed to drop its offer for Mesa only if Mesa sold its Cities stock back to Cities at cost, eliminating any chance for a profit. Pickens was incensed. He called Gulf's chief executive Jimmy Lee to see what he knew about Cities' proposal. Lee told Pickens that he wasn't aware of any proposal. He also told Pickens that Gulf was stretching to get to $63 per share for Cities and they weren't interested in Mesa. Pickens let Lee know that he would try to spoil Gulf's offer for Cities if Cities couldn't be persuaded to drop its bid for Mesa. Shortly after the conversation Cities' lawyer called back to offer to buy out Mesa's position for $55 per share, $8 per share less than Gulf's offer. Knowing that Gulf's offer was shaky, Pickens accepted. After costs, Mesa had made a $30 million profit on its position in Cities, representing a 25 percent return. It wasn't the blockbuster Pickens was hoping for, but it was solid return for the time spent. Six weeks later, Gulf pulled its offer for Cities and the stock crashed to the low $30s, below its pre-bid market price and effectively demonstrating the value of competition for control.

After the Cities bid, Pickens made several runs at undervalued oil companies, and lurked on the edge of several other contests. In each case, he was simply "an investor looking for a place to make a buck,"[15] and using the restructuring in the oil industry to do so. All of these smaller transactions were only "warm-ups . . . for the main event."[16] Pickens' next deal would be the most highly publicized of his career. It would, in his view, change the "whole dynamics of mergers and become a landmark in the history of acquisitions."[17] It was also the first time that Pickens would explicitly not seek control for its own sake, but to increase the share price by inducing the target to restructure or another acquirer to overbid Mesa's offer. The experience with Cities had prepared Mesa for something extraordinary, and the next project delivered on that promise.

Gulf Oil

Little Mesa Petroleum's run at the colossal Gulf Oil—20 times its size—was a takeover contest representative of the 1980s. Mesa's bid would lead to the largest corporate merger ever up to that time, and demonstrate that sheer size alone wasn't enough to protect an entrenched and underperforming management. Gulf had assets worth $20 billion, and earned $6.5 billion in profit on $30 billion in annual revenues. With a $7 billion market capitalization, it traded on an incredibly low price-to-earnings multiple of just over 1. It was even more undervalued than Cities. The conventional view was this was warranted because its enormous size protected it from hostile takeover. It was safe from corporate raiders and its share price therefore contained no takeover premium. Where analysts believed that Gulf was a highly risky proposition, Pickens saw that its huge discount limited his downside, and presented the potential for a very good return. As a deeply undervalued company in the public marketplace, Gulf was less risky than "exploring for oil and gas at a time of plunging prices and excess supply."[18] The problem was how to have the market recognize the underlying intrinsic value of a major oil company when the majors had been "undervalued for 50 years."[19]

Pickens' plan was not to actually acquire Gulf, but to have it restructure, either by repurchasing stock or reorganizing as a royalty trust—a more tax-efficient structure than the corporate form adopted by most oil and gas companies, and one that passed through cash flows directly to shareholders. Morgan Stanley prepared a detailed presentation for Mesa demonstrating that the royalty trust could increase the value of major oil companies by as much as 50 percent. Pickens hoped that, if implemented, the royalty trust would lead to substantially higher values for all stockholders, and the stock price would follow suit. He believed that Gulf's need for restructuring was self-evident. It was generating substantial cash flows, he wrote in his autobiography, but the prospects for reinvestment were poor. It was time to find a way to return the excess capital to shareholders.

Pickens considered several other possible targets, but kept returning to Gulf. Its overcapitalization and low returns on investment were characteristic of the industry. Importantly, it was trading at just a fraction of its intrinsic value; generating strong cash flow of $3 billion per year; and paying a substantial dividend—so substantial, in fact, that Mesa's carrying cost on the position was likely to be slightly positive, meaning it could hold out indefinitely if Gulf didn't cut the dividend. Pickens estimated that the underlying assets alone were worth $100 per share. The stock's all-time was $53, and in mid-1983 it languished in the low $30s with little prospect for trading higher. Crucially, from Pickens' perspective, was Gulf management's very poor reputation. Already a laughingstock following a series of scandals and blunders in the 1970s, they had badly burned a number of investors by backing out of the 1982 bid for Cities Service, killing any possibility for goodwill in the professional investment community. Despite its enormous size relative to Mesa, it was the epitome of a deeply undervalued takeover target, offering limited downside risk and huge upside potential.

By September 1983 Mesa had spent $350 million buying 8.5 million shares, representing 4.9 percent of Gulf Oil, and just below the 5 percent threshold that would require it to file with the SEC and disclose its holding to the market.[20] By the time Mesa filed with the SEC in October, it held 14.5 million shares, representing almost 9 percent of Gulf, acquired at a cost of $638 million. Mesa filed a 13G notice indicating a passive investment, but its reputation as a hostile bidder caused Gulf's management to panic. The board announced a special shareholders' meeting for December. Their plan was to have Gulf change its charter and bylaws to remove several shareholder rights and to move the state of incorporation from Pennsylvania to Delaware, which was friendlier to incumbent management teams. Pickens kept buying, and by the end of October held 11 percent of Gulf common. On October 31 Mesa announced that it intended to lead a proxy fight to block reincorporation.[21]

In the lead up to the special shareholders' meeting, Pickens pushed the merits of the royalty trust idea in the press and in meetings with the proxy committees of Gulf's large institutional shareholders. He argued that the royalty trust was the most efficient way of sharing Gulf's huge cash flows with its shareholders, and that it made no sense to eliminate shareholder rights and reincorporate just to prevent an activist investor from implementing the idea. Many investors were concerned that Mesa was seeking greenmail, so Pickens held a press conference in November to make it clear that Mesa intended to "participate in the enhancement of value of Gulf shares on an equal basis with all Gulf shareholders."[22] Mesa wouldn't take greenmail. Pickens also encountered difficulty selling the royalty trust idea, which was misconstrued as a means for liquidating the company. Pickens pointed out that Gulf hadn't replaced its reserves since 1971, and so was already in liquidation.[23]

By the time the shareholder meeting rolled around on December 10, Mesa held 12 percent of Gulf's common. From the pulpit, Gulf's chief executive Jimmy Lee opened the meeting by denouncing Pickens as a "shark," saying that he had a "history of hit-and-run tactics," and that the royalty trust would "cripple the company and severely penalize the majority of the stockholders."[24] He also said that Mesa would have to cut the Gulf dividend to pay for the royalty trust. When Lee had finished, Pickens was forced to speak from the floor, but turned it to his advantage by beginning, "I appreciate your giving me the chance to speak today from the same level as the Gulf employees and stockholders. Frankly that's where I feel most comfortable."[25] The line drew rousing applause from the audience. As they waited for the results of the meeting—it was expected to take several weeks to count the proxies from Gulf's 400,000 shareholders—Mesa continued buying Gulf stock, pushing its position to 21.7 million shares, or around 13 percent. When the results were finally tallied in late December, Gulf had received 52 percent of the votes, a win for Gulf, but a narrow one.

Pickens still believed that Gulf needed to restructure or sell out, and so Mesa kept pushing. First it detailed the benefits of restructuring Gulf as a royalty trust in a 57-page document delivered to each of Gulf's board members on December 29, 1983. Gulf dismissed the idea with a curt, two-page response. To maintain pressure, Mesa used the same tactic it had in its Cities Service contest, announcing in late January 1984 a partial tender offer for at least 13.5 million shares of Gulf at $65 per share. The stock price responded, jumping from $37 to $62. At noon on March 5 Pickens finally received the news he had been waiting for: Gulf announced that it had entered into a merger agreement with Socal, which provided for a cash tender offer of $80 per share, or $13.2 billion. If approved by shareholders, Mesa's investment group stood to make a $760 million profit on its 21.7 million-share position in Gulf. At a special meeting on June 15, Gulf's shareholders approved the merger with Socal. At Mesa's $45 per share average, Socal's $80 per share offer for Gulf represented an 80 percent return on an almost $1 billion investment in fewer than 12 months, a stunning return by any measure for an ostensibly failed takeover. For his part, Pickens wrote in his autobiography that "[t]his is what the Business Roundtable calls raiding:"[26]

> *The way I see it, when you invest $1 billion in a company's stock— as we did in Gulf's—you're not a raider, you're a very large stockholder. You should enjoy all the rights of ownership, including an open dialogue with management about changes that could benefit all shareholders. We weren't asking for anything special. We just wanted to talk.*

After Gulf, Mesa continued in its attempts to restructure the major oil companies, making hostile runs at majors Philips and Unocal. The recapitalization of Phillips and Unocal—both triggered by pressure from Mesa— resulted in significant gains to existing shareholders. In neither campaign did Pickens get control, but both times Mesa walked away with a sizeable return. Philips agreed to restructure by buying back 38 percent of its stock, delivering to Mesa in three short months a 40 percent gain worth about $90 million.[27] Unocal similarly agreed to buy back stock, delivering an $83 million gain on Pickens' $1 billion position.[28] In each case the companies also increased cash dividends, sold assets, and made major reductions in exploration and development expenditures. Pickens' thesis that oil and gas companies were overcapitalized and needed to reduce capacity was gradually accepted by industry and academics alike.

CAPITAL ALLOCATION AND RESTRUCTURING

Pickens' efforts to restructure the industry did eventually lead it to collectively return capital and become more efficient. In *The New Financial Capitalists*, George Baker and George Smith wrote that, while they adopted a different structure, Pickens' attempt to implement the royalty trust achieved the same end that leveraged buy-outs (LBOs) did:[29]

> *The companies that ended up owning the assets, including the oil reserves, had to take on large amounts of debt to finance their acquisitions, which always required huge cash payments to preexisting*

shareholders that had been driven up by the intervening bidding process. The payments were financed by liquidating the reserves, and thus served much the same function as the royalty trust, the underlying motive for which—the channeling of free cash flow to the shareholders—was the same as that of another technique for realizing value: the leveraged buyout.

Thus Pickens royalty trust was, like the LBO, simply another mechanism for solving what Michael C. Jensen—an economist who has undertaken research into agency theory and a professor emeritus at Harvard—described as the "agency costs of free cash flow."[30] Jensen proposed that excess free cash flow created a conflict of interest between shareholders and managers over payout policies. The problem, according to Jensen, was how to motivate managers to "disgorge the cash rather than [invest] it at below the cost of capital or wast[e] it on organization inefficiencies,"[31] a euphemism for high salaries and other perquisites. Promises to increase the dividends paid out were insufficient because they could be reneged upon at a later date, wrote Jensen. Rather, the solution was debt because it forced managers to guarantee that they would pay out future cash flows, thereby reducing the agency costs of free cash flow by reducing the cash flow available for spending at the discretion of managers. Jensen called this the "control hypothesis" of debt. Debt reduced the agency costs of free cash flow by reducing management's discretion in the allocation of it because it was apportioned at inception at the direction of the LBO firm shareholders to paying down debt.

Jensen also proposed that the "threat caused by failure to make debt service payments serves as an effective motivating force to make such organizations more efficient."[32] Managers were incentivized to "overcome normal organizational resistance to retrenchment which the payout of free cash flow often requires."[33] Buffett was less convinced about the use of debt as a motivational aid. In his 1990 *Chairman's Letter* he wrote that large debt loads caused managers "to focus their efforts as never before, much as a dagger mounted on the steering wheel of a car could be expected to make its driver proceed with intensified care:"[34]

We'll acknowledge that such an attention-getter would produce a very alert driver. But another certain consequence would be a deadly—and unnecessary—accident if the car hit even the tiniest pothole or sliver of ice. The roads of business are riddled with potholes; a plan that requires dodging them all is a plan for disaster.

Pickens' royalty trust idea cleverly avoided the LBO's dagger-on-the-steering wheel, while removing the temptation of excess cash flow. Jensen, in making his agency costs of free cash flow argument, cited two studies that had found the oil and gas industry had overinvested in exploration and development through the late 1970s and early 1980s. In the first study, the researchers examined 658 companies in the industry, finding that those announcing *increases* in exploration and development expenditures in the period from 1975 to 1981 saw systematic *decreases* in their stock price, and vice versa.[35] These results were striking because when industrial firms announced comparable *increases* in research and development expenditures their stocks enjoyed significant *positive* returns, and vice versa. A second study on the actual returns to exploration and development expenditures for the 30 largest oil companies found that on average the industry earned less than 10 percent before tax on their investments over the period from 1982 to 1984.[36] Jensen estimated that the net present value of future net cash flows of investments in the oil and gas industry at the time ranged from less than 60 cents on the dollar on the low side to as much as 90 cents on the dollar on the high side. It was capital misallocation on an industry-wide scale, but difficult for industry insiders to perceive, accustomed as they were to running on the reinvestment treadmill. The time was ripe for a Graham-style interloper—recall that Graham described rubbing shoulders with management as "self-help," and felt that an investor should be an outsider who confronted managements—to shake up the companies in the industry and point out the pervasive misallocation of capital. Pickens and Mesa stepped into that role, and made windfall profits as a result. It was a template that would eventually be replicated outside the oil and gas industry by other investors, many of whom were the forerunners to today's activist investors. While Pickens stood at the forefront of the takeover craze in the 1980s, he wasn't the first to recognize the value of using ersatz takeovers of over-capitalized companies as a means for catalyzing management to take share-holder friendly strides.

The Cigar Butt Berkshire Hathaway

In 1962, a fellow Grahamite value investor, Dan Cowin, alerted Buffett to a textile maker in New Bedford, Massachusetts, trading at one-third of its net current asset value of around $22 million, or $19.46 per share.[37] Buffett saw that he could either take it over and liquidate it, or sell his position back to the company when its then-president, Seabury Stanton, authorized one of its periodic buybacks. Stanton was in the habit of using extra cash not reinvested in the company's textile mills to self-tender for shares every couple of years. Buffett knew this, and reasoned he could buy ahead of Stanton's next tender offer, and resell to the company when it was announced.[38] His investment partnerships started accumulating shares of the textile manufacturer—which was, of course, Berkshire Hathaway—on December 12, 1962, paying $7.50 per share for 2,000 shares.[39]

Cowin was tasked with the role Henry Brandt would fulfill in Buffett's American Express investment, that of scuttlebutt acquisition. He discovered that Berkshire board member Otis Stanton was at odds with his brother Seabury because he had chosen his son, Jack, to succeed him as president.[40] Otis felt that Jack wasn't up to the job, and, in any case, didn't plan to cede control to him. Otis favored as Seabury's successor another employee of Berkshire Hathaway, Ken Chace, the vice president of manufacturing. Seabury, a graduate of Harvard, had been running Berkshire since 1934. He viewed himself as a hero who had saved the textile mills by pouring millions into modernizing them when others had "hesitated to spend stockholders' money on new equipment when business was so bad and the prospects were so uncertain."[41] Nicholas Brady, another graduate of Harvard's business school, and nephew to Berkshire's chairman Malcolm Chase—no relation to Ken—had written his thesis on Berkshire, and was so discouraged by the results of his research that he sold his shares.[42] Malcolm may have taken heed of his nephew's paper because he refused to go along with Seabury's modernization plans. Seabury's sense of his own destiny as savior of the textile mills won out, however, and he continued investing millions in the relentless modernization.[43] It didn't work, and, as the realities of the textile business's poor economics overwhelmed Seabury's limited managerial capabilities, he started drinking heavily, which Cowin duly reported to Buffett. Still, Seabury was sufficiently in command of his faculties to apprehend Buffett as an imminent takeover threat.

Seabury responded to Buffett's accumulating position in Berkshire by making several tender offers for the stock, one of the potential exits Buffett had considered before he starting buying. When Seabury's latest tender offer had pushed the Berkshire stock price to between $9 and $10 per share, Buffett decided to journey to New Bedford to meet Seabury, and discuss his plans for the next tender offer. Buffett later reported to his biographer, Alice Schroeder, that Stanton asked, "We'll probably have a tender one of these days, and what price would you sell at, Mr. Buffett?"[44]

> *I'd sell at $11.50 a share on a tender offer, if you had one.*
> *Well, will you promise me that if we have a tender offer you'll tender?*
> *If it's in the reasonably near future, but not if it's in 20 years from now. Fine.*

Shortly after the meeting, Berkshire Hathaway sent a letter to Buffett and the other shareholders offering $11 3/8 per share to anyone who tendered their stock.[45] The sum, 12½ cents per share less than Buffett and Seabury had agreed to, infuriated Buffett. He decided that, rather than sell his position back to Seabury and Berkshire Hathaway, he'd take it over.

Buffett approached Otis Stanton to make an offer for his stock. Otis agreed to sell out to Buffett on the condition that Buffett make the same offer to Seabury, a condition that Buffett readily accepted.[46] Otis's Berkshire Hathaway holding pushed Buffett's position to 49 percent, which was enough to control the board. Buffett was formally elected a director of Berkshire Hathaway at a special meeting convened in April 1965.[47] When Seabury and his son, Jack, resigned from the board at a board meeting a month later, Buffett was elected chairman. The *New Bedford Standard-Times* ran a story about the takeover. Buffett, seeking to avoid raising the ire of the townsfolk of New Bedford as he had the townsfolk of Beatrice following his attempted liquidation of Dempster Mill Manufacturing Company, was quick to assure the paper that he would run the business, rather than liquidate it. Buffett later said of Berkshire:[48]

> So I bought my own cigar butt, and tried to smoke it. You walk down the street and you see a cigar butt, and it's kind of soggy and disgusting and repels you, but it's free . . . and there may be one puff left in it. Berkshire didn't have any more puffs. So all you had was a soggy cigar butt in your mouth. That was Berkshire Hathaway in 1965. I had a lot of money tied up in the cigar butt. I would have been better off if I'd never heard of Berkshire Hathaway.

Later, writing in his 1985 *Chairman's Letter* about textiles, Buffett described a commodity-based industry in which substantial excess capacity existed similar to the oil and gas industry in the 1970s, and suffering from similarly endemic industry-wide capital misallocation. Buffett's insights into investment and proper capital allocation allowed Berkshire to avoid making large capital expenditures in its namesake textile operation, each of which looked like an "immediate winner . . . [m]easured by standard return-on-investment tests," but offered "illusory" benefits for the reasons Buffett describes:[49]

> Many of our competitors, both domestic and foreign, were stepping up to the same kind of expenditures and, once enough companies did so, their reduced costs became the baseline for reduced prices industrywide. Viewed individually, each company's capital invest-ment decision appeared cost-effective and rational; viewed col-lectively, the decisions neutralized each other and were irrational (just as happens when each person watching a parade decides he

can see a little better if he stands on tiptoes). After each round of investment, all the players had more money in the game and returns remained anemic. Thus, we faced a miserable choice: huge capital investment would have helped to keep our textile business alive, but would have left us with terrible returns on ever-growing amounts of capital. After the investment, moreover, the foreign competition would still have retained a major, continuing advantage in labor costs. A refusal to invest, however, would make us increasingly non-competitive, even measured against domestic textile manufacturers. I always thought myself in the position described by Woody Allen in one of his movies: "More than any other time in history, mankind faces a crossroads. One path leads to despair and utter hopeless-ness, the other to total extinction. Let us pray we have the wisdom to choose correctly."

Buffett did slowly liquidate Berkshire's textile business. At the time he took control, textiles were its only business. Rather than simply continue to reinvest in it, Buffett redirected to better prospects like insurance capital that would have otherwise funded inventories, receivables, and fixed assets. That decision, and others made for the same reason, eventually turned Berkshire into an investment powerhouse. Its competitors in the textile business that did not liquidate, but chose to stick it out, fared poorly. The experience of Burlington Industries—the largest U.S. textile company at the time Buffett got control of Berkshire Hathaway in 1964, and 21 years later after Berkshire Hathaway had exited the textiles industry—was, wrote Buffett, "instructive:"[50]

In 1964 Burlington had sales of $1.2 billion against our $50 mil-lion. It had strengths in both distribution and production that we could never hope to match and also, of course, had an earnings record far superior to ours. Its stock sold at 60 at the end of 1964; ours was 13.

Burlington made a decision to stick to the textile business, and in 1985 had sales of about $2.8 billion. During the 1964-85 period, the company made capital expenditures of about $3 billion, far more than any other U.S. textile company and more than $200-per-share on that $60 stock. A very large part of the expenditures, I am sure, was devoted to cost improvement and expansion. Given Burlington's basic commitment to stay in textiles, I would also sur-mise that the company's capital decisions were quite rational.

Nevertheless, Burlington has lost sales volume in real dollars and has far lower returns on sales and equity now than 20 years *ago. Split 2-for-1 in 1965, the stock now sells at 34—on an adjusted basis, just a little over its $60 price in 1964. Meanwhile, the CPI has more than tripled. Therefore, each share commands about one-third the purchasing power it did at the end of 1964. Regular dividends have been paid but they, too, have shrunk significantly in purchasing power. This devastating outcome for the shareholders indicates what can happen when much brain power and energy are applied to a faulty premise.*

Buffett concluded from his experience with Berkshire's relentlessly loss-making textile business that, "Should you find yourself in a chronically-leaking boat, energy devoted to changing vessels is likely to be more productive than energy devoted to patching leaks."[51]

Like Buffett in the textile industry, Pickens was unburdened by the oil and gas industry's notions of reinvestment. He saw the futility of allocating capital at below-market rates of return and, in the absence of better prospects, the opportunity for realizing a return by redirecting that excess capital into the hands of shareholders. Limited by his own investment capital, Pickens relied on ingenuity to achieve those ends, a crucial element of which was the market for corporate control—the market in which alternative management teams compete for the rights to manage corporations. By making possible an involuntary exchange of control of publicly traded companies, the stock market creates a competitive market for the management of corporations. Pickens never did get control of a major, or persuade one to restructure by specifically adopting his royalty trust idea, but he did prompt change at each of the companies that was subject to Mesa's attention. Many in the media interpreted his campaigns as quixotic tilts at unassailable windmills, misconstruing as failed takeovers his efforts to draw attention to deeply undervalued and poorly managed companies. Some investors, however, did take notice. What better platform than a well-publicized proxy fight and tender offer to highlight mismanagement and underexploited intrinsic value, and advocate for change? Just as Pickens' had in the oil and gas industry, they saw that the market for corporate control could be used as a catalyst to induce either a voluntary restructuring or takeover by a bigger player in other industries.

Observing that investors could capture investment returns by taking positions in undervalued stocks, and then precipitating a corporate catalyst like a takeover or liquidation, a group of so-called "takeover entrepreneurs" or "corporate raiders" started harassing companies in the 1980s. Often equipped with little more than ambition, they took advantage of the swathe of deeply undervalued companies and liquidity provided by the roaring market for control to generate outsized returns. Some sought to acquire companies whole in leveraged transactions; others sought board control and eventual liquidation or sale; still others sought only to create the illusion of pursuing control, hoping to be bought out by another acquirer at a premium after putting the company "in play." Most were either washed away by the 1987 stock market crash or couldn't find enough undervalued companies in the early 1990s to ply their trade, but a new breed emerged following the dot-com bust in 2000. They found a fertile investment landscape in which overcapitalized technology companies traded at a discount to liquidation value or, in some cases, cash backing. For the first time in more than a decade, the corporate raider was back, but now styled as an activist investor. Icahn again led the charge.

Notes

1. T. Boone Pickens, Jr. *Boone.* (Boston: Houghton Mifflin) 1989.
2. George P. Baker and George David Smith. *The New Financial Capitalists: Kohlberg Kravis Roberts and the Creation of Corporate Value.* (Cambridge: Cambridge University Press) 1998.
3. Pickens, 1989.
4. Ibid.
5. Ibid.
6. Ibid.
7. Michael C. Jensen, "Agency Costs of Free Cash Flow, Corporate Finance, and Takeovers." *American Economic Review*, May 1986, Vol. 76, No. 2, pp. 323–329.
8. Ibid.
9. Ibid.
10. Pickens, 1989.
11. Ibid.
12. Ibid.
13. Ibid.
14. Ibid.
15. Ibid.
16. Ibid.
17. Ibid.
18. Ibid.
19. Ibid.
20. Ibid.
21. Ibid.
22. Ibid.
23. Ibid.
24. Ibid.
25. Ibid.
26. Ibid.
27. Ibid.

28. Ibid.
29. Baker and Smith, 1998.
30. Jensen, 1986.
31. Ibid.
32. Ibid.
33. Ibid.
34. Warren Buffett. "Chairman's Letter." *Berkshire Hathaway, Inc. Annual Report,* 1990.
35. John J. McConnell and Chris J. Muscarella. "Corporate Capital Expenditure Decisions and the Market Value of the Firm." *Journal of Financial Economics.* Volume 14, Issue 3, September 1985, pp. 399–422.
36. Bernard Picchi. "Structure of the U.S. Oil Industry: Past and Future." *Salomon Brothers.* July 1985.
37. Alice Schroeder. *The Snowball.* (New York: Bantam Books) 2008.
38. Warren Buffett, "Chairman's Letter." *Berkshire Hathaway, Inc. Annual Report,* 1994.
39. Schroeder, 2008.
40. Ibid.
41. Ibid.
42. Ibid.
43. Ibid.
44. Ibid.
45. Ibid.
46. Ibid.
47. Ibid.
48. Ibid.
49. Warren Buffett, "Chairman's Letter." *Berkshire Hathaway, Inc. Annual Report,* 1985.
50. Ibid.
51. Ibid.

CHAPTER 9

How Hannibal Profits From His Victories

The Returns to Activist Investment

"*Vinse Hannibal, et non seppe usar' poi Ben la vittoriosa sua ventura.*"
[*Hannibal won battles, but he never knew how to profit from his victories.*]
— Petrach, *Sonnet 82(83)* from Screech, *Montaigne's Complete Essays*

"*The fact is that the Hypermodern Theory is merely the application, during the opening stages generally, of the same old principles through the medium of somewhat new tactics. There has been no change in the fundamentals. The change has been only a change of form, and not always for the best at that.*"
—José Raúl Capablanca, the "Human Chess Machine," in *Chess Fundamentals* (1934)

2009 was an *annus horribilis*—horrible year—for Genzyme Corporation, a giant biotechnology firm located in Cambridge, Massachusetts. The problems started in June when the company uncovered a viral contamination in its Allston Landing plant.[1] The U.S. Food and Drug Administration (FDA) had in February warned Genzyme that the plant needed to pass inspection in May as part of the approval process for a new drug candidate, *Lumizyme*, used to treat a rare condition called *Pompe* disease. With the contamination, the FDA delayed approval for *Lumizyme*, ordered the plant closed, and then subjected it to a five-week inspection and decontamination. As embarrassing as the contamination and delay were, Genzyme's troubles were just getting started. The five-week closure revealed problems with the stocking process for Genzyme's most important drugs. Genzyme had very little of the life-saving drugs in inventory, and the closure led to severe shortages. Stocks of *Cerezyme* and *Fabrazyme*, both used to treat rare genetic diseases, ran dry, leaving patients without the medicine they desperately needed. In *Cerezyme*, Genzyme had the only treatment for *Gaucher's* disease, a monopoly worth $1.25 billion annually.[2] To ensure supply, regulators allowed two of Genzyme's competitors to rush onto the market alternatives to *Cerezyme*, and its valuable monopoly was lost. The company also had to write off the value of its inventory in *Cerezyme*.[3] The source of the viral contamination was never identified.[4]

The aftershocks of the contamination extended beyond the end of the shutdown. In September the FDA rejected Genzyme's application for *Clolar*, a drug intended to treat leukemia, and in November finally rejected its application for *Lumizyme*. Genzyme also dropped a third candidate in November, a kidney drug that had failed to perform in Phase 3 of development. Just as the company was looking to put behind it the worst operational crisis in its history, a new, larger contamination was discovered. Doctors had found vials of some of the drugs coming out of the Allston Landing plant contained visible particles.[5] The particles were determined to be bits of steel, rubber, and fiber, remnants of old equipment and a sloppy manufacturing process.[6] The new contamination affected five of Genzyme's drugs, representing almost half of Genzyme's $4.6 billion in annual revenues.[7] CBS's Jim Edwards commented on *MoneyWatch*, "Genzyme could sure use some adult supervision right now."[8]

The crises hit Genzyme's business hard. In January 2009, the company had forecast earnings of $4.70 a share for the year, up from $4.01 a share in 2008.[9] As the contaminations came to light and the supplies of life-saving drugs ran dry, it was forced to cut its earnings and revenue forecasts four separate times. Finally, the company announced it expected earnings in 2009 to be down 43 percent from 2008, at $2.27 a share.[10] Genzyme's stock took a hit, tumbling 40 percent from its high of $80 per share to $48, its lowest level in five years. The stock lagged all of its large-capitalization biotechnology competitors in the NYSE Arca Biotech Index, which had risen 46 percent over the year.[11] Meanwhile, Genzyme's CEO Henri Termeer had a very good year, earning $35 million.[12] For his "epic mismanagement," *The Street* named him the Worst Biotechnology CEO of 2009.[13]

Shareholder anger was palpable. The contaminations, manufacturing shutdown, and the shortages were evidence, several claimed, that management had neglected Genzyme's best assets, underinvesting in its highly successful rare-disease business, while diversifying through acquisition into other businesses that were not as profitable.[14] A biotechnology analyst at Sanford C. Bernstein & Company said, "It's no surprise that that original business is starved for capital and you have all sorts of problems."[15] Genzyme needed "new management to reverse course," he said, "and break apart what had become a conglomerate."[16] Shareholders also complained that the company's accounting was opaque and that the financial reporting had not conformed to standard.[17] The board was simply too tightly knit, passive, and cowed by Termeer, an outsized personality who had run Genzyme for 25 years, building it from scratch into a giant with $4.6 billion in sales.[18] Sheridan Snyder, the founder of the company, called for Termeer's resignation. Termeer, revealing a tin ear, told CNBC that there was no reason for him to resign because the company would "recover through the first half of 2010 and return to the record-high share prices last seen in 2008."[19] Reuters reported that one portfolio manager holding 500,000 shares of Genzyme said, "In my opinion, and the opinion of Wall Street, Henri has failed to execute well over the past few years. I think there are certain investors who would welcome a management shake-up."[20]

Alex Denner, Icahn's biotechnology analyst, had been following Genzyme for years.[21] Icahn had held a passive 1 percent position in Genzyme in 2007, but sold out as the stock ran up. Denner let Icahn know that Genzyme was primed for his attention: its business was suffering through a series of crises caused by management missteps; the board had corporate governance issues; and shareholders were unhappy. The company was diverse, with many moving parts, some valuable, others less so. The opportunity was in Genzyme's undervalued jewel—its lucrative rare-disease business—hidden by muddy accounting in a thicket of bolted-on drugs and unrelated surgical and diagnostic products.[22] Denner believed the acquisitions, which generated $2 billion in revenue, contributed nothing to the bottom line.[23] Worse, they had drained capital away from the rare-disease business. Summing up the situation, Denner said:[24]

> *Genzyme had a golden goose. All you had to do was put a little hay in front of the goose in the morning, and they weren't even doing that.*

For his part, Termeer told *Forbes* that diversification was essential to survival and growth. "These products were highly profitable. Maybe [Icahn] couldn't see this in the [financial statements], but those assumptions were wrong."[25]

As Denner described Genzyme, Icahn peppered him with questions, "How broken was manufacturing? Could the FDA be so angry it would handicap Genzyme for years to come? With health care reform in the air, could Congress cap prices of its bestselling drugs?"[26] Satisfied with his answers, Icahn concluded Genzyme stock price was down "for the wrong reasons."[27] The manufacturing issues had scared investors for the near term, he said, "But for the long term I believed there was little problem. Additionally, Genzyme had a great pipeline no one was giving value to."[28] Icahn decided to take a position, "I said to Alex, 'This is a great one, this is a great opportunity for us. Just buy all we can buy.'"[29] By the end of the September 2009 quarter, he had spent $73 million to pick up 1.5 million Genzyme shares at an average price of $50.47. The stake amounted to just 0.5 percent of the company. Icahn kept buying. By the end of 2009 he had pushed his ownership stake to 4.8 million shares, or 2 percent, still too small to require the filing of a schedule 13D notice, but a toe hold.

AN IDEAL INDUSTRY

Icahn knew the biotechnology industry well before he and Denner went after Genzyme. He had found it a happy hunting ground since his first campaign begun in 2002 when he had targeted ImClone Systems. ImClone's stock had crashed from $74 per share to $15 when the FDA rejected its drug *Erbitux*, used in the treatment of colorectal cancer. Icahn had held a passive 5.1 percent stake in the company since 1995 due to his friendship with its founder and chief executive, Samuel D. Waksal.[30] Following the FDA's rejection of *Erbitux* and with the stock trading around $18, Icahn applied for, and received, approval from the Federal Trade Commission and the Justice Department to increase his stake to as much as 40 percent.[31] ImClone interpreted it as a vote of support in *Erbitux*.

When it later emerged that several ImClone executives, including Waksal, had sold stock prior to the announcement ImClone was hit by class action lawsuits and became the subject of informal investigations by a slew of Federal government agencies.[32] Waksal and the other executives were eventually convicted of insider trading, as was high-profile television personality Martha Stewart. The company announced an interim chief executive who Icahn opposed, and sought to merge with another company against Icahn's wishes. Shortly after the interim chief executive was installed, Icahn initiated an activist campaign with the filing of a 13D notice disclosing a $390.5 million position, representing 13.8 percent of ImClone. During the proxy fight, ImClone complained that Icahn had blocked a $36-per-share offer for the company that turned on Icahn's acceptance. Icahn had refused to agree, arguing that the "non-bid," as he described it, was too low, and made in "overpriced" bidder's stock. He kept up the pressure, and by October 2006, had been named chairman of ImClone's board. Four other Icahn nominees, including Denner, were named directors.

When in July 2008 Bristol-Myers Squibb announced a $4.5 billion, $60 per share bid for ImClone, Icahn ignored it for months and then, in September, finally rejected it. Although the bid offered Icahn a profit of about 80 percent over his purchase price, and valued his stake at $700 million, he claimed that a large pharmaceutical company—the name of which he refused to disclose—had offered $70 per share, subject to due diligence.[33] On September 22, Bristol-Myers responded by letter to Icahn as chairman of ImClone lifting its bid to just $62, implying that it either didn't believe Icahn or didn't regard the unnamed bidder's offer as serious.[34] (ImClone shares traded at $59.40, suggesting the market agreed with Bristol-Myers.[35]) In the letter containing the new $62 bid, Bristol-Myers also threatened to conduct a proxy contest to have Icahn and the other board members removed or to go directly to ImClone shareholders with a cash tender offer for their shares.[36] Both tactics were Icahn favorites, and the irony wasn't lost on the media that Icahn was feeling the sharp end of his own stick.[37] Icahn replied the next day in a short letter to Bristol-Myers, writing that its hostile offer of $62 was "absurd" given the presence of the $70 offer from the large pharmaceutical company, which was to complete due diligence on September 28, less than a week away.[38] True to his word, on October 6 ImClone announced a merger with Eli Lilly and Company at $70 per share in cash, for a total value of $6.5 billion.[39] Eli Lilly's offer represented a $34 premium to the 2006 offer, a $10 premium to Bristol-Myers' original $60 offer and an $8 premium to its tender offer price. In the press release announcing the transaction, Icahn said, "We feel that the Eli Lilly transaction vindicates our decision to oppose in 2006 a potential transaction in which the Company would have been sold at approximately $36 per share which the prior board favored."[40] The Eli Lilly offer gave Icahn a 109 percent cumulative gain on his position in ImClone, or 40 percent annualized, measured from the filing of the 13D notice in February 2006.

Icahn had closely followed the biotechnology industry since investing in a series of biotech firms before Genzyme, often highlighting in shareholder communications his success with ImClone. The next target after the 2006 proxy fight at ImClone was MedImmune, which sold out to AstraZeneca for $15.6 billion after a short struggle in 2007. He also challenged Enzon Pharmaceuticals in March 2008 and Amylin Pharmaceuticals in May 2008, with mixed success. Before the conclusion of the ImClone sales process in October 2008, Icahn had already moved onto Biogen Idec, disclosing a 6 percent position in the company in August. He challenged the board in a series of unsuccessful proxy contests in 2009 and 2010. In June 2011 after a run up in the stock, Icahn sold out with a 90 percent gain, but without ever getting control. Biogen-Idec, MedImmune, ImClone Systems, Amylin Pharmaceuticals, and Enzon Pharmaceuticals were all much smaller companies than Genzyme, but the opportunity was the same. Icahn was attracted to the biotech industry because, like the oil and gas industry in the 1980s and the textile industry in the 1960s, it was awash in capital, with wilting returns from new investments and larger, established pharmaceutical companies hungry for new treatments. The long lead-times for new drugs—biotechnology can take 12 to 15 years to bring to market—the high rates of failure in research trials, and the massive investment required to get from research to treatment meant that large pharmaceutical companies often found it less risky to buy new drugs than develop them internally.[41] The market rapidly sold down the stocks of biotechs with failed drug candidates, and Icahn used that fear to front-run the pharmaceutical companies who were eager to find new opportunities as older drugs became subject to competition from generic brands. Explaining his strategy, Icahn told *Forbes*, "These companies usually have management that has overspent and not enough funds to complete what they started. There's a suitor standing outside that can't get in the door. We help push that door open."[42] Genzyme was no different.

AN ARCHETYPAL TARGET

Genzyme was a classical Icahn target: deeply undervalued; a business stumbling from crisis to crisis; shareholders unhappy with management; weak corporate governance; and in an industry in need of restructuring. In February 2010, Icahn announced that he was nominating four directors to Genzyme's board.[43] In the announcement, Icahn laid out his plan and, as he had many times before, took the opportunity to highlight his success with ImClone:

> *Given that Genzyme's management has performed so poorly in the past, our first task will be to attempt to help fix what is broken. We have heard from a number of shareholders that they have very little faith in the current board and believe that there should be a major shake-up in its composition.*

Seeing the company as a new version of his ImClone successes, Icahn prepared himself to turn the company around before finding a buyer.

By the end of March 2010, he had picked up an additional 5.7 million shares, pushing his holding to 10.5 million shares purchased at an average price of $54.94.[44] Genzyme now represented 17 percent of Icahn's portfolio.[45] Genzyme, under pressure from Icahn, agreed to spend $2 billion to buy back its shares.[46] The move produced the desired effect: the company's stock spiked. Just as it looked like Genzyme might gain the advantage, the Allston Landing plant suffered a power outage, throwing the spotlight back on its manufacturing problems. The outage further limited the supplies of

Cerezyme and *Fabrazyme*. Compounding the issue, from Icahn's perspective, Genzyme failed to disclose the outage and its impact on the supply of the drugs until 21 days later.

In June, Icahn sent a letter to Genzyme's shareholders advocating for his slate of directors. The letter opened, "Are you as tired as we are of seeing your investment in Genzyme erode because of management's continuing track record of avoidable missteps and subpar performance in dealing with manufacturing problems at the company?" The main problem—capitalized in the letter—was that, "SEVERE PROBLEMS IN MANUFACTURING HAVE RESULTED IN A SIGNIFICANT DESTRUCTION OF NEAR-TERM AND LONG-TERM SHAREHOLDER VALUE." Icahn charged that the board was "asleep at the wheel" and described Termeer as "King of the Company." The company had "permanently lost revenues and profits to competitors from its 'cash cow' genetics disease franchise as a result of both manufacturing mismanagement and poor strategic planning. In addition, the company has lost significant credibility with patients, doctors and regulators, both in the U.S. and in Europe, two of its most critical markets for its life-saving drugs." The solution was "a major overhaul of Genzyme's management oversight through a reconstituted board that will work to resolve the manufacturing crisis and re-establish trust and credibility with stakeholders." And the people to do it were the so-called "Icahn Slate" who, while directors of ImClone "spearheaded a series of initiatives that resulted in a 126 percent gain in its share price from Oct. 2006 to Nov. 2008, when the company was sold to Eli Lilly & Co. The ImClone initiatives over a two-year period included recharging its partnership with Bristol-Myers Squibb that spurred sales of its flagship drug Erbitux; slashing expenses, reallocating resources and settling litigation. The Icahn team was integrally involved in lining up a counter-bidder to Bristol-Myers' $60 per-share offer, resulting in its sale at $70 per-share. All this is part of the public record."[47]

Genzyme responded in a proxy sent to shareholders that the Icahn Slate had a conflict of interest because Denner and Icahn sat on the boards of other biotechnology companies with drugs that competed with Genzyme's.[48] Some shareholders seemed to take the conflict seriously, enough that Icahn became concerned that the Icahn Slate wouldn't be elected to the board. Seeking to avoid defeat, Icahn contacted Genzyme director Ralph Whitworth, also an activist investor who had recently been added to the board, to see if he could get Denner on the board, too. Whitworth told him he couldn't have Denner, but he could pick two independent directors. Whitworth had already discussed the offer with Termeer, arguing, "You still have Carl out there, and he's pissed off now. Let's quiet things down and get everyone inside working [together]."[49] Icahn agreed to Whitworth's terms, withdrawing his slate a few days later when the two new directors were added to the board.

If Termeer felt any sense of relief, it was short-lived. Unbidden by Icahn, but apparently sensing the opportunity that the two activist investors had created in Genzyme, pharmaceutical giant Sanofi-Aventis started circling. In August, it made an informal approach, offering $69 per share, or $18.5 billion for the company. Genzyme's share price vaulted to $70, a 52-week high, on speculation in the press that an offer had been made. Genzyme rebuffed the offer. Sanofi-Aventis responded by unveiling a hostile bid for Genzyme at the same price, putting its offer directly to shareholders. In the October press release, the company explained that it had launched a hostile bid because its "attempts to [merge with Genzyme] have been blocked at every turn. Our recent meetings with Genzyme shareholders demonstrate that they support a transaction and are frustrated by Genzyme's unwillingness to engage in constructive discussions with us. This has left us with no choice but to present the offer directly to Genzyme's shareholders."[50]

Sanofi-Aventis' chief executive Chris Viehbacher approached Icahn, who told him, "Listen, this is a great company, you aren't going to get me fighting to sell it for less than 80. As far as I'm concerned we should get 80 bucks for the company, and if we don't I'm not going to support anything–in fact I'll be [Termeer's] ally."[51] Termeer was reluctant to sell, but met with Viehbacher in January 2011. There they agreed on the broad structure of a deal. Sanofi-Aventis would raise the price it would pay for Genzyme shares to $74 a share, or a total of $20.1 billion, plus a contingent value right. The contingent value right is a security that will trade through 2020, and which could be worth as much as an additional $14 per share, or $3.8 billion in total, if Genzyme can meet several ambitious sales targets.[52] Even without the contingent value rights, the takeover was the second largest in the history of the biotechnology industry.

Genzyme was vintage Icahn. He and Whitworth may have hastened it, but a sale became "inevitable," as one article described it, once Genzyme stumbled at its Allston Landing plant.[53] In an overcapitalized industry with falling returns, the precipitous dip in Genzyme's share price made it a clear target for a larger pharmaceutical company:[54]

That put them on the radar, and people started running the numbers. These deals are part of the ecology of this area. The big pharmaceutical companies are just dying for new sources of revenue, and biotechs are beautiful in that regard.

Icahn, along with Whitworth, had seen the possibility for a takeover, and moved to make the inevitable a reality. It was a successful campaign for Icahn, returning 40 percent on a $600 million position in under 18 months.

In the 40 years since Kingsley and Icahn set down the Icahn Manifesto, neither his philosophy nor his strategy have changed much. The name for his method evolved from corporate raiding to activist investing, and the targets have grown in size as his capital grew, but he still seeks to take "large positions in 'undervalued' stocks" and attempt to "control their destinies" as he had in the 1970s. He was active through the 1990s, where many of his contemporaries in the 1980s had fallen by the wayside, and he continued to agitate at companies consistently through the 2000s. His brand of activism has always had more than a shred of opportunism. He seeks out crises that force down share prices deeply below valuation, then harnesses the attendant shareholder frustration to gain control.

The strategy has worked. Icahn can lay claim to being one of the great value investors. His returns, measured from the date of his schedule 13D filings to his exit, are extraordinary: an annualized 29 percent through June 30, 2013, compared with 6.9 percent for the S&P 500 index, according to *13D Monitor*, a research service.[55] He continues to be active, seeking out new crises, not for their own sake, but because it creates urgency and opportunity. The uglier, the better. He bought another biotech, Forest Laboratories, in May 2012, two months after its top drug, the antidepressant *Lexapro*, went off patent. He bought back into Chesapeake Energy in May 2012 as natural gas prices nosedived and it looked as if the company might succumb to its debt load. After the stock had crashed 55 percent from its 52-week high, Icahn noted in a letter to the board attached to his schedule 13D filing that he believed Chesapeake had "collected some of the best oil and gas assets in the world" but "the low stock price today does not reflect the value of those assets; rather the stock price suffers because of the enormous risk associated with an ever changing business strategy, enormous capital funding gap, poor governance, and unchecked risk taking."[56] Icahn, as always, advocated for shareholder engagement, while taking the opportunity to point out a few of his successes:[57]

> We believe that shareholder representation on boards, even in a minority capacity, is an extremely powerful tool to instill accountability in a company. This has proven to be the case in numerous companies on which we had minority board representation, including Motorola, Biogen, Genzyme, and Hain Celestial to name a few.

RETURNS TO ACTIVISM

While Icahn's returns are particularly good, the returns to activism generally are also strong, significantly beating the market over both the short and long term. (In contrast to their reputation, activists tend to be long-term investors, with an average period of activism lasting just over two years in length.[58]) The filing of a schedule 13D notice—often the first public disclosure of an intention to engage in activism—tends to be a positive catalytic event, pushing up the stock of targeted companies in the short term. In 2007, finance researchers April Klein and Emanuel Zur found that "confrontational" activist campaigns—those where the activist filed a 13D notice stating that they intend to influence management's decisions—generated "significantly positive market reaction for the target firm around the 13D filing date" and "significantly positive returns over the subsequent year." On average, targeted stocks immediately return 7 percent in excess of the market return.[59] Target companies then return 10.2 percent over the market during the period after the filing of the schedule 13D notice, and an additional 11.4 percent over the market return in the following year.[60] In 2008 Alon Brav, Wei Jiang, Randall Thomas, and Frank Partnoy also measured the short-term impact of activism by examining the stock price performance around the filing of a schedule 13D notice, from 20 days prior to 20 days after filing.[61] They found that there is a runup of about 3.2 percent over the market between 10 days to 1 day prior to filing. The filing day and the following day see a jump of about 2 percent over the market. After filing, the stock price returns an additional 2 percent over the market for a total of 7.2 percent in the 20 days. Figure 9.1 shows the "abnormal" returns—the returns in excess of the market—around the filing window.

Returns vary by the type of activist campaign fought. Brav et al. find that campaigns seeking a sale of the target generated the highest return of 10.94 percent in excess of the market. Business strategy related activism—for example, agitating to have an over-diversified company refocus by spinning-off non-essential assets—also generated significant returns in excess of the market of 4.37 percent. Activist campaigns with no stated goal other than improving shareholder value, efficiency, or simple undervaluation, generated a return of 4.99 percent over the market. Brav et al. found that campaigns targeting capital structure and corporate governance issues generated little excess return. However, other researchers have found that corporate governance reforms led to the largest premia in a sale of the company.[62] This research examined activist strategies in the context of the ends sought, finding that the activists were on average successful in achieving their specific goals. For example, activist campaigns focused on business strategy produced profitable businesses, with revenue growth, increased margins, and improved returns on assets. Campaigns seeking a sale of the target succeeded in concluding a sale more than twice as often as the average target, and for higher prices. (A demand that a target put itself up for sale earned on average a 24.6 percent premium over the market.) Activism focused on the capital structure increased pay-out ratios by more than 10 percent and

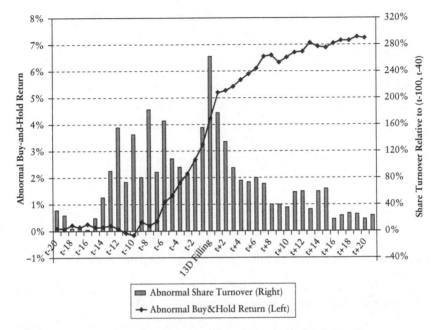

FIGURE 9.1 Excess Buy-and-Hold Returns Around Schedule 13D Filing
Source: Alon P. Brav, Wei Jiang, Randall S. Thomas, and Frank Partnoy. "Hedge Fund Activism, Corporate Governance, and Firm Performance (May 2008)." *Journal of Finance*, Vol. 63, pp. 1729, 2008.

reduced debt. Finally, corporate governance-related activism reduced agency costs as targeted companies tended to reduce assets compared to the average target. (Recall that Michael Jensen found that agency costs lead management teams to waste excess cash flow, growing assets at the expense of profitability.)

As we saw in earlier chapters, the returns to deeply undervalued stocks are very strong. To what extent are the returns to activism simply the returns to picking undervalued stocks? Asked another way, does activism create value, generating returns beyond the returns to cheap stocks? Benjamin Solarz at Yale University considered this question in 2009.[63] He examined the portfolios of activists and tracked the performance of "activist" campaigns, and "passive" investments—those investments that did not result in activism. Solarz concluded that activist holdings earn 3.8 percent greater returns than comparable passive investments over the first two months, and an astonishing 18.4 percent greater return over two years. Figure 9.2 shows the returns to activist and passive holdings over the short term (a 61-day window).

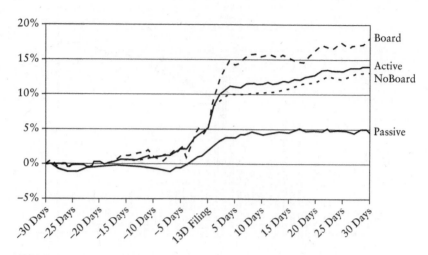

FIGURE 9.2   In the Short Run, Activist Investments Outperform Passive
Investments
Source: Benjamin S. Solarz. "Stock Picking in Disguise? New Evidence that Hedge
Fund Activism Adds Value." *Editorial Objective* 1001 (2010): 101.

Figure 9.3 shows the returns to activist and passive holdings over the
longer term (a 25-month window).

Brav et al. also examined this question, and found several indications
that activism adds performance beyond stock picking. First, they find that
hostile, aggressive, or confrontational activism—campaigns that employ
proxy contests, lawsuits, hostile takeover bids, threats to launch a proxy
fight or to sue, or public campaigns to criticize or even to replace the
management—generated higher returns than relatively friendly engagements (11.8 percent versus 5.3 percent). They also find that the market
reacts much more positively to an activist's announcement of specific plans
for the company—a change in business strategy or a sale—than to the activist's statement of belief that the company's shares are undervalued. This is
likely because, as Solarz found, activists sell targets more frequently, and for
higher prices than comparable firms. If activists were merely picking deeply
undervalued stocks, then we wouldn't expect such announcements to lead
to higher returns. Stocks targeted by activists do enjoy better stock-price
performance even after controlling for sales of targeted firms. Figure 9.4
shows that activism improves stock price performance beyond selling the
target, but that target sales generate very high returns.

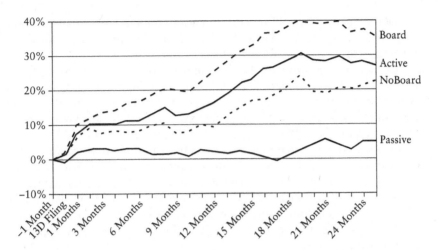

FIGURE 9.3   In the Long Run, Activist Investments Outperform Passive
Source: Benjamin S. Solarz. "Stock Picking in Disguise? New Evidence that Hedge
Fund Activism Adds Value." *Editorial Objective* 1001 (2010): 101.

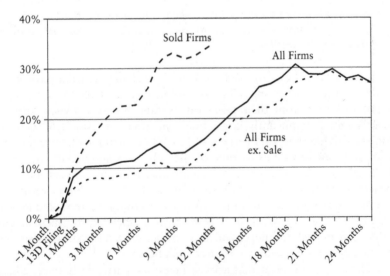

FIGURE 9.4   Activism Adds Value Beyond Selling Companies
Source: Benjamin S. Solarz. "Stock Picking in Disguise? New Evidence that Hedge
Fund Activism Adds Value." *Editorial Objective* 1001 (2010): 101.

Here, Solarz controls for undervaluation, finding that activism continues to produce outperformance over similar passive investments whether a sale occurs or not.

Do activists improve the fundamental performance of targeted firms? It seems that they do. Solarz finds improved margins and returns on assets, increased payout ratios, reduced leverage, and reduced assets. Brav et al. also found that targeted firms generated moderately improved returns on assets (defined as EBITDA/Assets), and significantly improved returns on equity, which suggests that they took on debt to lever the balance sheet. They also invest less in fixed assets and reduce capital expenditure. Brav et al. also note that activists are often successful in curtailing executive compensation and ousting CEOs, which has a considerable direct impact on shareholder gains. They demonstrate that chief executive pay drops by about $800,000 to $1 million annually after activism, and this has a significant impact on intrinsic value.[64]

> *Suppose all of the top executives combined are paid $4-$5 million less a year due to activism, and that this value goes to shareholders (assuming away tax issues, etc.), then the present value of such an income stream is on the order of magnitude of $50 million, which is a significant portion of the market capitalization of a typical targeted company (the average market capitalization of our sample firms is $706 million).*

Like Solarz, they observed a remarkable change in total payout policy before and after activism. While the total payout of the target companies is not different from their peers on average before activism, the difference becomes significantly larger one year after activism (1.66 percentage points). Defining the 14.5 percent of Brav et al.'s sample that are liquidated, sold, or taken private as a complete payout to existing shareholders, then the post-activism payout ratio is much higher than the conventional payout measures indicate. Boyson and Mooradian also found similar results, indicating that activists significantly improve both the short-term and long-term performance of targeted firms.[65] These performance improvements included reductions in cash holdings, which is further evidence that activists reduce the agency costs associated with free cash flows.

The research is clear that activist investors, particularly those who pursue aggressive, well-defined objectives, improve both the short-term market and longer-term operating performance of the companies they target.[66] In the process, they deliver strong returns for their own investors, in comparison to returns for less-aggressive activist investors and for comparable passive investors. While the filing of a schedule 13D notice heralds short-term market performance, the discipline applied by an engaged investor—improving corporate governance and reducing agency costs—leads to better long-term operating performance too. This is likely because agency costs—executive compensation, diversification, and cash hoarding—reduce the value of firms, and these are issues targeted by activists. Activist investors' interests are aligned with other shareholders, and so seek to unlock this hidden value.

Graham described a stock's market price discount from its intrinsic value as the barometer for assessing management's performance. If the stock trades at a steep discount to intrinsic value, management should "take all proper steps to correct the obvious disparity between market quotation and intrinsic value, including a reconsideration of its own policies and a frank justification to the stockholders of its decision to continue the business."[67] Where management was not forthcoming, shareholders should realize their rights as business owners and demand such a reconsideration of policies. A group of substantial stockholders with an important stake of their own to protect, acting in the interests of the shareholders generally should "gain a more respectful hearing from the rank and file of stockholders than has hitherto been accorded them in most cases."[68]

> *If they realized their rights as* business owners, *we would not have before us the insane spectacle of treasuries bloated with cash and their proprietors in a wild scramble to give away their interest on any terms they can get.*

The research on activism bears out Graham's thesis. An engaged shareholder can reduce agency costs by concentrating managers on creating shareholder value instead of pursuing other agendas. Any shareholder may do this, but, as Graham suggests, it does require that they realize their power as *owners*. Activist investors pressure boards to remove underperforming managers, stop value-destroying mergers and acquisitions, disgorge excess cash and optimize the capital structure, or press for a sale of the company, all of which are designed only to improve shareholder value. As a portfolio, companies with the conditions in place for activism offer asymmetric, market-beating returns. Activists exploit these properties by taking large minority stakes in these beaten-down stocks and then agitating for change, expecting a rapid resolution, and thereby a reduction in risk. This agitation—aggressive activism, with well-defined objectives—seems to improve both the short-term market performance and longer-term operating performance of the companies targeted beyond the mere mean reversion to deep value stocks. The market reacts as if this is the case, popping on the filing of a 13D notice. The opportunity is to identify these targets before activists arrive. We examine simple methods of doing so in the next chapter.

Notes

1. Jim Edwards. "Genzyme's Triple Screwup: Factory Problem Ends Its Monopoly and Puts NDA on Hold." *CBS News MoneyWatch*, September 1, 2009. Available at http://www.cbsnews.com/8301-505123_162-42842754/genzymes-triple-screwup-factory-problem-ends-its-monopoly-and-puts-nda-on-hold/?tag=bnetdomain.
2. Ibid.
3. Adam Feuerstein. "Genzyme's Termeer: Worst Biotech CEO of '09." *TheStreet.com*, November 17, 2009. Available at http://www.thestreet.com/story/10627877/1/genzymes-termeer-worst-biotech-ceo-of-09.html?cm_ven=GOOGLEN.
4. Edwards, September 1, 2009.
5. Jim Edwards. "Bring Me the Head of Genzyme CEO Henri Termeer!" *CBS News MoneyWatch*, November 17, 2009. Available at http://www.cbsnews.com/8301-505123_162-42843493/bring-me-the-head-of-genzyme-ceo-henri-termeer/?tag=bnetdomain.
6. Edwards, November 17, 2009.
7. Robert Weisman. "More contamination troubles for Genzyme." *The Boston Globe*, November 14, 2009.
8. Edwards, November 17, 2009.
9. Feuerstein, November 17, 2009.
10. Ibid.
11. Ibid.
12. Ibid.
13. Ibid.
14. Andrew Pollack. "After Genzyme's Stumbles, a Struggle for Control." *The New York Times*, February 22, 2010. Available at http://www.nytimes.com/2010/02/23/business/23genzyme.html?pagewanted=all.
15. Ibid.
16. Ibid.
17. Ibid.
18. Ibid.
19. Tracy Staton. "Genzyme founder calls for CEO change." *FiercePharma*, December 18, 2009. Available at http://www.fiercepharma.com/story/genzyme-founder-calls-ceo-change/2009-12-18.
20. Toni Clarke. "Icahn considering proxy battle at Genzyme: Source." *Reuters*, January 7, 2010. Available at http://www.reuters.com/article/2010/01/07/us-genzyme-icahn-idUSTRE60643J20100107.
21. Steven Bertoni. "The Raider's Radar" *Forbes*, March 9, 2011. Available at http://www.forbes.com/forbes/2011/0328/billionaires-11-profile-carl-icahn-biotech-twa-raiders-radar.html.
22. Ibid.
23. Ibid.
24. Ibid.
25. Ibid.

26. Ibid.
27. Ibid.
28. Ibid.
29. Ibid.
30. Andrew Pollack. "Icahn Seeking U.S. Approval for Big Stake in ImClone." *The New York Times*, February 16, 2002. Available at http://www.nytimes.com/2002/02/16/business/icahn-seeking-us-approval-for-big-stake-in-imclone.html.
31. Ibid.
32. Kim Kahn. "Icahn's ImClone Interest." *CNNMoney*, February 15, 2002.
33. Jacob Goldstein. "Bristol-Myers's Sweetened ImClone Bid Turns Tables on Icahn." *The Wall Street Journal Health Blog*, September 23, 2008. Available at http://blogs.wsj.com/health/2008/09/23/bristol-myerss-sweetened-imclone-bid-turns-tables-on-icahn.
34. Ibid.
35. Ibid.
36. Ibid.
37. Ibid.
38. ImClone Systems Incorporated, *Schedule 14D-9*, September 24, 2008 Available at http://www.sec.gov/Archives/edgar/data/765258/000104746908010243/a2188077zsc14d9c.htm.
39. ImClone Systems Incorporated, *Schedule 14D-9*, October 7, 2008. Available at http://www.sec.gov/Archives/edgar/data/765258/000114420408056317/v128157_sc14d9.htm.
40. Ibid.
41. Bill George. "Another View: Can Biotech Survive Icahn?" *The New York Times Dealbook*, June 3, 2010. Available at http://dealbook.nytimes.com/2010/06/03/another-view-can-biotech-survive-icahn/?ref=business.
42. Bertoni, March 9, 2011.
43. Carl Icahn, Schedule 14A Filing, February 23, 2010: http://www.sec.gov/Archives/edgar/data/732485/000091062710000037/dfan14a022210.txt.
44. Icahn Capital LP SEC Form 13F March 31, 2010 Available at http://www.sec.gov/Archives/edgar/data/1412093/000114036110021805/form13fhr.txt.
45. Ibid.
46. Howard Anderson. "Carl Icahn's Battle to Take Down Genzyme." *The Boston Globe*, June 2, 2010. Available at http://www.boston.com/bostonglobe/editorial_opinion/oped/articles/2010/06/02/carl_icahns_battle_to_take_down_genzyme.
47. Icahn Capital LP SEC Schedule 14A Filing Available at http://www.sec.gov/Archives/edgar/data/732485/000091062710000101/genzdfan14a060110.txt.
48. Genzyme Corporation SEC Form DEFA14A Available at http://www.sec.gov/Archives/edgar/data/732485/000110465910031820/a10-9595_20defa14a.htm.
49. Bertoni, March 9, 2011.
50. Sanofi-Aventis SEC SC To-T "Press Release." Available at http://www.sec.gov/Archives/edgar/data/732485/000119312510222490/dex99a5a.htm.

51. Bertoni, March 9, 2011.

52. Nina Sovich and Noelle Mennella. "Sanofi to buy Genzyme for more than $20 billion." *Reuters*, February 16, 2011. Available at http://www.reuters.com/article/2011/02/16/us-genzyme-sanofi-idUSTRE71E4XI20110216.

53. Robert Weisman. "Genzyme agrees to $20.1b sale to drug giant." *The Boston Globe*, February 16, 2011.

54. Ibid.

55. "Activist Profile: Carl Icahn." *13DMonitor.com*, June 30, 2013. Available at http://icomm-net.com/ActivistProfile.aspx?investor_id=32.

56. Carl C. Icahn, SEC Schedule 13D. May 25, 2012. Available at http://www.sec.gov/Archives/edgar/data/895126/000092166912000045/chk13d052512.htm.

57. Ibid.

58. Nicole M. Boyson and Robert M. Mooradian. "Corporate Governance and Hedge Fund Activism (June 1, 2010)." *Review of Derivatives Research*, Vol. 14, No. 2, 2011. Available at SSRN: http://ssrn.com/abstract=992739.

59. April Klein and Emanuel Zur. "Entrepreneurial Shareholder Activism: Hedge Funds and Other Private Investors (September 2006)." *AAA 2007 Financial Accounting & Reporting Section (FARS) Meeting* Available at SSRN: http://ssrn.com/abstract=913362 or http://dx.doi.org/10.2139/ssrn.913362.

60. Alon P. Brav, Wei Jiang, Randall S. Thomas, and Frank Partnoy. "Hedge Fund Activism, Corporate Governance, and Firm Performance (May 2008)." *Journal of Finance*, Vol. 63, pp. 1729, 2008.

61. Ibid.

62. Benjamin S. Solarz. "Stock Picking in Disguise? New Evidence that Hedge Fund Activism Adds Value." *Editorial Objective* 1001 (2010): 101.

63. Ibid.

64. Brav et al., 2008.

65. Boyson and Mooradian, 2011.

66. Ibid.

67. Graham and Dodd, 1934.

68. Ibid.

CHAPTER 10

Applied Deep Value

How to Identify Deeply Undervalued, Potential Activist Targets

Mr. Graham: "Management is one of the most important factors in the evaluation of a leading company and it has a great effect upon the market price of secondary companies. It does not necessarily control the value of the secondary companies for the long pull because if the management is comparatively poor there are forces at work which tend to improve the management and thereby improve the value of the company."

The Chairman: "When you go into special situations and buy large blocks, do you usually try to get control of the company?"

Mr. Graham: "No; that is very exceptional. I would say out of about 400 companies that we may have invested in in the last few years, there would not be more than 3 or 4 in which we would have had any interest in acquiring control."

—Benjamin Graham, *Stock Market Study. Hearings Before The Committee on Banking and Currency, United States Senate, Eighty-Fourth Congress, First Session on Factors Affecting the Buying and Selling of Equity Securities. (March 3, 1955)*[1]

Happy families are all alike; every unhappy family is unhappy in its own way.

— Leo Tolstoy, *Anna Karenina* (1877)

Like Tolstoy's happy families, Buffett's "wonderful companies" represent an ideal from which any deficiency creates a less-than-optimal intrinsic valuation, with a market price that is usually further depressed from

that suboptimal value. Activist investors seek these unhappy families—
"unwonderful" companies that do not possess all of the attributes of Buffett's
wonderful companies—where the opportunity exists to improve the intrinsic value by remedying the deficiency, moving the company's intrinsic value
closer to its full "wonderful company" potential, and eliminating the market
price discount in the process. Carl Icahn has described this as an arbitrage,
comparable to the arbitrage he undertook as an options trader:[2]

> *What I do today still is pretty much the same idea. You buy stocks
> in a company that is cheap and you look at the asset value of
> the companies that you buy the stocks in and it becomes a lit-
> tle more complex. Basically, you look for the reason that they're
> really cheap and the major reason is often–and usually–very poor
> management. In a sense, it's like an arbitrage. You go in; you buy
> a lot of stock in a company; and you then try to make changes at
> the company.*

The research shows that the typical company targeted by activists has
poor recent stock performance, a low valuation, a large cash holding, and
few opportunities for growth. Brav et al. examined activist engagements
over the period 2001 to 2005,[3] and found that the typical activist target
was deeply undervalued, and generating more cash than comparable firms
not targeted by activists. Though they generate relatively high cash flows,
they tended to have relatively low payouts measured by both dividend yield
and payout ratio, the amount of dividends paid out relative to the cash
generated by the business. Thus they built up large amounts of cash on
the balance sheet relative to the size of the other assets and of the business. Other researchers examining activist campaigns from 1994 to 2005
described the typical activist target in the same terms: A "a cash cow with
poor growth prospects, possibly suffering from the agency costs of free cash
flow,"[4] Michael Jensen's theory that free cash flow creates a conflict of interest between shareholders and management over payout policies. Jensen pos-
ited that management prefers to reinvest cash to grow assets, even when
the reinvested capital is likely to earn returns below the company's cost, or
waste it on "organization[al] inefficiencies," while shareholders prefer that
the cash be disgorged to them.[5] This problem plagued the textile industry in
the 1960s and induced Warren Buffett to target the then cigar butt Berkshire
Hathaway. It was also endemic in the oil and gas industry in the 1980s, leading to T. Boone Pickens' attempts to restructure Gulf Oil and others, and
Carl Icahn had the same complaints about the biotechnology industry in the
early 2000s. Two valuation metrics well-suited to identify the characteristics
that typically attract activists—deep undervaluation, large cash holdings,

and low payout ratios—are Graham's net current asset value rule and the enterprise multiple. Next we examine the returns to both, and apply them to identify deeply undervalued activist targets.

CIGAR BUTTS, NET CURRENT ASSETS, AND LIQUIDATIONS

David Einhorn founded Greenlight Capital in 1996 with just $900,000 under management. He found early success with the stock of a small Graham net net, C. R. Anthony, a retailer that had recently emerged from bankruptcy. Listed on the Nasdaq, little C. R. Anthony traded for half its $36 million in net current asset value. Einhorn put 15 percent of his fund into C. R. Anthony—about $135,000—at the end of May 1996, Greenlight's first month of operation. Fortuna smiled on Einhorn when Stage Stores, Inc. approached the company about a buyout shortly after Einhorn initiated the position. By the end of the year C. R. Anthony had returned 500 percent on Einhorn's 15 percent holding, and Greenlight, which returned 37 percent for the year, was on its way with $13 million under management.[6] While Einhorn's C.R. Anthony returns were exceptional, the returns to stocks meeting Graham's net current asset value criteria are typically very high. Recall from Chapter 2 that Graham estimated that his net net strategy had generated an average yearly return of 20 percent over the 30-year life of his investment management firm Graham-Newman, which turns a $10,000 investment into $2,374,000. Figure 10.1 shows the returns to Graham's net current asset value criteria over the full period of the data from December 1970 to December 2013.

At a compound annual growth rate of 38.7 percent, the net current asset value strategy turns $10,000 into an astonishing $12.7 billion in 44 years, while the comparable Small Firm Index, at a compound rate of 19.7 percent, can manage only $22.4 million. The compound returns to the net current asset value strategy are *unbelievable* in both senses of the word— they are as astronomical as they are unachievable. The problem with this strategy is that it is, in Graham's words, "severely limited in its application" because net current asset value stocks are too small, illiquid, and infrequently available. They tend to disappear in a pervasive bull market, and only become available in quantity at bear-market lows. As it does not need to actually buy the shares, the simulation in Figure 10.1 substantially overstates the capital that could be practically invested in the strategy. If we assume that the amount of capital invested in each net current asset value opportunity is equal, it would be very difficult to invest more than $1 million in 2014. Einhorn's $135,000 position likely represented most of

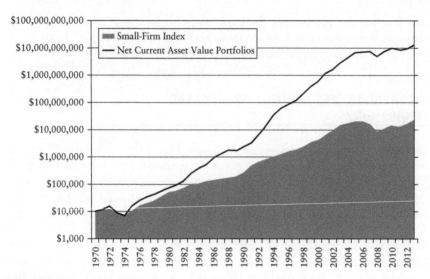

FIGURE 10.1 Returns to Graham Net Current Asset Value Rule and Comparable Small Firms Index (1970 to 2013)

the volume available in C. R. Anthony in May 1996, which was very little. Regardless, for individual investors managing personal accounts, the net net strategy remains, as Graham described it in 1976, "a foolproof method of systematic investment—once again, not on the basis of individual results but in terms of the expectable group outcome." It also remains a favorite valuation method for activist investors. Classic Graham net nets, though small and infrequently available, meet many of the criteria activists seek in targets. Graham intended the rule as a rough proxy for liquidation value, so a strong case can be made that a stock trading at a wide discount to this value is deeply undervalued. As most of the intrinsic value assessed on this measure is by definition found in the current assets—which includes cash and the other assets most readily turned into cash: inventories and receivables—they are also stocks with liquid balance sheets and low payout ratios. These attributes, combined with a shareholder base that is likely unhappy with management, make net nets attractive targets for activists.

Stocks trading at a discount to liquidation value are, in Graham's words, stocks that the market has determined are worth more dead than alive. The shareholders of net nets have therefore, implicitly or explicitly, expressed their extreme displeasure with the continued operation of the business. The most direct means by which an activist may remove the market price discount is through liquidation of the company, although this is typically a rare outcome, occurring in only about one-in-twenty net nets. A slightly more indirect method is a partial liquidation, which has the effect of improving the payout ratio. The research shows that investors targeting net nets with low payout ratios will outperform those targeting net nets with higher payout ratios. While Graham recommended that investors lean toward profitable, dividend-paying net nets, as we have seen, it is in fact loss-making net nets that tend to outperform profitable ones and non-dividend paying net nets outperform dividend-paying net nets. The primary problem with net nets is their scarcity and small size. They are hard to find, and when they do appear, they are often too small to absorb much capital. The second strategy—the enterprise or acquirer's multiple—embraces the same underlying philosophy as Graham's net nets—buying stocks with liquid balance sheets trading at a significant discount to intrinsic value—but has the benefit of scaling more readily, and identifying undervalued large-capitalization companies.

ACTIVISM AND THE ACQUIRER'S MULTIPLE

Daniel Loeb launched Third Point Management in 1995 with just $3.3 million in assets. He has since grown the assets under management to approximately $14 billion in 2013 with an extraordinary 17.8 percent annualized record.[7] Loeb is known for a method of agitation originated by another activist, Robert Chapman Jr., and which finds its roots in Icahn's media campaigns: Attaching to schedule 13D filings open letters to management. Written in vivid language and employing a scorching, sarcastic tone, the letters are intended to attract publicity for Loeb's campaigns. He has been described as the "Hunter S Thompson of activist letter writing," a reference to the American journalist and author who founded the "Gonzo" style of experimental journalism. Gonzo uses "wild invention and wilder rhetoric,"[8] as the author Tom Wolfe described it, in order to amuse and entertain while making biting social observation. Like Thompson, Loeb uses his caustic editorializing to help shine a light on whatever behavior or situation he finds objectionable. He has said he only resorts to poison-pen letters when other legal avenues are closed to him:[9]

> *Companies that have erected unnatural barriers such as "poison pills" and staggered boards make it impossible to call special meetings leave us with no alternative but to pursue the social-pressure angle, and that's a phenomenon of their own making. We would just as soon put it to a vote.*

The letters serve two purposes. First, they function like a marketing brochure, drawing other investors' attention to the company's undervaluation, and outlining various steps to eliminate the valuation discount, either through restructuring or returning capital. The other purpose of the letters is to embarrass management into taking the medicine prescribed by Loeb.

Loeb's first schedule 13D letter, sent in September 2000 to William Stiritz, the chief executive officer of Agribrands International, offers a study in the art form. Agribrands had agreed to merge with another firm, Ralcorp. Under the terms of the merger, Agribrands shareholders were to receive three shares for each share held in a new company representing the combination, and Ralcorp shareholders were to receive one share. The Agribrands shareholders could also opt to receive $39 per share cash, and Ralcorp shareholders $15 per share, giving Agribrands an implied acquisition price of $420 million. With $160 million in cash on its balance sheet, and earning $90 million per year in EBITDA, the acquisition valued Agribrands' business at less than three times EBITDA, a very low bid. Further, Loeb believed that the transaction had no strategic rationale.

In the letter, Loeb charged that the proposed merger price did not reflect full and fair value for Agribrands, demonstrated by the low enterprise multiple and price-to-earnings ratio:[10]

> [T]he current price represents only 2.9X Agribrands' Enterprise Value to EBITDA and only 9.2X Prudential Securities estimated earnings for the Fiscal Year ended August 31, [20]00 and 7.9X next year's estimated earnings. These estimates do not take into consideration the $10 million surrender value of the $102 million insurance policy taken out on your life, nor the potentially sizeable award Agribrands might be entitled to as part of the class entitled to the $242 million settlement of class-action claims against Roche Holding AG and five others in connection with their price fixing of vitamins used to fortify animal feeds and processed foods.

In an effort to raise the bid price, Loeb proposed a second sales process or several possible capital restructuring scenarios, including a leveraged recapitalization, Dutch tender offer, or special dividend. He concluded by pointing out that he had sufficient stock to block the merger, and called on management to consider the other possibilities for realizing value:[11]

> We are not alone in opposing the merger with Ralcorp. Based on our informal conversations with other large shareholders who share our frustration, we believe that it is unlikely that you will obtain the required 2/3 majority to approve the transaction. . . . Accordingly, we urge you to waive the $5.0 million break-up fee, to

officially put the company up for sale and to consider other alterna-
tives such as an LBO or recapitalization of the Company in order
to maximize shareholder value.

Loeb's letter had the intended effect. In December Agribrands broke
off its merger with Ralcorp, and entered into an agreement to be acquired
by Cargill for $54.50 per share, a 40 percent premium to the cash offered
in the Ralcorp merger. The new offer valued Agribrands at $580 million,
valuing Agribrands' business at closer to five times its EBITDA. The Cargill
offer delivered Third Point a $9 million profit on its $18.6 million position,
generating a 48 percent return in a little under 3 months. In April 2001 Loeb
sent a follow up letter to Stiritz offering his "praise and support for choosing a course of action consistent with the suggestions offered in my letter
of September 8, 2000."[12] While it's impossible to know the impact Loeb's
original letter had, his timing was uncanny, and certainly gave him grounds
to claim that he had in fact shot down the original merger and preempted
the final acquisition.

Loeb's analysis that Agribrands was undervalued at an acquisition price
representing less than three times its enterprise value was almost certainly
correct. As we saw in an earlier chapter, the enterprise multiple, whether
determined on an EBIT or EBITDA basis, is the most predictive fundamental measure of valuation. Figure 10.2 shows the market capitalization-
weighted returns to portfolios formed from the value decile of stocks ranked
on the enterprise multiple (enterprise value/EBIT) over the full period of the
data from January 1951 to December 2013. The stocks are selected annually from the largest 40 percent of stocks by market capitalization listed on
the NYSE, Nasdaq, or American Stock Exchange. For context, the smallest
stock by market capitalization in the available universe in December 2013
had a market capitalization of $1.8 billion, which makes it comparable to
the Russell 1000 Index. We require such a high market capitalization cut-
off and further market capitalization-weight the portfolio for two reasons.
First, smaller stocks can have wide bid-ask spreads, which makes it difficult
to trade them at the market price. More likely, the stocks are acquired at
a higher price, and sold at a lower price, overstating the returns that could
be obtained in the real world. Second, larger stocks are more likely to be
investable. The problem with the net net stocks is that they are too small,
and so the simulated returns don't reflect the experience of a real investor.
Larger stocks are more likely to offer sufficient volume for larger investors. We measured the one-year performance of the value portfolios from
January 1 of each year and compared it to the performance of the market
capitalization-weighted universe of stocks from which the value portfolios
are drawn ("All Stocks").

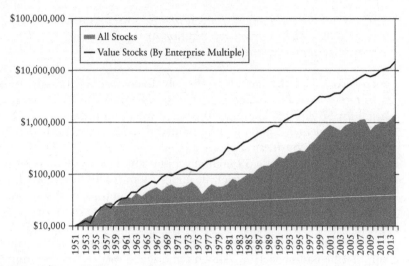

FIGURE 10.2   Performance of Value Stocks (by Enterprise Multiple) and All Stocks, Market Capitalization Weight (1951 to 2013)

Figure 10.2 demonstrates that the decile portfolios of value stocks substantially and consistently outperformed the comparably weighted All Stocks universe from which they were drawn. The portfolios of value stocks returned a compound annual growth rate of 12.50 percent annually over the full period, versus 8.36 percent for All Stocks. For context, this turns $10,000 in the value portfolios into $14.9 million over 63 years, versus $1.45 million invested in All Stocks.

The All Stocks portfolio, which stands in here for the market and represents the investable universe for the simulator, contains a large number of stocks. As at December 31, 2012, the last portfolio formed, the All Stocks universe contained approximately 1,140 stocks. This means that the portfolio formed from the value decile contained more than 100 stocks, which is too many for most investors. We want to find the stocks in the value decile that will perform best and avoid the ones that underperform. As we reduce the size of the portfolio, we run a risk that the performance of any given stock has a greater influence on the overall performance of the portfolio, whether it be good or bad. For the purposes of this examination, we'll simply divide the value portfolio into two halves of slightly fewer than 60 stocks to compare performance. While these are still very large portfolios—too large for most individual investors—they demonstrate the utility of a metric and no single stock will overly influence the results.

High- and Low-Quality Value Stocks

We can use any number of methods to whittle the universe down further to a more manageable portfolio. One possibility is that, like the Magic Formula, we employ a measure of Buffett-esque quality. We've already seen that return on invested capital—the measure of quality used in the Magic Formula—doesn't add to the performance of the enterprise multiple. Another metric of quality we can test that seeks to achieve the same end as return on invested capital is Robert Novy-Marx's ratio of gross profits-to-total assets, which is defined as follows:[13]

Gross profits-to-total assets = (revenue − cost of goods sold) ÷ total assets

In contrast to Greenblatt's measure, Novy-Marx finds that his ratio works on a stand-alone basis to identify stocks that outperform the market:[14]

[Gross profits-to-total assets] has roughly the same power predicting the cross-section of expected returns as book-to-market.

Novy-Marx's gross-profits-to-total-assets measure rewards stocks that generate more gross profit per dollar of total assets. This means that it uses different metrics to Greenblatt's return on invested capital measure to make a similar assessment of a business's performance. There are several subtle differences between the two ratios. First, Novy-Marx's gross-profits-to-total assets-ratio measures a business's profitability from the top of the income statement, where the return on invested capital ratio uses EBIT, which is reconstructed from the bottom of the income statement. Thus, argues Novy-Marx, gross profits is the "cleaner" measure of true economic profitability:[15]

The farther down the income statement one goes, the more polluted profitability measures become, and the less related they are to true economic profitability. For example, a firm that has both lower production costs and higher sales than its competitors is unambiguously more profitable. Even so, it can easily have lower earnings than its competitors. If the firm is quickly increasing its sales though aggressive advertising, or commissions to its sales force, these actions can, even if optimal, reduce its bottom line income below that of its less profitable competitors. Similarly, if the firm spends on research and development to further increase its production advantage, or invests in organizational capital that will help it maintain its competitive advantage, these actions result in lower current earnings. Moreover, capital expenditures that directly increase the scale of the firm's operations further reduce its free cash flows relative to its competitors. These facts suggest constructing the empirical proxy for productivity using gross profits.

The second difference is in the denominator of the ratios. Where Greenblatt's return on invested capital measure uses "invested capital," Novy-Marx's ratio employs total assets. Like Greenblatt's "invested capital," total assets is independent of the capital structure adopted by management, which makes it comparable to the gross profits measure, which is also independent of the firm's capital structure. Where it differs from Greenblatt's ratio is that it treats cash like any other asset, while Greenblatt deducts net cash to arrive at invested capital. This means that Novy-Marx's ratio penalizes companies carrying lots of cash relative to Greenblatt's measure, which rewards them with a better ratio. While Novy-Marx's penalization of companies holding cash might not make sense on a stand-alone basis, it might be useful in a group of value stocks selected using the enterprise multiple. Recall that one of the problems with the enterprise multiple is that it identifies many small "cash boxes"—companies with large net cash holdings relative to their market capitalization—often because the main business has been sold or the business is a legacy in run-off. While these stocks have very little downside because they are mostly cash, they also have little upside. The gross-profits-to-total-assets measure will penalize these companies for holding cash, thus it should be particularly useful at screening out the cash boxes and identifying undervalued, high-return businesses. The question is, do these slight differences make a significant difference to the returns of undervalued stocks? Figure 10.3 shows the performance of portfolios of stocks constructed from the value portfolios in Figure 10.2, and further divided using Novy-Marx's gross-profits-to-total-assets metric. The "High-Quality Value Stocks" portfolio contains half of the stocks from the value portfolio with the highest ratio of gross profits to total assets, and the "Low-Quality Value Stocks" portfolio contains the half with the lowest ratio.

As before, the All Value Stocks portfolio containing all 114 stocks in the value decile returned 12.50 percent compound, and All Stocks returned 8.36 percent compound. The low-quality value stocks underperformed the whole value portfolio, returning 10.79 percent compound over the full period. The high-quality value stocks outperformed, generating 13.37 percent compound over the full period. While the difference between the compound average performances is small, over the 63-year period under examination the high-quality value portfolio turns $10,000 into almost $24 million, while the low-quality value portfolio ends with just $5.7 million. The high-quality value stocks returned more than four times the capital of the low-quality stocks. Figure 10.3 seems to show that using Novy-Marx's

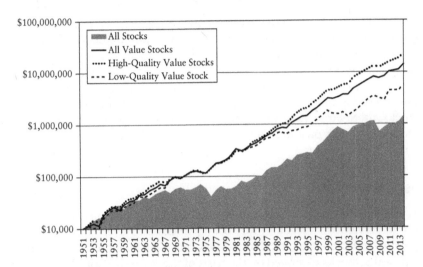

FIGURE 10.3 Performance of All Value Stocks Compared to High- and Low-Quality Value Stocks and All Stocks, Market Capitalization Weight (1951 to 2013)

gross profits-to-total assets measure to identify high-quality stocks in the value decile is a good idea. It would also seem inimical to the thesis of this book that that lower-quality stocks tend to outperform higher-quality stocks.

There are, however, several problems with this conclusion. First, the high-quality value portfolios do not consistently outperform the low-quality value portfolios. Figure 10.3 shows that they slightly underperformed the low-quality value portfolios to 1982, the entire first half of the period examined. All of the high-quality value portfolios' admittedly impressive outperformance occurs in the second half of the data. Further, the high-quality portfolios underperformed the low-quality portfolios in 27 of the 63 years examined, which means that the low-quality portfolios were a better bet fully 43 percent of the time. Strikingly, in the second half of the data—when the high-quality portfolios were outperforming the low-quality portfolios on a compound basis—the high-quality portfolios actually underperformed the low-quality portfolios in 17 out of 32 years, or more than half of the time. The high-quality portfolios also underperformed in 31 percent of rolling five-year periods. The lack of consistency in the performance of the high-quality value portfolios relative to the low-quality portfolios doesn't inspire confidence that the high-quality portfolios can be relied upon to outperform. The second problem with the performance of the high-quality metric is that it has not been replicable in international stock markets. This suggests the possibility that the relationship between quality and returns may be due to random chance. If we examine enough metrics, we expect to see several false positives—metrics that seem to predict returns, but are merely the result of chance—that won't persist outside the data tested. It is possible that this is one such spurious correlation. While there are good reasons why the gross-profits-to-total-assets measure should identify high-quality value stocks and there is some weak evidence for it identifying higher-quality value stocks, there's insufficient evidence, or outperformance, to definitively conclude that it will pick high-quality value stocks that beat low-quality value stocks in the future.

Deep Value Stocks

We already know that the enterprise multiple is the best metric for identifying undervalued stocks and for sorting stocks into over- and undervalued portfolios. With his metric, Novy-Marx only claims outperformance in line with value stocks identified on the basis of the price-to-book-value ratio. As we saw in Chapter 4, the price-to-book-value ratio is a middling predictor of returns and not particularly strong when sorting between over- and undervalued stocks. Perhaps the best solution is the simplest one: Sort the value portfolio on the basis of valuation using the enterprise multiple. Given that the enterprise multiple is so useful when identifying and sorting undervalued and overvalued stocks in the general stock market, it would be remarkable if it *didn't* work in the value decile to further identify undervalued stocks. Figure 10.4 shows the performance of portfolios of stocks again constructed from the value portfolios in Figure 10.2, and further divided into two halves using the enterprise multiple. We're going to define "deep value" here as the cheapest of the cheap—the cheapest half of the value decile. Thus the "Deep Value Stocks" portfolio contains the half of the stocks from the value portfolio with the highest ratio of EBIT to enterprise value, and the "Glamour Value Stocks" portfolio contains the half with the lowest ratio.

The All Value Stocks portfolio still returned 12.50 percent compound, against 8.36 compound for All Stocks. The Glamour Value portfolios—the more expensive half of the value stocks—underperformed the All Value Stocks portfolio, returning 8.84 percent compound over the full period. The Deep Value portfolios substantially outperformed, generating a compound return of 15.72 percent over the full period. The Deep Value Stocks portfolios' outperformance leads to a significant difference in ending capital. Over 63 years, $10,000 invested in All Stocks generates $1.45 million, in All Value Stocks $14.9 million, in Glamour Value Stocks $1.9 million, and in Deep Value Stocks an extraordinary $85.4 million. Table 10.1 contains the performance statistics for the All Value Stocks, Glamour Value, and Deep Value portfolios over the full period.

TABLE 10.1 Performance Statistics for All Value Stocks, Deep Value Stocks, and Glamour Value Stocks (1951 to 2013)

	Deep Value Portfolios	Glamour Value Portfolios	All Value Portfolios
Compound Annual Growth Rate	15.72%	8.84%	8.36%
Arithmetic Average	16.22%	9.61%	12.91%
Standard Deviation	13.63%	14.40%	14.35%
Sharpe Ratio	1.28	0.64	0.92

Data Source: Eyquem Investment Management LLC, Compustat.

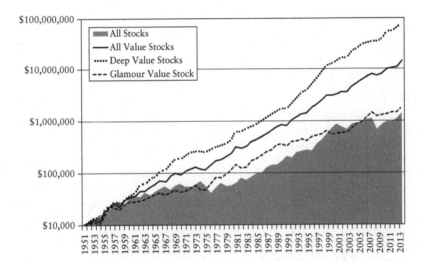

FIGURE 10.4 Performance of All Value Stocks Compared to Deep Value and Glamour Value Stocks and All Stocks, Market Capitalization Weight (1951 to 2013)

Figure 10.4 and Table 10.1 demonstrate that the Deep Value portfolios outperformed over the full period, but is this true for each decade? Where the quality measure failed, the value measure stands out, delivering an exceptionally consistent performance. Table 10.2 shows the performance statistics for the All Value Stocks portfolios, Glamour Value, and Deep Value portfolios broken out for each decade.

Figure 10.5 shows the compound annual growth rates for each of the portfolios in each decade.

TABLE 10.2 Performance Statistics By Decade for All Value Stocks, Deep Value Stocks, and Glamour Value Stocks (1951 to 2013)

	Deep Value Portfolios	Glamour Value Portfolios	All Value Portfolios
1951–1959			
Compound Annual Growth Rate	15.74%	12.30%	14.39%
Arithmetic Average Return	15.82%	14.34%	15.82%
Standard Deviation	20.40%	23.63%	21.47%
Sharpe Ratio	0.85	0.61	0.74
1960–1969			
Compound Annual Growth Rate	19.24%	5.90%	12.71%
Arithmetic Average Return	18.16%	4.65%	11.40%
Standard Deviation	15.42%	9.89%	14.38%
Sharpe Ratio	1.18	0.47	0.79
1970–1979			
Compound Annual Growth Rate	8.27%	9.13%	8.82%
Arithmetic Average Return	9.44%	11.12%	10.28%
Standard Deviation	7.86%	14.35%	11.30%
Sharpe Ratio	1.20	0.77	0.91
1980–1989			
Compound Annual Growth Rate	14.92%	13.10%	14.18%
Arithmetic Average Return	15.21%	13.14%	14.18%
Standard Deviation	11.69%	13.91%	12.55%
Sharpe Ratio	1.30	0.95	1.13
1990–1999			
Compound Annual Growth Rate	23.95%	6.92%	15.52%
Arithmetic Average Return	22.91%	5.09%	14.00%
Standard Deviation	10.99%	12.56%	14.68%
Sharpe Ratio	2.08	0.41	0.95
2000–2013			
Compound Annual Growth Rate	12.97%	8.00%	10.69%
Arithmetic Average Return	14.92%	9.73%	12.32%
Standard Deviation	12.97%	11.41%	12.27%
Sharpe Ratio	1.15	0.85	1.00

Data Source: Eyquem Investment Management LLC, Compustat.

Table 10.2 and Figure 10.5 show that the Deep Value portfolios consistently outperformed both the Glamour Value portfolios and the All Value Stocks portfolios. Only in the 1970 to 1979 period did the Deep Value portfolios underperform.

We can break out the average enterprise multiples for each portfolio in each year to better understand the drivers of performance. Figure 10.6

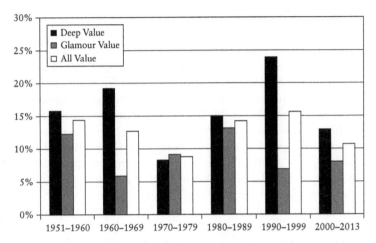

FIGURE 10.5 Compound Performance by Decade of All Value Stocks Compared to Deep Value and Glamour Value Stocks, Market Capitalization Weight (1951 to 2013)

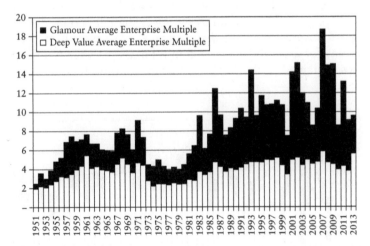

FIGURE 10.6 Average Enterprise Multiple for Deep Value and Glamour Value Stocks (1951 to 2013)

shows the average enterprise multiple for each of the Glamour Value and the Deep Value portfolios in each year of the study.

Figure 10.6 shows clearly why the Deep Value portfolios comprehensively outperformed the Glamour Value portfolios. In each year, the Deep Value portfolios were on average considerably cheaper on an enterprise multiple basis than the Glamour Value portfolios. On average over the full period the Glamour Value portfolios held stocks with an enterprise multiple of 8.2, while the Deep Value portfolios held stocks with an average enterprise multiple less than half of that multiple at 3.91. This chart may also explain the underperformance of the Deep Value portfolios relative to the Glamour Value portfolios in the 1970s. Both portfolios were close to valuation lows—only the early 1950s were lower—and the difference between the average enterprise multiples of the Deep Value portfolios and the Glamour Value portfolios was at its tightest. Contrast the 1970s to the 1990s. Through the 1990s, the spread between the enterprise multiples for the Deep Value and the Glamour Value portfolios was at its widest, and the Deep Value Portfolios enjoyed the largest outperformance.

Finally, we can examine the portfolios on the basis of Novy-Marx's gross-profits-to-total-assets ratio. Figure 10.7 shows the average ratios of gross profits to total assets for each of the Glamour Value and the Deep Value portfolios in each year of the study.

We can see from Figure 10.7 that the Glamour Value portfolios tended to contain slightly better stocks on the basis of Novy-Marx's measure. In 49 of the 63 years the Glamour Value portfolios contained stocks with a better ratio of gross profits to total assets. Over the full period, the Glamour Value portfolios owned stocks that generated an average of 43 percent in gross profits for each dollar invested in total assets, while the Deep Value portfolios contained stocks that generated gross profits on total assets of 39

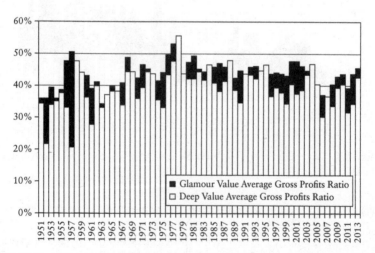

FIGURE 10.7   Average Gross Profits to Total Assets Ratio for Deep Value and Glamour Value Stocks (1951 to 2013)

percent on average. We can conclude from this analysis that the outperformance of the Deep Value portfolios over the Glamour Value portfolios was not a function of the Deep Value portfolios possessing higher-quality stocks. While the portfolios tended to contain stocks with broadly similar Novy-Marx measures of quality, the Glamour Value portfolios were slightly better in most years and on average, and yet underperformed.

We've examined the returns on a market capitalization-weighted basis because most stock market indices like the S&P 500 or the Russell 1000 are weighted by market capitalization. This means the All Stocks portfolio is a reasonable proxy for those market capitalization-weighted indices and the returns to the various portfolios are comparable. It makes sense to construct a stock market index that is weighted by market capitalization. We would not, however, construct a portfolio by market capitalization, which would mean that we allocate capital to each stock in the portfolio on the basis of how large or small it is. The simplest method of portfolio construction is to weight each stock equally. If, rather than weighting the stocks in each portfolio by market capitalization we weight each equally, we see substantially improved performance. Figure 10.8 shows the impact of equally weighting the Deep Value portfolios compared to weighting by market capitalization.

Simply equally weighting the same portfolios of Deep Value stocks generates an extraordinary compound annual growth rate of 21.30 percent

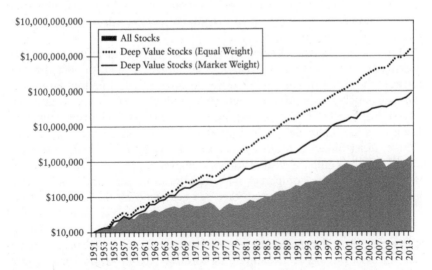

FIGURE 10.8 Comparison of Market Capitalization-Weighted and Equal-Weighted Performance of Deep Value Stocks (by Enterprise Multiple) and All Stocks (1951 to 2013)

for the full period, generating an average of 5.58 percent more return each year than the market capitalization-weighted portfolio. Over the 63 years examined, a $10,000 investment grows to a terminal capital of $1.6 billion, almost 19 times more than the comparable market capitalization-weighted portfolios. This is likely another example of the simulator getting ahead of reality. With this much capital, the equally weighted Deep Value portfolio would likely be pushing up against the limits of the strategy.

This examination demonstrates the utility of examining stocks on the basis of intrinsic value in general and the enterprise multiple in particular. We already know that the enterprise multiple is useful for identifying under-valued stocks in the general stock market. The decile portfolios of stocks formed on the basis of the enterprise multiple perform in rank order, with the most undervalued performing best and the most overvalued performing worst. We can now see that if we limit our examination to the value decile, we find that even there the portfolios of stocks with the lowest valuation ratios outperform the most expensive value stocks. The ratio of gross prof-its to total assets, Novy-Marx's measure of quality, seems to be one of the better measures of quality, identifying stocks in the general stock mar-ket that outperform the market. There is also some weak evidence in the data that it has identified high-quality value stocks that outperformed other value stocks, but it's not conclusive that it will continue to do so. In any case, it underperforms a comparably sized portfolio of stocks selected solely on the basis of valuation. This seems to confirm the thesis that valuation is a very powerful determinant of investment performance, and it is more important than quality.

Like Graham's net net rule, the enterprise multiple identifies stocks that meet many of the criteria activists seek in targets. Unlike the net net rule, however, the enterprise multiple has the advantage of scaling into large capi-talization stocks. Recall that the enterprise multiple seeks stocks with a high ratio of EBIT or EBITDA to enterprise value, which is the market capitaliza-tion less net cash plus debt, any preferred stock, minority interests, and may include underfunded pension costs, and is regarded as the true cost to an acquirer of the company in its entirety. The practical effect is that the enter-prise multiple favors companies with high levels of cash and low levels of debt in relation to the operating earnings generated by the business. While investors generally regard these attributes as positives, companies can build up too much cash relative to the size of the business. Jensen's agency costs of free cash flow illuminates the tension between managers wishing to retain cash for asset growth and maintaining too low payout ratios, versus share-holders preferring that the payout ratio be increased and the cash be paid out. Thus the enterprise multiple identifies many undervalued companies with so-called "lazy" balance sheets and hidden or unfulfilled potential. Activists target these undervalued, cash-rich companies, seeking to improve the intrinsic value and close the market price discount by increasing payout ratios.

Deep Value Activism

Cash hoarders looking to rationalize their hoarding like to postulate, "If you distribute cash to shareholders, doesn't that signal that you are no longer a growth company because you have no good use for the cash?" My first thought is, doesn't letting tens of billions of dollars accumulate on the balance sheet for years on end also reveal an inability to find good use for the cash?
—David Einhorn, iPrefs: Unlocking Value (2013)

The nature of the demands typically made by activists supports the view that activists seek undervalued companies with highly liquid balance sheets where increasing payout ratios will improve the intrinsic value and close the market price discount. While activists do not typically focus on a single flaw, using "poor management" as a proxy for a multitude of sins, Brav et al. found that the *primary* stated goal of activist campaigns typically fell into one of seven categories. Each centers on a distinct fault that can be remedied to improve the firm's intrinsic value and close the market price discount. The objectives are not mutually exclusive, meaning that a single activist campaign can address several problems. Here they are listed from most common to least common:

1. **Undervaluation:** The campaign is couched only in terms of "maximizing shareholder value." More than half—50.7 percent—of the engagements studied by Brav et al. fell into this category.
2. **Operational inefficiency:** The activist targets general operational inefficiencies, proposing cost cutting or tax efficiency.
3. **Low payout policy and overcapitalization.** The activists seek to reduce excess cash, increase leverage, or increase payouts to shareholders using either dividends or stock repurchases. Alternatively, they attempt to stop or reduce equity offerings and restructure debt.
4. **Excessive diversification.** Where the target is excessively diversified, the activists propose spinning-off divisions or refocusing the business strategy. Where the target is the subject of a merger or acquisition, the activist seeks either to stop the acquisition or seek a higher price for the target.
5. **Independence:** The activists attempt to take over the target or force a sale of it to a third party.
6. **Poor governance:** Activists seek to improve corporate governance by rescinding takeover defenses (either by declassifying the board or

revoking poison pills); ousting the CEO or chairman; challenging board independence and fair representation; seeking better disclosure and questioning potential fraud; and challenging the level or the pay-for-performance sensitivity of executive compensation.

7. **Undercapitalization:** Activists seek to provide finance for business growth or corporate restructuring arising out of bankruptcy or financial distress, in exchange for friendly board representation

Leaving aside the generic "undervaluation," and even "operational efficiency," which is typically a euphemism for cost cutting, the third most common activist demand was a higher payout, even to the extent of having the target assume more debt. The next most common complaint was excessive diversification, in which the activists either demanded a refocusing of the business, attempted to stop further diversification, or tried to stop the target firm from making acquisitions. These are all the demands we would expect to see if the issue was one of Jensen's free cash flow agency conflict. Brav et al. also cited general governance issues, including rescinding takeover defenses, ousting CEOs, promoting board independence, and curtailing executive compensation, as common reasons for activism.

In early 2013 David Einhorn began agitating to have Apple, Inc. pay out its enormous cash holding. Speaking at the Ira W. Sohn Conference, Einhorn noted that with close to $137 billion in cash on its balance sheet, it held more cash than "the market capitalization of all but 17 companies in the S&P 500," the size of which "reveal[ed] a basic flaw in Apple's capital allocation."[16] The problem with holding so much cash, according to Einhorn, was its opportunity cost. It earned only a small amount of interest, which meant a return below the rate of inflation. He likened it to "decaying inventory," arguing that the real value of it declined a little bit every day.[17]

> *Even worse, the return is far below the cost of capital. For companies with all-equity balance sheets, the cost of capital is particularly high, because expensive equity capital supports both the business and the foreign cash.*
>
> *Finance theory suggests that an unlevered or net cash balance sheet should be rewarded with higher P/E multiples. In practice, the market assigns a discount for this level of overly conservative long-term capital management.*
>
> *Not only does the cash earn a return below the cost of capital, it is evident that future profits will probably also be reinvested at a low return. As a result, the market not only discounts the cash sitting on the balance sheet, it also drives down the P/E multiple due to the anticipated suboptimal re-investment rate for future cash flows.*

Einhorn argued that, at a 10 percent cost of capital, the cash represented an opportunity cost of close to $13.7 billion per year, or $14 in earnings per share. His solution was for Apple to issue to existing shareholders "iPrefs"— high-yielding preference shares—which, said Einhorn, would allow Apple to "unlock significant shareholder value" by reducing the cash on its "bloated balance sheet."[18] He wasn't the only activist to complain about Apple's huge cash stockpile. Shortly after Einhorn unveiled his idea at the Ira W. Sohn Conference, Icahn would also propose in an open letter to Tim Cook, Apple's CEO, that Apple return cash through a $150 billion buyback:[19]

> *When we met, you agreed with us that the shares are undervalued. In our view, irrational undervaluation as dramatic as this is often a short-term anomaly. The timing for a larger buyback is still ripe, but the opportunity will not last forever. While the board's actions to date ($60 billion share repurchase over three years) may seem like a large buyback, it is simply not large enough given that Apple currently holds $147 billion of cash on its balance sheet, and that it will gener-ate $51 billion of EBIT next year (Wall Street consensus forecast).*
>
> . . .
>
> *With such an enormous valuation gap and such a massive amount of cash on the balance sheet, we find it difficult to imagine why the board would not move more aggressively to buy back stock by immediately announcing a $150 billion tender offer (financed with debt or a mix of debt and cash on the balance sheet).*

Icahn believed that if Apple decided to borrow the full $150 billion at a 3 percent interest rate to undertake a tender at $525 per share, the result would be an immediate 33 percent boost to earnings per share and, assum-ing no multiple expansion, a commensurate 33 percent increase in the value of the shares. Icahn saw the shares appreciating over the following three years from $525 to $1,250, assuming sustained 7.5 percent annual growth in Apple's EBIT and an EBIT multiple of 11 from Apple's 2013 EBIT mul-tiple of 7. In his presentation, Einhorn had also made an argument for Apple undertaking a buyback, although Einhorn's proposal was half the size of Icahn's and didn't require the company to take on debt. Why were Einhorn and Icahn fixated on Apple getting recognition for its cash holding?

An example demonstrates how overcapitalization can impact intrinsic value and simultaneously displays the utility of the enterprise multiple. Let's say we have a company, Orange, Inc., with a market capitalization of $500 million, earning $37 million per year, and generating $50 million in EBIT (assume also that capital expenditures match depreciation and amortiza-tion such that EBIT equates to operating cash flow and earnings represent

TABLE 10.3   Orange, Inc. Summary Financial Statements, Statistics, and Ratios

Summary Balance Sheet	
Net Cash and Equivalents	$150 million
Other Assets	$50 million
Total Assets	$225 million
Summary Income Statement	
Gross Profit	$70 million
EBIT	$50 million
Net Income	$37 million
Other Statistics and Ratios	
Market Capitalization	$500 million
Enterprise Value	$350 million
Price-to-Earnings Ratio	14×
Earnings Yield	7.4%
Enterprise Multiple	7×
Gross Profit on Assets	93%
Long Bond Rate	3%

free cash flow). On the balance sheet it carries $150 million in net cash and equivalents. Let's also say that the long bond earns 3 percent. Table 10.3 summarizes the financial statements, statistics, and ratios for Orange, Inc.

The price-to-earnings ratio of this company is 14 ($500 million ÷ $37 million). This equates to an earnings yield of 7.4 percent ($37 million ÷ $500 million), which is inexpensive given that it is more than twice the return available for long bond offers at 3 percent, albeit without taking on the peculiar risks of this company and its business. Its gross profit on total assets is a little over 31 percent ($37 million ÷ $225 million, where the $225 million comprises $150 million in net cash and equivalents and $75 million in other assets), which is excellent, again because it is more than 10 times the return available in the long bond. It is even more interesting on an enterprise multiple basis. It trades on an enterprise multiple of seven ($350 million ÷ $50 million). Given the very high proportion of cash on the balance sheet and the excellent cash flow generation, the company can comfortably return most or all of the cash to the shareholders.

Einhorn notes that to figure out how much value this would unlock, we have to guess how much credit the market already gives the company for its cash. If the market gives it no credit, and it does the restructuring through a return of all its cash, then the cash returned is found value, which means the dividend would unlock the whole $150 million. This might occur if the return on assets is boosted to more than 93 percent ($70 million ÷ $75 million), which likely justifies a price-to-earnings multiple of 14 or higher, meaning the market capitalization remains unchanged at $500 million. The shareholders receive $150 million and retain stock with the same market capitalization, $500 million. Although note that the extent to which the market already gives the company some credit for the cash, the amount unlocked would be reduced:[20]

> *There is no way to know for sure how much credit the market gives, so there is no way to know how much value will be unlocked. But the range is no less than zero and no more than [the value of the cash distributed].*
>
> *The caveat is that to the extent that this would reflect Apple adopting a better capital-allocation policy such that cash and future cash aren't trapped indefinitely, the market might reward Apple with a higher P/E ratio.*

Einhorn argues that this analysis is most useful for companies that are inappropriately capitalized because the concept of intrinsic value "presumes that the cash flows generated by the enterprise are optimally financed so as to minimize the firm's cost of capital." In practice, most publicly traded companies are appropriately capitalized, and consequently trade at market valuations commensurate with intrinsic value. This idea does not therefore improve the intrinsic value of most companies. However, where the company is not appropriately capitalized, where it is not minimizing its cost of capital, intrinsic value can be improved by reducing excess cash. In so doing, the market price discount is also likely to be removed, and the company trade closer to its fully realized intrinsic value. The utility of the enterprise multiple is that it identifies precisely this type of company, undervalued with an unexploited intrinsic value. If no activist emerges to improve the unexploited intrinsic value, other corrective forces act on the market price to generate excellent returns in the meantime.

The coda to Einhorn's and Icahn's campaigns to have Apple pay out $150 billion in excess capital clearly demonstrates the power of this idea. After both had prodded Apple for 6 months, writing letters and meeting with Apple chief executive Tim Cook, Apple initiated a buyback in 2013. By February 2014 it had repurchased $40 billion of stock, a record amount for any company over a 12-month span.[21] Shortly afterward, Icahn withdrew his plan to have the company undertake the bigger buyback he had proposed, writing in an open letter to Apple shareholders, "We see no reason to persist with our nonbinding proposal, especially when the company is already so close to fulfilling our requested repurchase target."[22] After Icahn had withdrawn his plan, Apple announced in April that it would in fact return $130 billion in capital through an increased buyback and a hike in its dividend. The stock price, which had already begun moving, leapt. After trading as low as $388 in May 2013, the April 2014 announcement of the return of capital pushed the shares to trade as high as $604, a 56 percent gain in one of the largest companies on the stock market in a little under a year. *The Wall Street Journal* noted in an article, "Carl Icahn has proved once again that even in defeat he can turn a tidy profit."[23]

CONCLUSION

> *"There is very little altruism in finance. Wars against corporate managements take time, energy, and money. It is hardly to be expected that individuals will expend all these merely to see the right thing done. In such matters the most impressive and credit-able moves are those made by a group of substantial stockholders, having an important stake of their own to protect and impelled thereby to act in the interests of the shareholders generally. Representations from such a source, in any matter where the inter-est of the officers and the owners may conceivable be opposed, should gain a more respectful hearing from the rank and file of stockholders than has hitherto been accorded them in most cases."*
> —Benjamin Graham. *Security Analysis*
> (New York: McGraw Hill) 1934.

Through his genius and his experience, Graham understood intuitively what others would demonstrate empirically 75 years later: That stocks appear most attractive at the peak of their business cycle when they represent the worst risk-reward ratio, and least attractive at the bottom of their cycle when the opportunity is at its best. Though they appear intensely unappealing— perhaps *because* they appear so intensely unappealing—deeply undervalued companies offer very attractive returns. Often found in crises, they have tanking market prices, receding earnings, and the equity looks like poison. At the extreme, they might even be headed for liquidation and losing money in the process. That's why they're cheap. As Graham noted in *Security Analysis*:[24]

> *If the profits had been increasing steadily it is obvious that the shares would not sell at so low a price. The objection to buying these issues lies in the probability, or at least the possibility, that earnings will decline or losses continue, and that the resources will be dissipated and the intrinsic value ultimately become less than the price paid.*

For the investor who ignores the precise ills of the stock under consideration, and refers to the base case—undervaluation—they know that Fortuna's wheel is more likely to lift these stocks than crush them. This is mean reversion, and it is pervasive, even if we are not particularly good at intuiting its influence. It is, as Graham testified, one of the mysteries of the business, as much a mystery to him as it is to everybody else.[25] Rather than focus on the experience of deeply undervalued stocks, we are distracted by the crisis. We make cognitive errors. They are easy to make because the incorrect decision—rejecting the undervalued stock—feels right, while the correct decision—buying stocks with anemic, declining earnings—feels wrong. Extrapolation is instinctive, while mean reversion is not. And when we extrapolate the fundamental performance of stocks with declining earnings, we conclude that the intrinsic value will ultimately become less than the price paid. But this is not what the data show.

The research shows, first, that valuation is more important than the trend in earnings. Cheap, low, or no-growth portfolios systematically outperform expensive, high-growth portfolios, and by wide margins. The second, more counterintuitive finding of the research is that, even in the value portfolios, high growth leads to underperformance, and low or no growth leads to outperformance. For many value investors, this is an unexpected finding. Intuitively, we are attracted to high growth and assume that high-growth value stocks are high-quality stocks available at bargain prices. We might also assume that a high return on invested capital meets Buffett's requirements for a high-quality business. The problem is that the data show that high-growth and high-return stocks tend to disappoint. Competition acts on high returns to drag front-runners back to the pack. It is the rare business that can resist competition, and the research shows that they are extremely difficult to identify *ex ante*—before the fact. Warren Buffett has shown an extraordinary ability to find sustainable economic moats and sustainable high returns on capital, one of the conditions, along with a competent and honest management, for his "wonderful companies." The data show, however, for those of us who don't have Buffett's talent, that the low- or no-growth value stocks are the more consistent bet. It seems that the uglier the fundamental business trend, the better the return, even when the valuations are comparable. This is deep value investing.

Deep value stocks are often found in hairy situations—think of Buffett's pursuit of American Express in his Buffett Partnership days—and some are mired in scandal. But scandal and crisis don't connote distress. These companies aren't distressed—they tend to be cash rich and profitable—but they're not growing or the earnings trend is unsatisfactory, and they're deeply undervalued as a result. They have unfulfilled potential. This is why deep value investment and activism go hand in hand. In 1934 Graham saw deep undervaluation as a prod impelling "stockholders to raise the question whether it is in their interest to continue the business," and "management to take all proper steps to correct the obvious disparity between market quotation and intrinsic value, including a reconsideration of its own policies and a frank justification to the stockholders of its decision to continue the business."[26] Graham exhorted investors to become "ownership conscious."[27]

The research on activism bears out Graham's thesis. An engaged shareholder can reduce agency costs by concentrating managers on creating shareholder value instead of pursuing other agendas. Shareholder activists may pursue a multitude of agendas, not necessarily seeking to improve intrinsic value or remove a market price discount, but activist investors seek only to deliver a return. The difference between activist investing and other forms of shareholder activism is the difference between whaling and whaling on the *Pequod*. The mandate is whales—deep undervaluation—not white whales—shareholder activism. This leads activist investors to seek different ends to other shareholder activists. Activist investors pressure boards to remove underperforming managers, stop value-destroying mergers and acquisitions, disgorge excess cash and optimize capital structures, or press for a sale of the company, all of which are designed only to improve shareholder value.

As a portfolio, companies with the conditions in place for activism offer asymmetric, market-beating returns. Activists exploit these properties by taking large minority stakes in these beaten-down stocks and then agitating for change. This agitation seems to improve both the short-term market performance, and longer-term operating performance of the companies targeted beyond the mere returns to deep value. The market reacts as if this is the case, popping on the filing of a 13D notice. Activists, by investing in target companies and then supplying the catalyst, capture this return. The more "aggressive" the activism—sale of the company, stock repurchases, asset spinoffs, ousting the CEO—the quicker and better the returns. The best returns are associated with an outright sale of the company, which delivers a full control premium. The activists who succeed in getting control then undertake many of the basic steps private equity firms would undertake if the company was taken private, typically changes the old management could have made, too. Icahn brags, "We do the job the LBO guys do, but for all the shareholders."[28]

Icahn has been described as the "ultimate contrarian," and "the contrarian to end all contrarians,"[29] and his preferred targets have been described as looking "as appetizing as roadkill."[30] Ken Moelis, an investment banker and founder of Moelis & Company, an independent investment-banking firm, has said of Icahn that he goes beyond betting against trends:[31]

> *He'll buy at the worst possible moment, when there's no reason to see a sunny side and no one agrees with him.*

As we've seen, the research supports such a bet. In this light, Icahn's holdings are perfectly rational, as he explains:[32]

> *The consensus thinking is generally wrong. If you go with a trend, the momentum always falls apart on you. So I buy companies that are not glamorous and usually out of favor. It's even better if the whole industry is out of favor.*

In July 2013, some 38 years after he and Kingsley sat down at 25 Broadway to hash out the *Icahn Manifesto* activist strategy, Icahn appeared at the Delivering Alpha conference to discuss his latest investment. The interviewer, CNBC's Scott Wapner, asked Icahn why he was pursuing Dell, Inc., the "build-to-order" personal computer manufacturer, in the midst of a buyout offer from its founder Michael Dell, "There are those who are looking at this entire situation and saying, 'Carl, you don't really want Dell, do you? Why do you want this business? It's a dying business. Are you just trying to get to [Michael] Dell to bump his offer?'" Asserting that his investment philosophy remained unchanged at 77 years of age, he said:[33]

> *My whole history if you look at it, is not to buy businesses that are great. I don't pay retail. I go in when people say they're terrible. It's really the old Graham-and-Dodd philosophy. You go in when nobody likes it, but it's still ok.... A lot of analysts miss this stuff.*

As he had many times before, Icahn again acknowledged the intellectual underpinnings of his *Icahn Manifesto* strategy as Benjamin Graham and David Dodd's *Security Analysis*, and revealed that his brand of deep value activism is as old as value investing itself.

Notes

1. United States Government Printing Office. Washington. 1955. Available at http://www4.gsb.columbia.edu/filemgr?file_id=131668.
2. Carl Icahn and Robert Shiller. "Financial Markets (ECON 252) Guest Lecture." *Yale University*, November 19, 2008.

3. Alon P. Brav, Wei Jiang, Randall S. Thomas, and Frank Partnoy. "Hedge Fund Activism, Corporate Governance, and Firm Performance (May 2008)." *Journal of Finance*, Vol. 63, pp. 1729, 2008. Available at SSRN: http://ssrn.com/abstract=948907.

4. Nicole M. Boyson and Robert M. Mooradian. "Corporate Governance and Hedge Fund Activism (June 1, 2010)." *Review of Derivatives Research*, Vol. 14, No. 2, 2011. Available at SSRN: http://ssrn.com/abstract=992739.

5. Michael C. Jensen. "Agency Costs of Free Cash Flow, Corporate Finance, and Takeovers." *American Economic Review*, May 1986, Vol. 76, No. 2, pp. 323–329.

6. David Einhorn. *Fooling Some of the People All of the Time, A Long Short (and Now Complete) Story*. (Hoboken: John Wiley & Sons) 2010.

7. Augustino Fontevecchia. "Billionaire Dan Loeb's Big 2013: Third Point Is Up 18% As It Unveils Nokia Stake And Returns 10% Of Capital." *Forbes Magazine*, October 22, 2010. Available at http://www.forbes.com/sites/afontevecchia/2013/10/22/billionaire-dan-loebs-big-2013-third-point-is-up-18-as-it-unveils-nokia-stake-and-returns-capital-to-investors.

8. Tom Wolfe. "A Gonzo in Life as in His Work." *The Wall Street Journal*, February 22, 2005.

9. Katherine Burton. "Hedge Hunters: Hedge Fund Masters on the Rewards, the Risk, and the Reckoning." *Bloomberg Press*, 2007.

10. Daniel Loeb, "Schedule 13D Exhibit 3. Letter To Chief Executive Officer." Securities and Exchange Commission, September 15, 2000. Available at http://www.sec.gov/Archives/edgar/data/1040273/000089914000000393/0000899140-00-000393-0003.txt.

11. Ibid.

12. Daniel Loeb, "Schedule 13D/A Exhibit 2. Letter to Chief Executive Officer." Securities and Exchange Commission, September 15, 2000. Available at http://www.sec.gov/Archives/edgar/data/1040273/000089914001500023/tmp889727c.txt.

13. Robert Novy-Marx. "The Other Side of Value: Good Growth and the Gross Profitability Premium" (April 2010). NBER Working Paper No. w15940. Available at SSRN: http://ssrn.com/abstract=1598056.

14. Ibid.

15. Ibid.

16. David Einhorn. "iPrefs: Unlocking Value." *Greenlight Capital*, 2013. Available at https://www.greenlightcapital.com/905284.pdf.

17. Ibid.

18. Ibid.

19. Carl Icahn, "Letter to Tim Cook." *Icahn Enterprises*, October 8, 2013. Available at http://www.scribd.com/doc/178753981/Carl-Icahn-s-Letter-To-Apple-s-Tim-Cook.

20. Einhorn, 2013.

21. David Benoit. "Icahn Ends Apple Push With Hefty Paper Profit." *The Wall Street Journal*, February 10, 2014.

22. Steven Russolillo. "Carl Icahn: 'Agree Completely' With Apple's Bigger Buyback." *The Wall Street Journal*, April 23, 2014.
23. Benoit, 2014.
24. Benjamin Graham and David Dodd. *Security Analysis*. (New York: McGraw Hill) 1934.
25. United States Government Printing Office. Washington. 1955. Available at http://www4.gsb.columbia.edu/filemgr?file_id=131668.
26. Graham and Dodd, 1934.
27. Ibid.
28. Shawn Tully. "The Hottest Investor in America." *Fortune Magazine*, May 30, 2007. Available at http://money.cnn.com/magazines/fortune/fortune_archive/2007/06/11/100060832/index.htm.
29. Ibid.
30. Andrew Feinberg. "Carl Icahn: Better Investor Than Buffett." *Kiplinger*, February 2013. Available at http://www.kiplinger.com/article/investing/T052-c100-S002-carl-icahn-better-investor-than-buffett.html.
31. Tully, 2007.
32. Ibid.
33. Scott Wapner. "Icahn: Really would love to own Dell." *CNBC*, July 17, 2013. Available at http://video.cnbc.com/gallery/?video=3000183755.

Index